ON SELF AND SOCIAL
ORGANIZATION

THE HERITAGE OF SOCIOLOGY

A Series Edited by Donald N. Levine

Morris Janowitz, *Founding Editor*

CHARLES HORTON COOLEY

ON SELF
AND SOCIAL
ORGANIZATION

Edited and with an Introduction by

HANS-JOACHIM SCHUBERT

THE UNIVERSITY OF CHICAGO PRESS
Chicago and London

Hans-Joachim Schubert, lecturer in the Department
of Sociology at the University of Potsdam,
Germany, is the author of *Demokratische Identität:
Der soziologische Pragmatismus von Charles
Horton Cooley* (Suhrkamp, 1995).

The University of Chicago Press, Chicago 60637
The University of Chicago Press, Ltd., London
© 1998 by The University of Chicago
All rights reserved. Published 1998
Printed in the United States of America
07 06 05 04 03 02 01 00 99 98   1 2 3 4 5
ISBN: 0–226–11508–9 (cloth)
ISBN: 0–226–11509–7 (paper)

Library of Congress Cataloging-in-Publication Data

Cooley, Charles Horton, 1864–1929.
    On self and social organization / Charles Horton
  Cooley : edited and with an introduction by Hans-
  Joachim Schubert.
        p.   cm. — (The heritage of sociology)
    Includes bibliographical references and index.
    ISBN 0-226-11508-9 (hardcover : alk. paper). —
  ISBN 0-226-11509-7 (pbk. : alk. paper)
    1. Social psychology. 2. Social groups. 3. Social
  change. 4. Self. 5. Individualism. I. Schubert,
  Hans-Joachim. II. Title. III. Series.
  HM251.C83   1998
  302—dc21   98–13172
                                                  CIP

♾ The paper used in this publication meets the minimum
requirements of the American National Standard for
Information Sciences—Permanence of Paper for Printed
Library Materials, ANSI Z39.48–1992.

Contents

III THE SELF, SOCIAL ORDER, AND SOCIAL CHANGE

The Looking-Glass Self

Social Order and Democracy

Social Change and the Pragmatic Method

Acknowledgments

I would like to thank Donald Levine for his trust, support, and encouraging criticism. I would also like to thank Katharina Ruerup and Peter Rigney for translating the introductory essay, and Mary Caraway for her conscientious editorial work.

Hans-Joachim Schubert
Potsdam, 1997

Introduction

It is almost impossible now to imagine the prestigious position Charles Horton Cooley (1864–1929) held within the founding generation of American sociologists. Yet when Luther Bernard solicited autobiographical sketches from more than 250 of these scholars in 1927 (Levine 1975–76), Cooley was named more often than any other author in the field as having exerted a significant influence. His seminal formulations on human communication, the primary group, the looking-glass self, social organization, and public opinion stimulated and guided a good deal of early sociological thought in the United States. Above all, he was a significant mentor of the pathbreaking theorists of the Chicago school of sociology (Harvey 1987, 154–57).

With the ascendance of quantitative research methods and other analytic frameworks in the decades after World War II, Cooley's work was nearly forgotten, although Cooley himself continued to be remembered—along with George Herbert Mead—as one of the founding fathers of symbolic interactionism (Farberman 1985; Meltzer, Petras, and Reynolds 1980) and for his pioneering work on primary groups (Cooley was especially esteemed by Edward Shils, Robert Merton, and their students).

Perhaps only now, with the opening up of new interpretative methodologies and a renewed concern for civil society, can the enduring importance of his work be appreciated. His formulations relating self and community and proposing what he called a "pragmatic approach" to social change appear, under our vastly different circumstances, more relevant than ever to the problems of understanding and directing modern democratic societies. It was Cooley's aim and achievement to apply the ideas of pragmatism in developing a sociological theory of social action, social order, and social change that could serve as his instrument for analyzing the social problems and cultural crisis of the age. In the process, he was able to deduce from his sociological theory cautious normative assumptions on the meaning of democracy.

The goal of the present compilation of texts is to reconstruct Cooley's comprehensive perspective. He published his first major book in 1902; from that time on he never changed the basic foundations

1

and main features of his sociological theory. Indeed, his extensive conceptions were already in place at the turn of the century, when he first
planned to write a trilogy—a project he eventually accomplished with
his *Human Nature and the Social Order* (1902), *Social Organization*
(1909), and *Social Process* (1918).

During his formative years, between 1864 and 1902 (see part I),
Cooley devoted his attention primarily to three subjects and problems.
First of all, his youth and early adulthood were characterized by a
tension between the Reconstruction era's individualism and materialism, on the one hand, and the competing ideals of transcendentalism,
on the other (see chapters 1 and 2). Second, he dealt intensively with
questions concerning transportation that were of central importance
in the rapidly industrializing United States (see chapters 3 and 4). And
third, Cooley participated in the widespread discussion on Darwinism,
which in America became extremely controversial (see chapter 5).

In the second phase of Cooley's career, the foundations of his sociology and social psychology were set (see part II). Cooley's anthropological reflections articulate and verify the "plasticity of human nature"
(see chapter 6): he thereby uncovers the conditions for the possibility
of human freedom of action. Only by examining the coordinating
"mechanisms" of communication and understanding (see chapters
7–9), however, can he explain, without falling back into "mere individualism" or collectivism, the simultaneous development of self and
social ties that creates the "vital unity" of individual and society (see
chapters 10–12).

Basing his inquiry on those general concepts, Cooley developed in
his major works a coherent theory integrating the self with social order and social change (see part III). In his first book, *Human Nature
and the Social Order,* he formulated a theory of the self. His famous
"looking-glass self" describes neither an "oversocialized self" nor an
"unencumbered self"; rather, it represents an open but distinct self-
image formed through interaction and communication with others (see
chapter 13). In *Social Organization,* Cooley developed his theory of
social order, based on his concepts of the primary group, public opinion, institution, classes, and democracy. Democracy, for Cooley, is not
simply a form of government but a form of life rooted deeply in the
social nature of humankind (see chapters 14–17). Finally, in his *Social
Process,* he introduced what he called a "pragmatic method"—his theory of social change. According to Cooley, social change cannot be
predicted through the scientific study of evolutionary trends, nor can
history be subjected to an instrumental rationality. Social change is a
fragile and unending interactive process that, due to constantly arising

"problems of action," requires permanent scrutiny and redefinition by the public (see chapters 18–22).

With his last book, *Life and the Student* (1927)—a collection of aphorisms and personal, as opposed to sociological, reflections— Cooley retired from professional social science and returned to Emerson, Thoreau, and Goethe and the beginning of his own creative phase.

Part I: Early Writings

Transcendentalism

Charles Horton Cooley was born on 17 August 1864, in Ann Arbor, Michigan, the fourth child of Thomas McIntyre Cooley and Mary Horton Cooley. That same year, his father was elected to the Michigan Supreme Court. This was only one of many successes in the remarkable life of Thomas McIntyre Cooley; the son of a large, poor farming family, he became dean of the University of Michigan Law School, reporter of the supreme court of the state, a university professor, author of standard law works, respected judge, and popular speaker. All this professional and social success he reached solely as a result of his astonishing industriousness and inexhaustible energy, without any social patronage or financial aid whatsoever (Cheever 1898). Charles Horton Cooley reports almost incredulously, considering his father's social background, about his career and scholarly achievements. His father, as he noted in his journal, had fifteen siblings, of which he was the only one who fully learned how to read and write (Cooley 1895, 21 July). It is clear from his many letters to his son that the course of Thomas McIntyre Cooley's professional career, flush with the sense of success, provided him with a wider general orientation. Success meant material profit but, above all, it meant an improvement in social position, higher prestige, and the accumulation of greater power, offices, and technical competence than his competitors acquired.

Thomas McIntyre Cooley's rise in the world and his philosophy of life can surely be seen as expressions of an important aspect of American culture—utilitarian individualism. As a youth, Charles Horton Cooley without doubt tried to follow the example of his father and fulfill his high expectations. Reading between the lines of his journal, which he kept from his early adolescence until his death, we can see that his father was omnipresent, primarily in the form of Charles's own extremely high self-expectations. However, he also expressed needs in his journal that stood in complete opposition to the demands made upon him.

As this internal division continued, he became more and more entangled in contradictions. His journal documents over many pages the strong conflicts he was involved in as a boy and as a young man. For example, he repeatedly claimed to have taken a leadership role among his peers, only to admit later to having been introverted and an outsider. He also often forced himself to appear as a speaker and man of the world at formal occasions but then confessed to being a poor speechmaker who felt uncomfortable in official company and preferred a more casual atmosphere. In addition, his journal is full of confessions of shyness. Although he undertook travels and sought adventure, he clearly was very bound up with his hometown and longed for a sense of community and belonging. Above all, he repeatedly expressed dissatisfaction with his own performance. On the one hand, he would have liked to read many books and memorize many texts. On the other hand, he believed that success could not be measured quantitatively but, instead, depended on how he related to his work and how the results correlated with his ideas of balance, truth, and authenticity. His early journal entries fluctuated constantly between euphoric prospects of success and depressive feelings of self-doubt.

Despite his numerous efforts to fulfill the high self-expectations stemming from his father's example, he also diagnosed many pathological consequences of what he called the "strenuous life." Cooley believed his aging father's physical frailty and mental restlessness to be a result of his longstanding utilitarian orientation. In 1895, he writes in his journal:

> My father is miserable partly because his body is broken, partly because he has come by lifelong habit to care only for action and applause, and now he cannot have these. To avoid the same misfortune the receipt would seem to be; preserve your body and accustom yourself to desire things that are good in themselves, like beauty, truth, sympathy, whatever is common rather [than] private. (Cooley 1895, 21 July)

As a prescription, he suggests a morality whose point of departure is not private success but, rather, overall ideals such as "beauty, truth, [and] sympathy." Cooley thus developed an alternative outlook that followed his critique of utilitarianism. He found this morality and philosophy further articulated in another American sociocultural tradition, one that competed with utilitarianism: the transcendentalism of Emerson and Thoreau.

The writings of Emerson and Thoreau provided him with a historical and practical paradigm that appeared to be opposed to and nobler than the utilitarianism of his father. Through the influence of Emerson,

Cooley was able to take the offensive and intellectually criticize his father's worldview. Emerson wanted to be socially influential as a "representative character," much like Cooley's father was as a judge; on the other hand, Emerson rejected the utilitarian tools of power, money, and influence insofar as they contribute nothing to introspective self-fulfillment or successful communitarian life. The transcendentalist person finds his orientation through contemplation. He intuitively discovers, through the example of nature, what is meant by beauty, truth, honesty, as well as independence. Though the transcendentalist can communicate important insights to society, he does not expect power, social reputation, or wealth in exchange. Compared to the materialism of economic individualism, transcendentalism postulates the superiority of the moral realm and, at the same time, tries to provide a practical, political example for strengthening the social world.

For Cooley, the work of Emerson and Thoreau took on a significant meaning. Young Cooley believed, as did the transcendentalists, that contemplation of the inner life, of the sort he practiced in his journal, was not only the definitive method of attaining self-perception and self-realization—the "cultivation of the self"—but also a "contribution to the art of life" (Cooley 1893, 296) and the only possible method of realizing universal truths.

For Cooley, such contemplation in the spirit of Emerson and Thoreau was, in fact, until about the turn of the century the decisive path to self-fulfillment, one which, at the same time, called for a specific way of life—namely, that of the hero, artist, or hermit (Schwartz 1985). The "beauty" of life was to be explored through an inward approach to life; in an outward orientation this beauty remains unknown. In 1889, he wrote in his journal: "Life is embosomed in beauty. Why can we not always see it? The principle of beauty is within us like the principle of life in a seed. . . . We must live from within then. When we see and feel that our outward action is shaped after our inward guidance we are content" (Cooley 1888–90, 8–9). Five pages later, Cooley posed the central question of transcendentalism, the question of the possibility of individual autonomy in light of social constraints and normative bonds: "Who are slaves? Those whose life is determined by immediate externals or by their own past thoughts?"

In the eyes of the transcendentalists, the expanding industrial economy had produced, more and more, an uninspired society of profit maximizers. For this reason, transcendentalists sought to withdraw from that society and develop instead the creativity intrinsic to the individual mind but stunted and buried by commerce with industrial society. However, their critique remained inadequate since transcendentalism, with its solipsistic epistemology, was more caught up with exploring personal self-definition than with explaining human association in society.

Transcendentalism therefore shares with utilitarianism a basic individualistic tendency, although each conceived the term "individual" differently. In utilitarianism, the self-realization of the individual is achieved by maximizing private ends. In transcendentalism, on the other hand, individualism is suspended in the universality of nature. In both schools of thought, the individual must prevail in his private objectives against the influence and competition of others. Though Emerson, too, says, "a man must be a non-conformist" (Cooley 1887, 5), this is not homologous to the individualism of the Jacksonian era. A transcendentalist is not one who pursues his own interests against another's but one who follows in a universal way the ideals inherent in nature (Kateb 1984).

Cooley's strong roots in the transcendentalist tradition can be seen in the style and topics of his journals, in various essays he published in the student journal *Inlander,* as well as in his membership in the artistic circle of the Samowar Club (Coser 1977, 326). His veneration for the transcendentalists climaxed during a trip to Concord in 1891, where, in conversation with local residents and relatives of Emerson and Thoreau, he tried to learn more about the heroes of his youth.

Although Cooley, with the help of transcendentalism, was able to replace his father's utilitarian frame of reference with a loftier view, he ultimately found it much more difficult to reconcile the contradictory demands of transcendentalism for a contemplative, lonely way of life and for a broad-based and effective artistic efflorescence than to meet utilitarianism's demands of performance, success, and influence. In 1890, he wrote in his journal:

> Our part is to build up in our hearts by solitary thought a glorious ideal of life and[,] holding it firmly in our sight[,] build such a likeness to it as we may. . . . I have courage. I have a spirit that needs but to see the banner flying and I will follow it or die. Can I also hold the banner? (Cooley 1890)

The pages that followed this entry in this volume of his journal were carefully cut out. The next five years are entirely absent; not until 1895 do the journal entries resume, in another volume. The destruction and hiatus could be seen to coincide with a strong crisis of orientation, caused by the excessive demands he made upon himself during this period.

After the turn of the century, Cooley finally overcame transcendentalism by finding his own path toward self-fulfillment beyond the problematic individualism of both utilitarianism and transcendentalism. His sociological and sociopsychological theory grew to be more strongly rooted in the communally oriented, sociocultural republican tradition, the "great humanistic traditions" (Cooley 1918, 2), and in the philosophy of pragmatism. A central statement in his first major work, *Human Nature and the Social Order,* is that the self is not simply given, as the utilitarians believed, nor can it be set by contemplation, as the transcendentalists believed; rather, the "looking-glass-self" can develop only by communicative interaction with its social surroundings.

Theory of Transportation

In 1888, following the completion of his undergraduate studies in the Department of Philosophy at the University of Michigan, Cooley went to Washington, D.C., for two years to work first for the Interstate Commerce Commission and later for the Bureau of the Census. There, in contrast to the student milieu of Ann Arbor, he was directly confronted with the political, economic, and social problems of the Gilded Age. His job was to investigate the transportation system—particularly, the railroads, which most clearly showed the massive social impact of the nation's rapid industrialization. This expansion caused wide-ranging debates over the alternatives for economic policy: state intervention versus laissez-faire approaches. "In this country there is no example so important and so familiar as that of the State and national laws designed for the regulation of railways" (Cooley and Cooley 1894, 81), Cooley wrote in "Transportation," an Interstate Commerce Commission report that he coauthored with his father. While this essay portrayed current, practical, financial, and political problems, his monograph, *The Theory of Transportation* (1894), which was accepted as his doctoral dissertation, in political economy, analyzed the relevance of the transportation system for the structuring of societies and drew from a wide range of historical studies.

In 1894, Cooley's *Theory of Transportation* was a unique project. Only later would the "territorial demography" (Schnore 1968) Cooley initiated become an area of broad research in sociology. What was new about Cooley's theory of transportation? In contrast to the first generation of sociologists, Cooley did not represent an organicist position. He chose a very different theoretical starting point. In organicism's thought, social order and historical changes are analyzed analogously to the biological structure and the organic development of plants and animals, in conformity with natural law. For Cooley, however, social order and social change are based on processes of communication and interaction between social actors. In his "organic view," institutions are therefore spheres of action, connected by transportation and communication, not by natural laws.

In *The Theory of Transportation,* Cooley examined the role played by the various modes of transportation and communication in the structuring of the economy, politics, culture, and the military. The specific form of these social institutions is—from Cooley's perspective of interaction theory—closely tied to the changing means of transportation and communication. Whether new technological developments (for instance, faster transportation links or the introduction of the telephone) contribute to democratization or to an increased surveillance of the population was an open question for him. However, he contended, transportation and communication cannot be subjected to any purpose whatsoever but, instead, constitute a limited range of possibilities for development, thereby specifically influencing the generation of new ideas and the formulation of new objectives. The usage of new technologies within the transportation and communication systems essentially involves a process of social redefinition.

The conclusion Cooley reached in *The Theory of Transportation* was thus sobering in relation to the study's explanatory power: although he was, by his own judgement, able to ascertain many connections between the constitution of social structures and the transportation system, this endeavor alone could contribute little to the actual analysis of societal processes of definition. According to Cooley, this analysis should not only consider the conditions of material distribution that are controlled through the transportation system but should explicate thoroughly the function and effect of symbolic interaction and communication.

> Transportation is physical, communication psychical. The latter belongs to a distinct branch of study of immeasurable importance and complexity, namely, social psychology. It cannot profitably be dissociated from that field of inquiry which embraces language as an instrument of social organization and all the material agencies that language employs.
>
> I think, then, that a separation can advantageously be made between the theory of transportation and the theory of communication, notwithstanding that they use, in part, the same vehicles, have a common aim in the overcoming of space, and exert in many ways an analogous influence upon social development. A study of communication from the point of view of place relations may be undertaken in connection with the study of transportation; but such a study cannot penetrate more than

skin-deep into the social meaning of communication. (Cooley [1894] 1969, 61)

Cooley's main interest after he completed *The Theory of Transportation* was to investigate the "social meaning of communication." The task which Cooley set for himself was the elaboration of the specific character of human communication and its meaning for the identity of the individual and for the structures of society. "Communication," according to Cooley in his 1928 autobiographical retrospective, "was thus my first real conquest, and the thesis a forecast of the organic view of society I have been working out ever since" (Cooley [1928] 1969, 8).

Darwinism

Rather surprisingly, Cooley was given the opportunity to professionally employ his interest in sociology, which had been increasing since his study of the transportation system. In 1890, when he was working at the census bureau in Washington, D.C., Cooley talked about the problem of transportation at a meeting of the American Economic Association, where he met Lester Frank Ward and Franklin Giddings. Both urged him to go into the new field of sociology.

Cooley followed their advice and in 1892 began to study political economy and sociology at the University of Michigan, where sociology was not yet established as a separate department. Henry Carter Adams, professor of political economy and an advocate of institutionalism, asked Cooley to become an instructor in sociology while he was still nominally a student in political economy. Sometime between 1892 and 1894, Cooley met George Herbert Mead, in Ann Arbor, who since 1891 had been lecturing on psychology at the University of Michigan and had studied with John Dewey. While in Ann Arbor, Dewey had begun to turn away from speculative philosophy—which he later called the "Hegelian bacillus"—and started to develop his pragmatic philosophy (Westbrook 1980). Very carefully, Cooley recorded Dewey's lectures entitled "Political Philosophy" (1893) and "Several Lectures on Anthropological Ethics" (1894). In these talks, Dewey discussed the Darwinian paradigm, and he presented the beginnings of a pragmatic theory of "social sensorium," action, and communication.

Like many early social scientists, Dewey and Cooley thought that with Darwin's theory of evolution through natural selection, both Hume's behaviorism and Hegel's metaphysical idealism could be overcome. Darwinism had indisputably caused a revolution within the humanities—without, however, establishing a new paradigm (Hofstadter

1962; Russett 1976; Bannister 1976). At the turn of the century, Cooley was confronted with a variety of different interpretations of Darwinism; basic concepts, such as adaptation, selection, evolution, and chance variation, were used very differently. William Sumner, who originated the notion of *social* Darwinism in the United States, saw in the unrestrained "struggle for existence of natural evolution" the only true mode of social change that could secure the permanent social integration of human societies. Lester Frank Ward, in complete contrast, maintained that "natural evolution" had come to a standstill and that rational action had become the means for "social evolution." In turn, Herbert Spencer, in contrast to Ward, portrayed evolution as a functional process of differentiation beyond all rationality of action.

Cooley participated in this vigorous discussion of Darwinism (Cooley 1897). His interpretation of the theory of natural selection, however, differed fundamentally not only from both Sumner's social Darwinist theory of the struggle for survival and Ward's rationalist theory of social evolution but also from Spencer's theory of teleological differentiation. Cooley believed, like Darwin and unlike Ward, that environmental "problems of action" triggered processes of change that could not rationally be fully anticipated. For example, if you want to leave a room but you can't because the door is locked and you discover you don't have the key, you are faced with a "problem of action," because you can't immediately act as you would have liked to act, according to your preliminary orientation and objective. Pragmatists consider this type of situation very important because it motivates us to devise new ways of conceptualizing the problem at hand. To solve the problem, social actors must continually create new orientations and objectives and choose the ones most likely to succeed. Cooley maintained, unlike Sumner, that this selection process is not decided by a struggle of competition and survival but, rather, that such situational problems can be overcome through creative, tentative, and cooperative responses to them. Unlike Spencer, who thought the surmounting of problems and the establishment of new objectives and new institutions were bound to a teleological process of differentiation, Cooley saw this as an open development. For Cooley, the revolutionary character of Darwinism lay in its interpretation of modernity, which allowed for the conceptualization of both individual freedom and individual contingency (particularly, the individual's dependence upon the larger environment). The theory of natural selection served, on the one hand, to explain the expansion of freedom of action (through the concept of the individual's direct, active confrontation with the social surroundings), while, on the other hand, it helped to demonstrate the chances and the risks involved in pursuing various options of action (through the concept of the social environment's constant, constraining reactions). Darwinism was for Cooley (1897) as well as for Dewey (1951) the decisive intellectual means of avoiding all empirical and idealistic pitfalls. It pointed a way to make not mind (as in idealism) nor environmental circumstances (as in naturalism) but, rather, social action the starting point of their theories.

Part II: The Foundations of Cooley's Sociology and Social Psychology

The philosophical starting point of Cooley's thought was not Descartes's epistemological doubt, which had characterized wide areas of Western philosophy for hundreds of years. At the end of the nineteenth century, a "revolt against dualism" (Lovejoy 1955) arose, triggered by the Darwinist revolution and by massive social changes—a revolt that Cooley joined. Descartes's distinction between two autonomous spheres, the human will (*res cogitans*) and the objects of the outer world (*res extensa*), was increasingly called into question. In the first pages of *Social Organization,* Cooley emphatically made clear the limitations of the dualistic perspective of Descartes's famous dictum, "I think, therefore I am." Motivated by radical epistemological doubt, Descartes held the mind of the individual to be the foundation of scientific knowledge: the appearance of the empirical world cannot serve as the foundation for our perception, since that world is constantly subject to change; only the mind of the individual, contemplatively explored through introspection, can provide an invariable basis for true perception. Consequently, the separation of body (empirical world) and mind (will) is a constitutive principle of Cartesianism. For Descartes, individualism—in the form of the singular mind—is an unavoidable epistemological authority.

For Cooley, however, individualism ("I") and rationalism ("I think") cannot be the foundation of philosophy. In dealing with the contemplative methods of Emerson's and Thoreau's transcendentalism, Cooley recognized that the self is constituted through interaction with its surroundings and that the mind is established within that process of interaction. Hence, the self-regarding method of introspection cannot be the starting point of a scientific process of inquiry. According to Cooley, every act of introspection is, in fact, not simply a private matter but, rather, an act of public communication. Cooley substitutes the Cartesian preconditional singular mind with *processes* of understanding, triggered by problems of action, that create the option of subjectivity. Thus, in place of the a priori, given self, we have instead a socially constituted, "looking-glass self."

> Introspection is essential to psychological or social insight, but the introspection of Descartes was, in this instance, a limited, almost abnormal, sort of introspection—that of a self-absorbed philosopher doing his best to isolate himself from other people and from all simple and natural conditions of life. The mind into which he looked was in a highly technical state, not likely to give him a just view of human consciousness in general. (Cooley [1909] 1963, 6)

Because, according to Cooley, the foundation of the individual is social, Descartes's radical doubt as well as the resulting body-mind dualism he propounded become meaningless: in order to make up our own mind, we invariably consult our store of knowledge about the previous opinions and actions of others faced with a similar dilemma. The existing world, with all its familiar certainties and conditions, is the necessary starting point for our capacity to take action. Radical Cartesian doubt is therefore only a fiction; the epistemological process is carried out not through a bracketing of the empirical world but through a communicative understanding of empirically given contents. For Cooley, what is constitutive of the self is not the separation between an empirical and a spiritual (or mental) world but, rather, a process of interaction between people, out of which can develop what we consider body and mind. The self is not an a priori, given entity, since it develops only through contact with others, just as social structures do not exist independently of the interaction of acting individuals. Self and society are merely two sides of the same coin.

> Self and society go together, as phases of a common whole. I am aware of the social groups in which I live as immediately and authentically as I am aware of myself; and Descartes might have said "We think," *cogitamus,* on as good grounds as he said *cogito.* (Cooley [1909] 1963, 8–9)

Cooley shares his critique of Descartes's epistemology with all the other pragmatists. For Charles Saunders Peirce, it was Descartes's achievement "to (theoretically) permit scepticism and to discard the practice of the schoolmen of looking to authority as the ultimate source of truth. That done, he sought a more natural fountain of true principles, and thought he found it in the human mind; thus passing, in the directest way, from the method of authority to that of apriority" (Peirce [1893] 1996, 249 §1.391). According to Peirce, Descartes teaches that philosophy, in contrast to scholastic reasoning, "must begin with universal doubt," and that "the ultimate test of certainty is to be found in the individual consciousness." The founder of pragmatism did not want to fall behind the enlightened philosophy of Descartes in its rejection of authority as the ultimate touchstone of reason. Nevertheless, we cannot, Peirce stated, go along with Descartes: "We cannot begin with complete doubt. We must begin with all the prejudices which we actually have when we enter upon the study of philosophy. These prejudices are not to be dispelled by a maxim, for they are things which it does not occur to us *can* be questioned" ([1868] 1996, 156 §1.265). Individuals can by no means call into question the truth of theories or assertions without reference to a community, since all assertions are always made against the background of familiar certainties within a collective communication process. For this reason, as Cooley suggests, Descartes should have said *cogitamus* instead of *cogito*.

Descartes's individualism is also rejected by Peirce, who refers to the communitarian basis of validity for all theories. "We individually cannot reasonably hope to attain the ultimate philosophy which we pursue; we can only seek it, therefore, for the *community* of philosophers" ([1868] 1996, 157 §1.265). Peirce overcame Cartesian dualism in a comprehensive manner, by theoretically reconstructing the problem of rationality. In accordance with his pragmatic maxim, the validity of a statement is decided only by anticipating the consent of a universal community of communication. The practical relevance of a concept must prove itself in its use, as well as through every conceivable and potential consequence. "Consider what effects, that might conceivably have practical bearings, we conceive the object of our conception to have. Then, our conception of these effects is the whole of our conception of the object" (Peirce [1893] 1996, 258 §1.391).

Although John Dewey attacked the "bifurcation of nature" at various points of his work (1949, 36), it was George Herbert Mead more than all the other pragmatists who called for "intolerance" toward Cartesian dualism ([1929] 1964, 343). Like Peirce, however, he did not do this without emphasizing Descartes's great achievement, which in Mead's eyes lay in the establishment of a freedom of inquiry against the dogmatism of theories claiming to represent a unified higher authority. Nevertheless, Mead argued, the Cartesian philosophy was a hindrance to the development of free thought, as its dualism created a dogmatism of its own. In the dominant philosophic current since Descartes, Spinoza, and Leibnitz "lies the implication of some structure of reality which the structure of thought undertakes to reflect or sets up as a postulate, a structure, whatever it may be, that has the immutability and irrevocability of the past" ([1929] 1964, 343). The foundation of pragmatism, by contrast, lay not in an "immutable and irrevocable order" (343). "The most distinctive mark of the Pragmatic movement" is, according to Mead, "the frank acceptance of actual ongoing experience, experimentally controlled, as the standpoint from which to interpret the past and anticipate the future. So far as I can see this acceptance must recognize as ruled out any absolute order within which is to be placed a final concatenation of events past, present, and future" (344).

The disintegration of the dualistic Cartesian structure of consciousness and object is accounted for by all pragmatists, as it is by Cooley, via a theory of action. The pragmatists recognized that human beings cannot conceive the outer world independently of human action—just as the identities of human social actors in the process of social action do not exist separately and fully formed but, rather, constitute themselves in that process.

In his *Human Nature and the Social Order,* Cooley takes up with utmost consistency all of the problems which arose with the decline of Cartesian philosophy. In the book's introduction, "Heredity and Instinct," he analyzes the meaning of these factors for human development. If the mind is no longer seen as independent of the body, natural circumstances, and the process of human action, then environmental circumstances and human biological preconditions inevitably come to the fore as crucial issues. Only if it can be shown that a person is not programmed by his surroundings or by his innate disposition can the possibility of individual freedom of choice arise. If the role of the subject in the historical process is decentralized, then automatically the relationship between sociability and individuality becomes important, as Cooley discusses in the book's first chapter, "Society and the Individual" (see chapter 10 below). If consciousness or will is not the decisive authority, then the tension between consciousness and the subconscious, between "suggestion and choice," as well as between "sociability and personal ideas" becomes a problem (see Cooley [1902] 1964, chapters 2 and 3). Cooley subsequently shows in the two central chapters of the book—"Sympathy or Understanding as an Aspect of Society" and "The Social Self—The Meaning of 'I'"—how Descartes's solipsistic contemplation or introspection must be replaced, through an interactionist conception of consciousness, with a method of intersubjective understanding (see chapter 7 below), which then provides the foundation for his theory of identity. The "plasticity" of human nature makes possible the creation of personal identity "through the looking glass"—that is, through the integration of other peoples' judgments and perspectives (see chapter 13 below). In the last seven chapters of *Human Nature and the Social Order,* Cooley creates an "empirical ethic," based on his communication and identity theory, which pursues the goal of overcoming the dualism between societal coercion and individual freedom.

In his work, Cooley systematically untangles all the problems which arose with the critique of Cartesian epistemology and individualism. Fundamental to his method are his anthropological reflections on the biological preconditions of man (see chapter 6 below), his examination of the "mechanisms"—suggestion, imitation, communication, and understanding—which coordinate action (see chapters 7–9 below), and his explanation of the relationship between individual and society (see chapters 10–12 below). In all his books and essays, Cooley furthers these three approaches, themes which resulted directly from his anti-dualistic, action-centered and intersubjectivist perspective.

The Plasticity of Human Nature

Under the banner of Darwinism, the developing disciplines of sociology and psychology were characterized, above all, by the search for the fundamental mechanism in the relationship of human beings to their surroundings. Many sociologists and psychologists, guided by the example of the natural sciences, did not go beyond a positivist examination of human instincts. Eugenics, criminology, and the psychology of instincts attributed the possibilities of human action to rudimentary, biologically determined dispositions. Cooley's anthropological reflections, however, proceed in a completely different direction.

According to Cooley, humans are determined neither by their environmental surroundings nor by their biological dispositions. Rather, only a person's "lines of teachability" are predetermined through what Cooley calls "heritage," (Cooley 1923, 454), and these lines are merely evoked in a person's confrontations with his surroundings in daily life. He possesses no repertoire of instincts which can serve as a guide for solving problems; human problem-solving abilities develop only with reflection or reference to familiar habits. This "plasticity" and openness of human nature is therefore the condition for the constitution of social rules and institutions, which, in turn, allow humans to control their surroundings. Paradoxically, it is a biological weakness—the lack of extensive instincts—which places humankind in the position to react more effectively to threatening changes than any other species can.

> The distinctive thing in human evolution . . . is the development of
> a process which is not fixed but plastic, which adapts itself directly to
> each particular situation, and is capable of an indefinite number of ap-
> propriate and successful modes of action. (Cooley [1918] 1966, 199)

People do not achieve their uniqueness, in comparison to animals, by
simply adapting to the norms, values, and customs of their surroundings. Rather, the human being must make the environment accessible
through intelligent experimentation in concrete situations. "The human process . . . involves a plastic heredity prepared to submit itself
to the guidance of environment as interpreted by intelligence" (200).

With this, Cooley, first, shows his opposition to dispositional determinism, which causally traces human action to inborn characteristics
and attributes—as we find, for example, in Lombrosos's criminology
or Galton's eugenics. Second, Cooley rejects the environmental determinism of materialism and naturalism, which attribute no constitutive
power to human action and see the human spirit merely as an empty
vessel. Third, he also dismisses a rationalism which neglects all subconscious factors and reduces the natural foundation of humankind to the
unspecified motive of the individual pursuit of pleasure. According to
Cooley, none of these theories could sufficiently explain the connections between individual and society. These unsolved problems stimulated Cooley's vision of an interactionist social psychology.

Communication and Understanding

The path to an interactionist social psychology led Cooley to reject
introspective methods and the philosophy of mind, on the one hand,
and biologistic and behavioristic approaches such as eugenics, criminology, mass psychology, the theory of imitation, and the psychology
of instinct, on the other. To establish itself on a firm theoretical foundation, interactionist social psychology needed to determine the
"mechanism" of social *integration*. Cooley was not able to proceed
beyond the futile alternatives of "heredity and environment," "imitation and innovation," and "suggestion and choice"—key terms in his
early thinking—until he discovered the basic elements of his envi-
sioned theory: communication and understanding. The basic medium
of social integration, according to Cooley, is not the mental mechanism
described by mass psychology (Le Bon [1899] 1974), not imitation
(Tarde 1903), not instincts (McDougall 1921), not social control in
the form of habits (Ross 1929), and not a consciousness of kind (Giddings 1903) but, rather, communication based on "standardized symbols."

Human beings have to "understand" each other if they are to create both a manifest social order and autonomous selves. "Without communication the mind does not develop a true human nature, but remains in an abnormal and nondescript state neither human nor properly brutal" (Cooley [1909] 1963, 62). Only through communication can individuals develop distinct identities as well as social ties to far-reaching normative values. Only if symbols are available which can be understood independently of a single, concrete situation by all interacting participants in the same way can a common orientation toward a generally valid pattern of behavior come about. Only if the symbols used by one social actor mean the same thing for that actor as they do for any partner in social interaction are both actors able to anticipate each other's reactions and thus adjust their own actions to accord with this perceived expectation.

> The growth of personal ideas through intercourse . . . implies a growing power of sympathy, of entering into and sharing the minds of other persons. To converse with another, through words, looks, or other symbols, means to have more or less understanding or communion with him, to get on common ground and partake of his ideas and sentiments. (Cooley [1902] 1964, 136)

Through language, social actors are no longer limited to concrete experiences; they do not necessarily need to duplicate others' experiences to be able to understand them. Rather, through a common background of symbolically structured social knowledge, they can mentally discover the meaning of specific situations outside their direct personal experience. "Social experience," according to Cooley, "is a matter of imaginative, not of material, contacts" (139). "Social and spatial knowledge" is therefore always part of a "mental-social complex" (Cooley [1926] 1969, 298). Every individual perception—whether of symbols or of objects—is thus always a mental process registered against the background of a stock of social knowledge.

The use of significant symbols, however, gives rise not only to the formation of reciprocal expectations of behavior but also to the constitution of distinct identities. This is a paradoxical problem: the problem of intersubjectivity. It means, for starters, that the subjects must be able to subordinate themselves to one social category while, at the same time, they must also realize that they are absolutely distinct from one another.

The use of significant symbols is a decisive factor in the overcoming of this paradox—in making oneself into an object, interpreting one's own expectations in light of the anticipated expectations of others.

Cooley illustrates how identities constitute themselves within the framework of speech-acts.

> That the "I" of common speech has a meaning which includes some sort of reference to other persons is involved in the very fact that the word and the ideas it stands for are phenomena of language and the communicative life. It is doubtful whether it is possible to use language at all without thinking more or less distinctly of some one else, and certainly the things to which we give names and which have a large place in reflective thought are almost always those which are impressed upon us by our contact with other people. ([1902] 1964, 180–81)

In every sentence ("common speech"), the "I" is always in relation to a second person ("reference to other persons") and to objects ("things"). Only through the forming of such relationships does the establishment of intersubjectivity become possible, the process in which the identity and, simultaneously, the nonidentity of the self are mutually defined.

The identity of the self/speaker is created and manifests itself only through an active reference to objects which the speaker can legitimate before a listener or a community of interpretation. Within this tripolar situation, the identities of speaker and listener are formed and clarified, as are the communitarian ties between the interactive agents and the meaning of the objects.

As early as his *Human Nature and the Social Order,* Cooley worked with a pragmatic theory of meaning and identity. His central terms "understanding," "communication," and "sympathetic introspection" ground and substantiate his radical denouncement of the dualism between nature and nurture, heteronomy and autonomy, human nature and social order, and individual and society.

Individual and Society

With his "organic view," Cooley claims to integrate the unity of society and the autonomy of the self. "The organic view," he said, "stresses both the unity of the whole and the peculiar value of the individual, explaining each by the other" ([1902] 1964, 36). According to Cooley, society is neither the sum of autonomous action (as many utilitarians believed) nor an entity distinct from the action of individuals; rather, it manifests a "collective aspect" enlightening the constitution of habits and rules, structures and institutions. Its "distributive aspect," on the other hand, manifests the constitution of the self, of personal abilities and tastes, through interaction with others. Cooley analyzed how the autonomy of the self and the structures of society evolve jointly through the processes of communication. The experience of difference—a prerequisite for the development of an autonomous self—is possible only in reference to common orientations. Likewise, social habits and structures can survive only if and as long as they are reproduced through collective action.

> Social consciousness, or awareness of society, is inseparable from self-consciousness, because we can hardly think of ourselves excepting with reference to a social group of some sort, or of the group except with reference to ourselves. The two things go together, and what we are really aware of is a more or less complex personal or social whole, of which now the particular, now the general, aspect is emphasized. . . . Self and society are twin-born, we know one as immediately as we know the other. (Cooley [1909] 1963, 5)

On the one hand, Cooley's organic view is opposed to the organicism of Comte, Spencer, and others, as well as to all idealistic concepts of a "social consciousness." On the other hand, Cooley did not defend any specific form of individualism. First of all, he rejected the "mere individualism" of the *homo economicus* ideal. Utilitarianism is not able to reconcile the ability of the individual to pursue his own ends with the binding character of social structures. For this reason, social structures appear negatively, as restrictions or merely as necessary forces of order. According to Cooley, utilitarian individualism can only define freedom negatively, namely, as an absence of social constraint.

> The common notion of freedom is negative, that is, it is a notion of the absence of constraint. Starting with the popular individualistic view of things, the social order is thought of as something apart from, and more or less a hindrance to, a man's natural development. There is an assumption that an ordinary person is self-sufficient in most respects, and will do very well if he is only left alone. ([1902] 1964, 422)

Furthermore, Cooley rejected the concept of double causation—a notion that signifies the idea of a free individual, on the one hand, and an extramundane entity, on the other. He also disliked an evolutionary theory of individualization that he called "a crude evolutionary philosophy," the "primitive individualism" of which Herbert Spencer was an advocate. Finally, he dismissed the "social faculty" view, which discriminated between biologically given social faculties (herd instincts) and individualistic faculties (egoistic instincts). Further articulating his theory of understanding and communication, Cooley illustrates how individual orientations and social organizations, socialized individuals and social institutions can develop *simultaneously*. Cooley develops this "organic view" in his books with great resolution. It was his goal, through his theories of identity, the primary group, the public, the institution, democracy, and social change, to achieve an integration of the sociological microlevel, mesolevel, and macrolevel.

Part III: The Self, Social Order, and Social Change

The Looking-Glass Self

Influenced by the pragmatist philosophy that John Dewey was teaching in Ann Arbor and by William James's *Principles of Psychology,* Cooley was in sharp opposition to a formalist and economic utilitarianism that gave priority to the autonomy of the individual without researching the anthropological, rehabilitational, communal, and cultural preconditions of individuality. In his *Human Nature and the Social Order,* Cooley analyzed these preconditions in connection with his theory of the "looking-glass self." Identity, he concluded, is created out of the tension between natural impulses that the individual must actively develop and social structures that he must actively appropriate. The given social structures are transformed through this process of appropriation, which is simultaneously a process of self-development, thereby leading to the formation of distinct individualities.

Cooley's approach, however, was not received without controversy. For George Herbert Mead, the critical point of Cooley's theory was that he represents the development of identity as a mental process rather than as a phase of objective experience. "The crucial point, I think, is found in Cooley's assumption that the form which the self takes in the experience of the individual is that of the imaginative ideas which he finds in his mind that others have of him. And that others are the imaginative ideas which he entertains of them" (Mead [1929] 1964, xxxiv). In Cooley's eyes—according to Mead—the sole origin of identity lies in "psychical experience." Mead, in contrast, maintained that the mental imagination of judgments about oneself is preceded by an "objective phase of experience" that is formed in the process of action. "The locus of society is not the mind, in the sense in which Cooley uses the term, and the approach to it is not by introspection, though what goes on in the inner forum of our experience is essential to meaningful communication" (xxxvi). Mead's reproach of "mentalism" refers to such statements by Cooley as "society is mental" (Cooley [1902] 1964, 81); "imaginations . . . are the *solid facts* of society" (121); "we know persons . . . as imaginative ideas in the mind" (120); "*[t]he immediate social reality is the personal idea*"

(119); "[s]ociety . . . *is a relation among personal ideas*" (119); and "Mind or Imagination . . . is the *locus* of society" (134). However, only when they are taken out of context do these statements warrant the charge of mentalism.

Cooley was not a mentalist; he describes in detail, in *Human Nature and the Social Order,* his understanding of "Mind" and "Imagination." Imagination is not a force isolated from the empirical world but, rather, a practical "intercourse," an intersubjective "communication." Mind is not a solipsistic capacity but an "inner experience" created in conjunction with the outside world. "The mind," according to Cooley, "lives in perpetual conversation" ([1902] 1964, 90). Cooley insists that "society is mental" because "the human mind is social" (81). The human mind forms itself in the process of action, but it cannot be reduced simply to automatic reactions to problems in its immediate environment. It is possible for a person, through the power of imagination, to generate new ideas in response to problems of action that do not stem directly from anything in those particular circumstances.

Cooley gives two reasons why problems of action arise in social situations: either we are mistaken about the expectations and prognoses derived from our reservoir of images concerning the actions of our partners, or we are mistaken about the presupposed communality of meaning of those images. When our suppositions prove to be fallacious, the stored images are not sufficient to effectively judge the situation or form an effective course of action. If the actor has no coinciding images from which to create a secure sense of expectation, then what is required for solving the problem of action is a reorganization of the images or the formation of wholly new patterns of interpretation. The analysis of such situations is a central theme of *Human Nature and the Social Order* ([1902] 1964; see, especially, chapter 8, "Hostility"), since these objective conflicts of action are for Cooley (as well as for Mead) the point of departure for the creation of identity.

Cooley without doubt recognized that we are constantly exposed to conflicts, the resolution of which makes up the core of the process of experience. Conflicts are the result of differing attitudes and expectations in specific practical situations of action. They can be resolved if the images used by the respective actors can be reduced to their common experiential content, synthesized to new concepts, and, finally, applied to the situation at the root of the conflict. Accordingly, Cooley labels the dynamic of conflict between individuals as "hostile sympathy," because "this opposition . . . is . . . dependent upon a measure of community between one's self and the disturbing other" ([1902] 1964, 130–31). Deceptions, animosities, and conflicts do not simply threaten social certainties; they are also the condition for the creation of the individual mind—that is, of identity—and of new patterns of behavior.

From the social actor's perspective, which Cooley reconstructs in *Human Nature and the Social Order,* the development of identity is linked to the creation of social structures. Cooley shows that the actors can define their identity only within the framework of a social community. The starting point of this process is the mother-child dyad. In the framework of this relationship, a growing solidarity between mother and child parallels the child's increasing competence in using significant symbols. This simultaneous development is itself a necessary prerequisite for the child's ability to adopt the perspectives of other participants in social relationships and, thus, for the child's capacity to develop a social self. The reciprocal attainment of understanding and interpretation enables individuals to connect with each other in a "vital whole" and, at the same time, to distinguish themselves from others, to develop a distinct "looking-glass self." The means of socialization are therefore simultaneously the means of individualization. One's social identity develops itself through symbolically mediated interaction with one's surroundings.

Cooley reconstructed three progressive phases of the evolving self: (1) the "sense of appropriation," which is the expression of a biologically manifested spontaneity and activity; (2) the "social self," which is developed by taking in the attitude of others; and (3) the famous "looking-glass self," which describes neither an "over-socialized self" characterized by passive internalization of given habits and values nor an "unencumbered self" cut loose from all social constraints. The metaphor "looking-glass self," as Cooley explicitly declared, is meant to represent an open but distinctive self-image created through the imagination and interpretation of the world we inhabit. A "looking-glass self," Cooley said,

> seems to have three principal elements: the imagination of our appearance to the other person; the imagination of his judgment of that appearance; and some sort of self-feeling, such as pride or mortification. The comparison with a looking-glass hardly suggests the second element, the imagined judgment, which is quite essential. The thing that moves us to pride or shame is not the mere mechanical reflection of ourselves, but an imputed sentiment, the imagined effect of this reflection upon another's mind. ([1902] 1964, 184)

Like William James (1890) and James Mark Baldwin (1900), Cooley considered the development of the self to be a process of interaction between it and the surrounding world. But unlike James—who saw this process as just the self's "appropriation" of the world—and unlike Baldwin—who held the methods of "ejection," "accommodation," and "imitation" responsible for the constitution of the self— Cooley presented the mechanisms that mediate between self and society as formative activities, of communication, sympathetic introspection, and understanding. According to Cooley, the self gains its autonomy when the rules of social control are subject to deliberation by social actors. Cooley's theory of the self is therefore inextricably linked to his concept of social order and democracy.

Social Order and Democracy

In *Human Nature and the Social Order* ([1902] 1964), Cooley shows how identities develop in a social context. He pursues this theme in *Social Organization* ([1909] 1963), although in this work he is no longer examining the creation of the self but, rather, the generation of institutions and social organizations through the collective action of individuals. In *Social Organization,* Cooley is interested in constructing a meaningful concept of community, as well as formulating a theory of public opinion, institutions, classes, and democracy that builds upon this concept.

Cooley's first step toward his theory of social order is his conception of the "primary group" (see chapter 14 below). It is very important to note that this term is defined neither by racial characteristics, nor by culturally given traditions, nor by narratively transmitted rituals or myths; Cooley realized, instead, that the basic means for creating communities is communication in the form of dialogues. He is, in the first place, interested in articulating the universal rules that simultaneously enable both socialization and individualization. This conception of *continuity* between personal identity, primary group (or community), and social organization (or society) is altogether unprecedented. Ferdinand Tönnies ([1887] 1979), for example, differentiated in a dualistic way between *Gemeinschaft* (community) and *Gesellschaft* (society). Tönnies defines *Gemeinschaften* as thick organic unities, characterized by hierarchies, habits, moral orientations, and emotions. *Gesellschaft* is, in every sense, just the opposite of *Gemeinschaft: Gesellschaften* are controlled by conventions, laws, and public opinion.

It is not possible to subsume Cooley's ideas in this European scheme. Tönnies's dualism—which was motivated by a philosophical dualism between British natural right theory and attempts to historicize German idealist philosophy—is accompanied by a similarly dualistic theory of action. *Gemeinschaften* are organized by normative action; *Gesellschaften* are integrated by rationality of means and ends. However, for Cooley—whose concept of the primary group was motivated, above all, by the new social psychology theories of William James and James Mark Baldwin—the basic mode of action that underlies *Gemeinschaften* and *Gesellschaften*—or, primary groups and social organizations—is communication:

> Although "group," in ordinary usage, often denotes a mere assemblage of persons or things[,] it is commonly understood in sociology to mean a social group, that is[,] a number of persons among whom is some degree of communication and interaction. Moreover this must be reciprocal and not in one direction only. . . . Evidently the conception is a very general one, and groups may vary indefinitely in size and character. Any two persons conversing make a group, and, on the other hand[,] the word might be applied in some connections to the whole population of the earth, since there can be few persons, if any, who do not directly or indirectly receive and give influence. (1895[?], index card)

The difference between Cooley's and Tönnies's respective conceptions of community leads to very different social-political theories. Cooley analyzed the deep-rooted democratic aspect of primary groups. In his theory, the enlargement of primary-group ideals involves by necessity the enlargement of democracy, whereas no theory of democracy derives from Tönnies's conception of *Gemeinschaft*. Cooley's examination of primary-group communication reveals the intrinsically social nature of mankind. He reformulates the postulates of enlightenment, freedom, equality, and solidarity not as natural rights, and not as "popular impressions," but as "sure and sound" sentiments based on experiences available to every member of a primary group (Cooley [1909] 1963, 122–25).

Thus, we find at the very heart of Cooley's sociology the question of democracy. His normative demand is to enlighten the democratic options and prerequisites of the constitution of the self, social organizations, and the social process. Democracy, Cooley concluded, cannot be vital solely by means of laws and institutions, and it does not presuppose a common will: democracy needs a culture rooted in authentically organized primary groups and associations. According to Cooley in his *Social Process* ([1918] 1966), the dissolution of the dualism between individual and society lies in the establishment of a "culture of individuality," which would allow for the development of individual possibilities within the framework of supportive social groups.

The culture of individuality, the need of which we are beginning to recognize, cannot go far except as we also foster distinctive groups. We
need many kinds of family, of school, of church, of community, of occu-
pational and culture associations, each with a tradition and spirit of its
own. (369)

From his concepts of the looking-glass self and the primary group,
Cooley developed a normative model of democracy. On the one hand,
modern societies consist of different classes; numerous professional,
political, and social associations; and a multitude of cultural groups
which are not united in a higher identity. But on the other hand, the
unity of a society cannot simply be dissolved into subjectless forms of
communication and procedures (electoral procedures, for example)—
Cooley's respect for the experience of individuals in primary groups
is much too strong for that. In Cooley's special way of thinking, the
symbolic place of social power is neither occupied by a substantive
candidate (a certain class or social movement, for example) nor dissolved into universalistic formal procedures (laws and rules, for example). The central arena of power is one of conflict between different
groups, associations, parties, civil leagues, and so on, which inces-
santly define the social meaning of important issues and concerns. This
process also involves the ongoing change of collective and personal
identities; the creation of new normative rules; and the formation, destruction, and reconstruction of organizations and institutions.

Social Change and the Pragmatic Method

Society's method of creating new moral orientations and new social
institutions is the main topic of Cooley's third major book, *Social Process* ([1918] 1966). Cooley defined this "pragmatic method" as the
solution of action problems through the invention of new ways, new
norms, and new ends. Normative forms of action (action following
norms—eating with silverware, not stealing) and teleological forms of
action (action following ends, aims, or goals) may therefore be seen
as working themselves at via a pragmatic method (see chapters 18–
22 below). But, according to Cooley, it is important to realize that the
solution of action problems through the implementation of a new social rule or habit is not just a compromise of incompatible interests.
Cooley is not an advocate of "mere pluralism." In fact, it is interesting
from a sociological perspective that no new level of social understanding is without consequence for the identities of the persons involved or
for societal rules and structures. Using his pragmatic theory of action,
Cooley conceptualized social change as a fragile process of interaction

that is potentially open to permanent reconstruction of personal identities, institutions, and moral orientations.

In his *Social Process,* Cooley discusses terms such as "intelligence," "reconstruction," "anticipation," and "creativity." These terms possess central importance for all pragmatists, since a theory of social change, in tandem with a critique of ontological and teleological theories of action, is at the core of pragmatism. Social change is triggered when habits are called into question by conflicts. The destabilization of social structures is followed by a phase of reconstruction, in which new orientations and patterns of behavior are created.

> We get on by forming intelligent ideals of right, which are imaginative reconstructions and anticipations of life, based upon experience. And in trying to realize these ideals we initiate a new phase of the social process, which goes on through the usual interactions to a fresh synthesis. ([1918] 1966, 358)

What Cooley sees as most important in this "tenative process" is the phase of "imaginative reconstruction": in the forming of ideals through a "creative synthesis" of experience lies the possibility of developing improved social rules, the chance of shaping stronger identity, as well as the option of producing human action that is rational.

Cooley defines intelligence as the ability to find solutions for problematic situations: "The test of intelligence is the power to act successfully in new situations" ([1918] 1966, 351). However, this should not be understood in a social-engineering context. "Intelligent behavior" does not mean mastering anticipated problems of action but, rather, generating inventive solutions for unanticipated conflicts through a creative synthesis of the widest range of personal perspectives. By tapping the knowledge inherent in our realm of experience, we can solve problems of action through fashioning prospectively new interpretations and syntheses, which can, in turn, be applied to the conflict situation.

Intelligent action can thus be described primarily as the discovery of unknown goals, not as the achievement of anticipated ends. "Behavior which can be formulated in advance is not, in any high sense, intelligent," Cooley declared (353). Intelligence manifests itself in action problems via the actor's power of interpretation. Accordingly, intelligence is

> the power to anticipate how . . . elements will work in a novel combination: it is a power of grasp, of synthesis, of constructive vision. . . .
>   Intelligence, then, is based on memories, but makes a free and constructive use of these, as distinguished from a mechanical use. By an act

of mental synthesis it grasps the new combination as a going whole and foresees how it must work. It apprehends life through an inner organizing process of its own, corresponding to the outward process which it needs to interpret, but working in advance of the latter and anticipating the outcome. (351–52)

The rationality of the social world, and hence also of the social sciences, is grounded, according to Cooley, in the creative rather than in the mechanistic or technical development of behavioral patterns.

Cooley's theory of action, particularly the rationality of action, forms the background to his normative concepts of an authentic self which gains consistency through communicative contact with its surroundings; of primary groups, "where . . . we get our notions of love, freedom, justice, and the like which we are ever applying to social institutions" (Cooley [1909] 1963, 32); of a "democracy, in the sense of an active participation of the common people in the social process" ([1918] 1966, 248), in which minorities have the chance to call into question the existing norms of the majority; and of a "process of culture . . . [which] is one of enlarging membership in life through the growth of personality and social comprehension" ([1918] 1966, 68). "No culture," according to Cooley, "can be real for us that is not democratic" (1918, 3).

* * *

Although he received offers from other universities, Cooley spent his entire academic life at the University of Michigan in Ann Arbor. He "became an assistant professor in 1899, an associate professor in 1904[,] and full professor in 1907" (Cooley [1928] 1969, 10). While he held tenure there, he was responsible for directing a number of important doctoral dissertations, among them those of Red Bain, Walton Hamilton, and Robert Cooley Angell. During his time at the University of Michigan, however, no large department of sociology was established. Nevertheless, over the course of his career, Cooley found widespread acceptance within the expanding field of American sociology and in 1918 was elected president of the American Sociological Association. When they were released, his books were widely reviewed, not only in academic journals but also in popular newspapers and magazines (Schubert 1995).

The same holds true for his last book. *Life and the Student: Roadside Notes on Human Nature, Society, and Letters* (1927) is not a sociological work in the strict sense of the word; rather, it is composed of aphorisms and epigrams which Cooley had written over the years on very different topics. With *Life and the Student,* Cooley returns to the beginning of his literary creativity, that is, to concerns of the transcendentalists and romantics. Released from the constraints of a conventional systematic, the form of the presentation emerges on its own out of Cooley's intense and creative treatment of his subject matter. "All original masterly work has form; second hand or uninspired labor can never create it. It is what Goethe meant when he wrote 'I will rest no more until it is no more word and tradition but living conception' (*Lebendiger Begriff*)" (62).

In *Life and the Student,* Cooley demonstrates again his main concern, that democracy alone can become the normative core of American identity without requiring communities to surrender their cultural characteristics in order to attain it. The reader of *Life and the Student* gains insight into the idea of tolerance. This, according to a reviewer writing in the journal *The New Student* (4 January 1928), is the decisive tenor of Cooley's thinking: "If there is a predominant characteristic, it is that of tolerance in its broadest and truest sense, based upon a wise and thoughtful sympathy." Cooley understands tolerance not as relativism, not as disinterested acceptance of dissenters, nor as what Herbert Marcuse called "repressive tolerance" but instead as a discourse in which everyone can participate, from which no questions are left out, and which seeks true solutions for conflicts.

People say, "We must not be *too* tolerant," and call for suppression of what strikes them as dangerously wrong. But tolerance does not mean indifference to wrong, or diminished vigor in combating it; rather, that the conflict should go on with all possible vigor, openly, fairly, and under such condition that the right may be free to prevail. (Cooley 1927, 21)

References

Baldwin, James Mark. 1900. *Mental Development in the Child and the Race.* New York: Macmillan.

Bannister, Robert C. 1976. *Social Darwinism, Science, and Myth in Anglo-American Social Thought.* Philadelphia: Temple University Press.

Cheever, Noah W. 1898. "The Author of Constitutional Limitations." *The Inlander: A Magazine by the Students of Michigan University* 11.

Cooley, Charles Horton. 1885[?]. Miscellaneous Papers. Charles Horton Cooley Collection, box no. 3. Bentley Historical Library. University of Michigan, Ann Arbor.

———. 1887. "Some Teachings of Emerson." Unpublished Manuscript.

Charles Horton Cooley Collection, box no. 2. Bentley Historical Library. University of Michigan, Ann Arbor.

———. 1888–90. Journal. Charles Horton Cooley Collection, box no. 2. Bentley Historical Library. University of Michigan, Ann Arbor.

———. 1890. Journal. Charles Horton Cooley Collection, box no. 2. Bentley Historical Library. University of Michigan, Ann Arbor.

———. 1893. "On Autobiographies." *Inlander: A Magazine by the Students of Michigan University* 7:295–97.

———. [1894] 1969. "The Theory of Transportation." In *Sociological Theory and Social Research: Selected Papers of Charles Horton Cooley*, ed. Robert Cooley Angell. New York: Kelley. First published in *Publications of the American Economic Association* 9, no. 3 (May 1894).

———. 1895. Journal. Charles Horton Cooley Collection, box no. 2. Bentley Historical Library. University of Michigan, Ann Arbor.

———. 1897. "The Process of Social Change." *Political Science Quarterly* 7, 1: 63–81.

———. [1902] 1964. *Human Nature and the Social Order*. New York: Schocken.

———. [1909] 1963. *Social Organization: A Study of the Larger Mind*. New York: Schocken.

———. 1918. "A Primary Culture for Democracy." Pp. 1–10 in *Papers and Proceedings: Thirteenth Annual Meeting, American Sociological Society*. Chicago: University of Chicago Press.

———. [1918] 1966. *Social Process*. Carbondale and Edwardsville: Southern Illinois University Press.

———. 1923. "Heredity and Instinct in Human Life." *Survey* 49: 454–69.

———. [1926] 1969. "The Roots of Social Knowledge." Pp. 289–309 in *Sociological Theory and Social Research: Selected Papers of Charles Horton Cooley*, ed. Robert Cooley Angell. New York: Kelley. First published in *American Journal of Sociology* 32, no. 1 (July 1926): 59–79.

———. 1927. *Life and the Student: Roadside Notes on Human Nature, Society, and Letters*. New York: Alfred A. Knopf.

———. [1928] 1969. "The Development of Sociology at Michigan." Pp. 3–14 in *Sociological Theory and Social Research: Selected Papers of Charles Horton Cooley*, ed. Robert Cooley Angell. New York: Kelley.

Cooley, Thomas McIntyre, and Charles Horton Cooley. 1894. "Transportation." Pp. 65–134 in *The United States of America*, ed. Nathaniel Southgate Shaler. Vol. 2. New York: Appleton Press.

Coser, Lewis. 1977. "Charles Horton Cooley." Pp. 305–30 in *Masters of Sociological Thought*. 2d ed. New York: Harcourt Brace Jovanovich.

Dewey, John. 1949. *Logic: The Theory of Inquiry*. New York: H. Holt.

———. 1951. *"The Influence of Darwin on Philosophy" and Other Essays in Contemporary Thought*. New York: H. Holt.

Farberman, Harvey A. 1985. "The Foundations of Symbolic Interaction: James, Cooley, and Mead." *Studies in Symbolic Interaction,* supplement 1: 13–27.

Giddings, Franklin. 1903. "A Theory of Social Causation." *Publications of the American Economic Association* 5, no. 2.

Harvey, Lee. 1987. *Myths of the Chicago School of Sociology.* Brookfield, Vt.: Aldershot.

Hofstadter, Richard. 1962. *Social Darwinism in American Thought.* Rev. ed. Boston: Beacon.

James, William. 1890. *The Principles of Psychology.* 2 vols. New York: Macmillan.

Kateb, George. 1984. "Democratic Individuality and the Claims of Politics." *Political Theory* 3: 331–60.

Le Bon, Gustave. [1899] 1974. *The Psychology of Peoples.* New York: Arno Press.

Levine, Donald. 1975–76. "Simmel's Influence on American Sociology, pt. 1." *American Journal of Sociology* 81:813–45.

Lovejoy, Arthur O. 1955. *The Revolt against Dualism: An Inquiry Concerning the Existence of Ideas.* La Salle, Ill.: Open Court.

McDougall, William. 1921. "The Use and Abuse of Instincts in Social Psychology." *Journal of Abnormal Psychology and Social Psychology* 16.

Mead, George Herbert. [1929] 1964. "A Pragmatic Theory of Truth." Pp. 320–44 in *Selected Writings of George Herbert Mead,* ed. Andrew J. Reck. Chicago: University of Chicago Press.

———. [1930] 1964. "Cooley's Contribution to American Social Thought." Foreword to *Human Nature and the Social Order,* by Charles Horton Cooley. New York: Schocken.

Meltzer, Bernard N.; John W. Petras; and Larry T. Reynolds. 1980. "Charles Horton Cooley." Pp. 8–15 in *Symbolic Interactionism: Genesis, Varieties, and Criticism.* Boston: Routledge & Kegan Paul.

Peirce, Charles Sanders. [1868] 1996. "Some Consequences of Four Incapacities." In *Collected Papers of Charles Sanders Peirce,* ed. Charles Hartshorne and Paul Weiss, 5:156–89. Cambridge, Mass.: Harvard University Press.

———. [1893] 1996. "How to Make Our Ideas Clear." In *Collected Papers of Charles Sanders Peirce,* ed. Charles Hartshorne and Paul Weiss, 5: 248–71. Cambridge, Mass.: Harvard University Press.

Rosenwald, Lawrence A. 1988. *Emerson and the Art of the Diary.* New York: Oxford University Press.

Ross, Edward A. 1929. *Social Control: A Survey of the Foundations of Order.* Boston: Beacon.

Russett, Cynthia E. 1976. *Darwin in America: The Intellectual Response, 1865–1912.* San Francisco: W. H. Freeman.

Schnore, Leo F. 1968. "Cooley as a Territorial Demographer." Pp. 13–31 in *Cooley and Sociological Analysis,* ed. Albert J. Reiss, Jr. Ann Arbor: University of Michigan Press.

Schubert, Hans-Joachim. 1995. *Demokratische Identität: Der soziologische Pragmatismus von Charles Horton Cooley.* Frankfurt am Main: Suhrkamp.

Schwartz, Barry. 1985. "Emerson, Cooley, and the American Heroic Vision." *Symbolic Interaction* 8: 103–20.

Tarde, Gabriel. 1903. *The Laws of Imitation,* trans. Elsie Clews Parsons. New York: H. Holt.

Tönnies, Ferdinand. [1887] 1979. *Gemeinschaft und Gesellschaft: Grundbegriffe der reinen Soziologie.* Darmstadt: Wissenschaftliche Buchgesellschaft.

Westbrook, Robert. 1980. *John Dewey and American Democracy.* Ann Arbor: University of Michigan Press.

I

EARLY WRITINGS

Transcendentalism

1

Some Teachings of Emerson

I do not know what it is that should make a writer's words of lasting value unless it be that they are such as other men must always find profit in reading. If they contain this element of permanent interest, it will not matter very greatly what else they contain or lack. It is the affirmative, not the negative, that is in the end important. In pursuit of that ideal beauty and simplicity, beyond the attainment of our time and people, which we think we perceive in the Greek sculpture, men are willing to give themselves much trouble, nor is any figure rejected because it is found imbedded in earth or because it lacks arms, legs, or head. So in literature, it seems to me, we should estimate a man by what he is rather than by what he is not, by the light that is in him and not by the darkness.

Three or four years ago the first of English critics came to this country and gave us a talk upon our Emerson which many Americans found very irritating. Few accepted the critic's decision, and it was even thought that he took a true British satisfaction in giving our conceit a set down. Yet it seems to me that if there is injustice in his criticism, it lies rather in what is omitted than in what is said. He tells us much about what Emerson is not and little about what he is. Our attention is called with great emphasis to the want of legs and arms in our statue, but the wonderful beauty of the torso seems neglected. We are told he is neither a great poet, a great philosopher, nor a great man of letters; only, like Marcus Aurelius, "the friend and aider of those who would live in the spirit." This phrase may, no doubt, mean much, but certainly there was no great enthusiasm shown in expanding and illustrating it.

Without accepting or attempting to controvert this literary estimate of Emerson, I propose to offer a few somewhat general remarks upon his influence as a "friend and aider."

To everyone puzzled by the conflicting claims of reason and authority, hesitating, perhaps, between friends, interest, and peace, on the

From "Some Teachings of Emerson." Unpublished manuscript, 1887. Charles Horton Cooley Collection. Box no. 2. Bentley Historical Library. University of Michigan, Ann Arbor.

one hand, and his own intractable instincts, on the other, Emerson offers his calm, clear, and unmistakable counsel of self-reliance. "Trust thyself."

"Whoso would gather immortal palms must not be hindered by the name of goodness but must explore if it be goodness." He does not say "follow your own instincts unless they seem to conflict with what the world recognizes as right and proper" but "trust thyself" always, implicitly, and everywhere. This is his bottom fact; if this is not true, nothing is. A man's first duty is to live not according to the world but according to himself. If there still linger, in this generation, the notion that the divine light is in some way outside of man and not within him, at that Emerson strikes as at the root of all evil. How this mild-mannered descendant of many clergymen admires strong and independent men; hardly less than Carlyle himself.

But this vigorous and uncompromising declaration of independence is not enough. He asserts that this self-guidance is the most difficult of attainments, only to be gained by him who is ready to sacrifice much for it. "Society," he points out, "everywhere is in conspiracy against the manhood of everyone of its members." "The virtue in most request is conformity. Self-reliance is its aversion." "Whoso would be a man must be a non-conformist." I am ashamed to think how easily we capitulate to badges and names, to large society and dead institutions. A favorite thought with him is the contrast between the simple, straightforward independence of inanimate things or of young children, and man's cringing submission to others. In "The Sphinx," his first poem, the waves are "unashamed" but man "crouches and blushes, absconds and conceals."

Another fundamental doctrine of Emerson's ethics is that this uncompromising struggle must be carried on with temperance and composure. Quarrel and controversy are, perhaps, a little better than apathy but not much. They defeat the real end. How can the "still small voice" be heard amid the tumult of party conflict? Noisy people, however good their ostensible purpose, were his aversion. He had no faith whatever in such.

His temperament enabled Emerson to practice a composure in trying circumstances which his friend Carlyle admired but did not attain. Early in his career he was invited to address the students of the Divinity School at Cambridge. He consented, and with the calm and innocence and audacity peculiar to him the "gentle iconoclast" presented views on religious matters that must have made his hearers' blood run cold. Yet nothing more wholly uncontroversial in its tone than this address can be imagined. There is not a word to indicate that Emerson sup-

posed it possible that anyone could take his opinions amiss. Bigotry
and intolerance were things he hardly comprehended.

The unresenting silence with which he took the abuse that New
England orthodoxy heaped upon the author of this lecture proved that
he could live as nobly as he wrote. Even in the outward result he was
well justified. It takes two sides to make a quarrel, and those whom
an angry reply would have made bitter enemies soon grew ashamed
of themselves. By the next spring he is able to write Carlyle that "The
ill wind is blown over." His lack of contentiousness enabled this formidable heresiarch, more dangerous than a thousand noisier men, to live
and die in perfect personal amity with the New England clergy.

This composure of Emerson's must be not only outward but real
and internal, controlling the whole conduct of life. An artist in ethics,
if not in literature, his test of behaviour is beauty. We must not strive
too hard. No man must exaggerate his part. "Zeus hates busy bodies
and those who do too much." We are to be masters of life, not its
slaves. "A man should give us a sense of mass." Truly great men, he
declares, are much greater than their deeds. "We cannot find the smallest part of the personal weight of Washington in the narrative of his
exploits." Caesar, who seems great without effort in everything he at-
tempted, was profoundly admired by Emerson.

Nor are we to trouble ourselves too much about to-morrow. The
present is always the critical moment. He has a great deal to say about
the Day. He alone is rich who owns the Day. "Devastator of the Day"
he calls the unlucky celebrity-hunter who bores him. None of his
poems, in my opinion, is more perfect in its way than that beginning
"Daughters of time the hypocritic Days." It is one of those few produc-
tions of Emerson's which he seems to have conceived as a whole and
not in fragments. The days march past in an endless procession offering the poet such gifts as he chooses to take, "diadems and faggots."
Choosing too hastily, he forgets his morning wishes, selects a few
"herbs and apples," things of no value, and the Day departs in silence.
Too late he sees how she scorns him for his choice.

Perhaps, after all, the chief benefit we derive from a writer like Emerson is his companionship. Our daily life does not always offer the
most inspiring company, but in reading we may always "hold converse
with the wise." I do not know a writer with whom this sort of converse
is closer or more elevating than with Emerson. Here is a man who,
having a noble idea of life, lived up to it. Confiding his thoughts to
paper as they occurred to him without attempt at system or literary
form, he made up his works by collecting these fragments; "each," he
confesses, "an infinitely repellant particle." Books so composed are,

no doubt, seriously defective, but they lend themselves in a wonderful way to desultory reading. You cannot go wrong in opening Emerson. Every paragraph, almost every sentence, is a little essay by itself, always suggesting much more than it says. Such reading, it seems to me, brings us very close indeed to the personality of the author.

Such, I take it, is an outline of Emerson's teaching on a few questions of daily importance. I imagine that there is scarcely anyone who has felt his influence deeply who does not stand ready to say that he could better do without many poets, philosophers, and men of letters than without this "friend and aider."

2

On Autobiographies

All men of every sort who have done anything worthy, or that
even approaches worth, ought, supposing them good and
truthful folk, to describe their life with their own hand; but
this excellent enterprise should not be undertaken before
passing the age of forty years.

—Benvenuto Cellini

It will be seen that Benvenuto, though only a simple craftsman, prom-
ulgated a bold and comprehensive theory of autobiographies. He was
in fact peculiarly suited for this work as he was altogether free from
that false reluctance to speak frankly of one's self that many feel. Most
people praise their own virtues by indirection, Benvenuto openly, as
any one can see on almost any page of his narrative.

Beside the narrative autobiography, of which Benvenuto's may
serve as the type, there is another sort of literary performance, of close
kin with it, namely, the diary, which might be characterized as an ejac-
ulatory autobiography. There have been many illustrious keepers of
diaries, but certainly the philosopher and protagonist of diary writing,
the man who holds the same place in relation to them as Benvenuto
to autobiographies, is our Emerson. He practiced and taught this habit
that many look upon as unsocial and self-conceited. "Pay so much
honor" he says "to the visits of truth to your mind as to record them."
Holding that "He who writes for himself writes for an eternal public"
he wrote down day by day the thoughts he needed for his own use
and afterward arranged them into essays as best he might. He gives
his own experience as a student and practitioner of life and pretends
to do no more. Perhaps this fact is a reason both of his exhaustless
interest and suggestiveness and of his being misunderstood by those
who do not appreciate his method nor sympathize with his personality.

From "On Autobiographies," *Inlander: A Magazine by the Students of Michigan University* 3, no. 7 (April 1893): 295–97.

The views of these men are worth considering. Why may not, why ought not, one who has dreamed, planned, striven, lost and won, write his autobiography; not necessarily under that name, but leave for others' use some simple record of his more inward self, his aims, methods and results?

One answer to this might be that he may and ought if he can, but that few are capable of it; few can so record the results of their own lives that others can understand and use them; it needs an openness, a mastery over the instinct to seem other than one is, that is all but unattainable. It needs power of expression—in a word, self-record is not so simple a matter as one might suppose but calls for the whole armory of literary faculties.

One thing is certain: we do not like that a writer should too grossly presume upon our interest in him. We desire to know what sort of man he is; perhaps even that he should make it his business to tell us; but we desire that he should do it by such delicate innuendoes as shall reveal his sense of our extreme condescension in taking any interest in him whatever. Egotism is not the sort of autobiography here meant, nor is it sufficient for fame that a man write himself down an ass.

Even this, however, is as it may be. Not all self-assertion, even extravagant, is ridiculous. We glory in it when it comes from the right men at the right times. Dante demanding "If I go who stays?," Landor declaring of his fame "I shall dine late but the guests will be select," Wordsworth commiserating the generation that did not understand him, John Quincy Adams rising at a critical moment when the House hesitated before a great responsibility and declaring "*I* intend to put the question", these are not ridiculous. We like this magnificent self-trust of real greatness and feel that such men spoke not from vanity but from a consciousness that they stood for something worthy. They were on our side, standing up for things that we wish to see stood up for. But this we endure only from great men at great moments. For the most part this style of expression must either be entirely unconscious, like the diary of the Emperor Marcus Aurelius, or the touch must be very delicate indeed. Few writers can talk of themselves with perfect grace, only peculiarly select and genial spirits. From most men, even of genius, such familiarity has something repugnant.

There is one kind of literature that has always been written very much in the autobiographical manner and apparently always must. I mean that which relates to the conduct of life. There is no well-settled science of personal conduct and there has always been objection to general and dogmatic propositions on this subject. But experience has the greatest value and suggestiveness and this is most accessible in the

self-records of a few wise and good men. The writings of Marcus Aurelius, of Epictetus, of Thomas à Kempis, of Emerson, and of Thoreau,
may be regarded from one point of view as a sort of empirical ethics,
but certainly they are much more than this. Their greatest use is as a
contribution to the art of life. We need these facts for their beauty and
inspiration; and the facts are in their very nature autobiographical.

Theory of Transportation

3

Transportation and Organized Society—General

The character of transportation as a whole and in detail, at any particular time and throughout its history, is altogether determined by its inter-relations with physical and social forces and conditions. To understand transportation means simply to analyze these inter-relations. So far, attention has been fixed as much as possible on the simpler and more obvious conditions, the physical. We now approach the more complex question of the social relations of transportation.

The need for the movement of things and persons underlies every sort of social organization, every institution whatever. It is equally necessary to that economic organization which supplies society with food and other material goods, and to those psychical organizations, the church, education, research and the like, which, though ideal in their aims, require material instruments. The transfer of books, of scientific instruments and, above all, of men charged with multifarious social functions, is as necessary to society in its way as the transfer of grosser material substances. There can be no adequate theory of transportation which has regard only to some one aspect of its social function, as the economic aspect. That is not the only aspect, nor can one truly say that it is more important than the others. All are co-ordinate, equally indispensable to social progress.

Precisely because transportation underlies social development it is in turn determined by that development. It is a tool of the economic, the political, the military organizations, and the character of the tool varies with their needs. The most permanent conditions of its progress are the natural obstacles it has to overcome and the natural forces it employs; but even these in their practical bearings are relative to social development. The art of scientific sailing converts a contrary wind form an obstacle into an assisting force. When men discover how to

From "The Theory of Transportation," in *Sociological Theory and Social Research: Selected Papers of Charles Horton Cooley,* ed. Robert Cooley Angell (New York: Kelley, 1969), 39–42. First published in *Publications of the American Economic Association* 9, no. 3 (May 1894).

utilize coal through steam and the steam-engine, it is as if there were
a new and ample creation of natural power. The natural forces were
always there, but they exist for man only as they are discovered and
used by art. The mechanical arts, again, do not advance in an accidental manner, but are intimately associated with economic and political
conditions as well as with the progress of physical science. We have
the railroad not only because of the ingenuity of men like Stephenson,
but because the great economic need of the time was back of that ingenuity urging it on. The chief characteristic of the economic revolution
begun in the latter part of the previous century, was industrial concentration and specialization. These could not go far without better means
of land movement, and the canals first and then the railroads supplied
that means. The railroad is inseparably bound up with the other
changes of the time, in part their cause, in part their effect.

What, in general, is the social function of transportation?

Sociologically considered it is a means to the physical organization
of society. Development or evolution, the organization of social forces,
implies unification of aim, specialization of activities in view of a common purpose, a growing interdependence among the parts of society.
Such organization, such extension of relations, involves a mechanism
through which the relations can exist and make themselves felt. This
mechanism is Communication in the widest sense of that word; communication of ideas and of physical commodities, between one time
and another and one place and another. These are the threads that hold
society together; upon them all unity depends. And transportation, the
means of material communication between one place and another, is
one of the strongest and most conspicuous of these threads.

Following this conception we may analyze communication or the
mechanism of social organization as follows:

> The mechanism of material communication:
> Place communication—transportation.
> Time communication—storage and the like.
> The mechanism of psychical communication:
> Place communication—gesture, speech, writing, printing, telegraphs,
> mails, etc.
> Time communication—writing and printing regarded as means for re-
> cording and preserving thought for considerable periods of time;
> custom, imitation and heredity as conservative agents.

However imperfect this analysis may be it shows sufficiently well
what is here held to be the part played by transportation in the social
mechanism as a whole. It is a universal organizing machinery, variously specialized to suit various sorts of organization. I shall attempt

to throw some light on these more special relations in the succeeding chapters.

It follows from the intricacy of these relations, from the fact that transportation is but one pigment of the social picture, that the test of its efficiency is a variable one. The only perfectly general criterion is that it is efficient in proportion as it furthers the actual type of social development. This criterion continually means more and more as progress goes on and conditions become more complex. At bottom are the mechanical tests stated in the first chapter—that transportation is efficient in proportion as it has speed, cheapness or economy of force, and independence of natural obstacles. Taking the social point of view, security becomes a very important and ever present requirement,—security to the persons and things transported from all loss or injury whatever. The means, very highly developed, for meeting this requirement are seen in all those complicated modern arrangements that aim not only at safety but at obviating all the smallest inconveniences of travel and of the movement of goods. To these general tests each variety and stage of social progress adds appropriate details. A system of military conveyance must be carefully adjusted to actual and possible military conditions. In societies chiefly industrial, where the principles of freedom and equality have gained recognition, it becomes a fundamental requirement of transportation that it do justice among individuals—the requirement underlying the present railroad problem.

In order, therefore, to develop a theory of transportation that shall be at all adequate, one must examine severally its relations to various social institutions. For this purpose I shall for convenience classify those institutions as military, political, economic and ideal, including among the last all forms of organization having primarily religious, ethical, intellectual or artistic purposes. It is a sufficient defence of this classification that it corresponds well with the concrete facts of history. These classes of institutions are those which are in fact most obvious in the study of the past. As soon as institutions begin to differentiate at all they differentiate in this way. Other classifications may very probably be found preferable for other inquiries. The study of society has many aspects, and each aspect may call for a new classification of social facts.

In discussing the relation of the means of conveyance to any particular phase of society the inquiry may be looked upon as two-fold: first as to arrangements of a certain character found in transportation itself, and second as to the relation of transportation to institutions of this character is society at large. The several sorts of activity characterized as military, political, economic and ideal, work themselves out not only through great specialized organizations like the army, the state, economic exchange, science and art, but also in a greater or less degree through subordinate arrangements existing in all social institutions, among others in the institutions of transportation. It is obvious, for example, that a highly developed agent of transportation, like a railroad system, requires an internal political organization of much complexity and importance. And it is quite the same with other kinds of activity.

4

Transportation and Economic Organization

In this essay the economic idea is held to be, at bottom, the nourishment idea, using the word nourishment in a wide sense to include the getting and using of all material commodities whatever. As all forms of social organization require nourishment in this sense, so all have some kind of economic structure. Organizations devoted primarily to other ends, as the family, the state, schools, need material commodities and so must have, secondarily, an economic organization of one sort or another. There is also a great and general organization that is primarily economic and only secondarily anything else. This rests upon the division of labor, territorial and personal, and embraces the whole mechanism of production and economic exchange.

Theoretically, therefore, the study of the economics of transportation covers two fields, that of the economic structure existing within transportation itself and that of the relation of transportation to the economic organization of society at large. The former subject, as well as the latter, is one of very great importance, including as it does the private or internal aspect of all the problems of transportation—such questions, for example, as that of the theory of railroad rates regarded as a means of getting the greatest possible private revenue. In practice, however, it will be convenient to treat the two together, taking chiefly the public standpoint but referring to the private where it seems important to do so. We come, then, to the relation of transportation to economic society.

We strike the key-note of this matter when we say that the study of economic transportation is equivalent to the study of economy in its place relations. Transportation is a mechanism for moving things and persons from one place to another, and so far as economic phenomena are related to this movement they are related to transpor-

From "The Theory of Transportation," in *Sociological Theory and Social Research: Selected Papers of Charles Horton Cooley,* ed. Robert Cooley Angell (New York: Kelley, 1969), 62–75. First published in *Publications of the American Economic Association* 9, no. 3 (May 1894).

tation. Whatever is connected with territorial conditions, with the surface of the earth considered as an area, is connected with transportation, which is a mechanism conformed to these conditions.

The whole matter, then, of the distribution of population, wealth and industries over the face of the earth is in one of its aspects a matter of transportation. We have before us such great questions as that of the territorial division of labor, general and local, the concentration of population in cities, the location of cities, and the relation of territorial conditions to prices, markets, competition and other phases of economic exchange. These are, to be sure, questions of transportation in only one of their many aspects; but that one is important, perhaps as important as any.

The best plan of procedure in discussing these questions will be to begin with their simpler, more physical or mechanical, aspects, and then go on to those that are more complex or symbolic. Commencing, then, with the segregation of population as a merely physical matter, we shall pass first to some discussion of the territorial division of labor and of the theory of cities, and then to the relation of transportation to a complex system of commercial exchange.

Without transport mankind would necessarily be pretty uniformly distributed over the surface of the arable earth, the main irregularities being those due to differences in the fertility of the soil. The earth is the only primary source of food, and man must stay where the food is produced unless he can have it brought to him. The existence of the smallest village involves the movement of commodities to and from it, the beginnings of social transportation. Side by side with this general fact we have the fact, equally general, that development is dependent upon differentiation, upon the breaking up of uniformity and the redistribution into a complex and interdependent system of centers of mass and force. Or, to be more specific, any efficient organization of industry is quite inconceivable without the concentration of men and other industrial forces in cities and other foci of industrial activity. Economy of force and concentration are inseparable. All kinds of industry except agriculture are distinctly and directly centralizing in their tendency. Nor is agriculture a real exception, since efficient agriculture means specialized agriculture, and specialization implies centers of collection and distribution.

Apparently this tendency to industrial concentration must continue to be an accompaniment of industrial progress. It is sometimes said in a speculative way that the present industrial concentration is the concentration incident to the generation of power from coal through steam, and that if electricity, for example, should accomplish the economical distribution of power from a central plant over wide areas, industrial concentration would diminish. As to this it may be said that, even though power could be distributed indefinitely without loss, this distribution could by no means produce the effect suggested. The division of power is the simplest of many questions of division that must first be solved. How divide expensive machinery, such as steam-hammers, rolling mills and the like? Production is daily becoming more dependent upon complicated and costly pieces of machinery to multiply which would be quite out of the question. If this problem could conceivably be solved there would still arise the more difficult one of the division of the social machinery of collection, distribution and economic exchange that must ever accompany complex industry.

The point here is, of course, that transportation is the instrument of all social specialization in place. Just in the degree that transportation is mechanically efficient can this segregation of men and things in accordance with various laws of economic progress, take place.

It is also true, however, that since the aim of transportation is to set men free in respect to place relations, to make these relations more plastic to social needs, it can mitigate or do away with those aspects of concentration that are socially undesirable. The extreme concentration of population at centers, has, for example, deplorable effects upon the health, intelligence and morals of persons who have to live in such places. Transportation having rendered extreme concentration possible now turns around and by means of street railways and other forms of urban travel endeavors to mitigate its evils. Humanity demands that men have sunlight, fresh air, grass and trees. It demands these things for the man himself and still more earnestly for his wife and children. On the other hand, industrial conditions require concentration. It is the office of urban transportation to reconcile these conflicting requirements; in so far as it is efficient it enables men to work in aggregates and yet to live in decent isolation. The greater its efficiency in speed, cheapness and convenience, the greater the area over which a given industrial population may be spread.

The development of transportation and of the territorial division of labor must ever proceed side by side. Neither can be said to go before the other, since they are mutually dependent. The only source of local or international trade in ancient or modern times is international or local specialization in production—something is produced in one place which is lacking in another. In the presence of an active demand for these distant commodities they tend to move from the place where they are produced to the place requiring them; transportation is set up. On the other hand, the transportation resulting from these forces is by no means a mere passive effect but becomes in turn a very active cause of counterchanges. It enormously stimulates and greatly modifies that specialization to which it owes its origin. Under the spur of transportation existing differences in production are increased and new ones are introduced that could not well have been maintained previously. Amid the complication of causes and effects, of reiterated interaction, from which economic life as a whole results, transportation, determined in great measure by permanent natural conditions, has its firm position as one of the fundamental and comparatively independent causes. There is no first cause: this one is as early as any.

On account of its peculiar relation to place-specialization in industry transportation increases more rapidly than production. As the efficiency of productive processes is multiplied by the division of labor, the bulk of goods carried is increased not only proportionately but far more than proportionately. A greater share of the whole product must be conveyed from one place to another. Thus in a somewhat simple state of society, where half of what is consumed is produced at home, the other half only will require transportation. If owing to greater territorial division of labor nine-tenths of what is consumed comes from abroad, transportation must increase in the same ratio, independently of that general increase of production which goes on, of course, at the same time. Conveyance, then, is an industry that must ever grow much more rapidly than industries in general. One puts the matter forcibly if not accurately when he says that transportation increases as the square of production.

For the closer study of the relation of conveyance to the territorial division of labor we must turn to the latter and observe that there are two underlying reasons for it. Place-specialization in industry is necessary, first, because of the economy inherent in the principle of the division of labor; second, because of the existence of local facilities for production. These causes, though everywhere in operation—sometimes in harmony, sometimes at variance—are in theory quite distinct. If the surface of the earth could be conceived as perfectly uniform, offering nowhere peculiar natural encouragement to the development of particular kinds of production, men would yet find their advantage in local specialization because specialization saves force. On the other hand, even though there were no economy in the territorial division of labor as such, yet the face of the earth being diversified as it is, territorial division would result from that diversity. Even in the first case men would aggregate in towns, cities and factories; even in the second they would produce wheat in one place, cattle in another and metals in a third. It will be worth while to divide these two principles in thought and to glance at their separate operation.

First, then, is place-specialization in industry regarded simply as an economic distribution of force and without reference to differing natural facilities.

I have already remarked, in a general way, that transportation, in the absence of marked diversity in the earth's surface, tends to take on a complex radial form, the primary roads converging to central points which are themselves connected by secondary roads with other and more important centers. In its operation this tendency is closely associated with the principle of local division of labor, and the two acting together bring about that primary separation into town and country everywhere observed. The tendency of society to divide into town and country comes from the economy of division of labor; the size and location of towns is determined largely by transportation. The blacksmith, the miller, the carpenter, etc., are required in every agricultural community; convenience of access to them and other craftsmen calls for the formation of a village at a point easily reached by converging roads. The question whether this division and concentration of labor shall be carried so far as the building of large towns depends upon the facilities of movement to and from the center.

If those facilities permit we have, situated near the center of a group of country villages, a large town connected with them by converging highways. The country villages themselves, instead of being simply centers where the farmers and craftsmen meet and exchange products, now become the starting point and end of longer movements between the villages and the town. They become centers of collection for such commodities as are produced in the neighborhood and of distribution for such as are brought in from abroad. The division of labor in them is increased by the addition of a class that occupies itself with buying, selling and storing the goods that go abroad or come thence. The formation of the large town is due to precisely the same forces as the formation of the village; the higher division of labor requires factories and other forms of concentrated production which call together a large population and must be located with reference to the conditions of transportation. And these large towns are again connected with great cities whose existence is due to the same general causes.

In the larger town we see another sort of local division of labor introduced in the specialization of the various parts of the city. The separation between city and suburbs, between the portions assigned to residence and to business, is an example. It is this that chiefly determines the character of local passenger movement by street and elevated

railways and other forms of rapid transit. Here also we see at work
the general principle that the degree of specialization is determined by
the efficiency of transportation. Only as the machinery of this local
movement is developed can we have that separation between the place
of living and the place of working that permits certain parts of cities
to be devoted wholly to industry. The speed of street-cars determines
the distance from his work at which a man can conveniently live. Another form of place-specialization in cities is the setting apart of different quarters for different industries. This existed in mediæval cities,
and is quite marked in modern ones.[1] The wholesale and retail quarters
are commonly quite distinct, while the chief establishments in each line
of industry may be found grouped together. Only restaurants, retail
provision and drug shops, and other places where small and frequent
purchases must be made, are without this segregation.

The larger the city the greater the part played in it by those industries that are concerned with movement. At an important center we
have radial movements in and out—centrifugal and centripetal—of a
very complex character. There is, to begin with, the local or primary
movement of commodities to and from the country in the immediate
vicinity. This is of the same sort as that about a country village and
is effected chiefly by the teams and wagons of the farmers, gardeners,
etc. Next is the other local movement peculiar to the large centers of
population and exchange. To accomplish this we have for commodities a countless multitude of trucks, wagons, etc.; for persons, hacks,
omnibuses, street, elevated and underground railways of all sorts, bicy-
cles and the like. Even the movement up and down becomes here so
important that we cannot well omit freight and passenger elevators
from the list of means of transportation. All of these devices, of course,
have their numerous *personnel* and their important and costly mechanism—tracks, overhead and underground structures, wires, cables,
power-plants and barns. Together they make, as any one may see, an
industry that takes up a great part of the labor and wealth of the city.

Not only the local movement but the longer movement connecting
the city with other towns and cities, requires its own complex machinery. The terminal structures of railroads for the accommodation of
passengers and freight, offices, storage-warehouses, hotels, grain elevators, docks and the like, are an important and conspicuous part of city
structure on the material side and the people connected with them are
equally important on the personal side. All industries concerned with

1. In the middle ages this segregation appears often if not usually to have been compulsory. See Ashley, *English Economic History,* ii, p. 19.

the collection of commodities and persons in the city for shipment away from it, in the distribution of commodities and persons coming in from without, or in the transfer and storage of what is passing through the city, are a part of the machinery of this secondary or dis-·tant movement. Nor should it be forgotten that the whole mechanism of commercial exchange,—wholesale and retail shops and stores, banks and other instruments of trade,—is in one sense a part of the means for the movement of commodities and persons. The relation of transportation to exchange will presently be examined more closely.

All those forms of place-specialization that have been described can be conceived to exist in a country without natural diversity of surface. They would grow up out of the economy resulting from the division of labor even were they not, as in fact, stimulated and modified by a difference in the natural capabilities of places. As a matter of fact they do take place in regions where there is almost no perceptible diversity in natural conditions. This is the case over wide areas in certain of the western states of this country, where the land is flat and of uniform fertility, the rivers too small to be navigable, and irrigation unnecessary. The railroad alone enters to disturb the prevailing homogeneity. A considerable town grows up at a central point whose position is often determined by the accidental circumstance that it is near the center of a county and therefore chosen for the county seat. This slight advantage gives it a start, and population and industry accumulate around it simply because economic progress requires industrial centers. About such centers the roads exhibit much of that radial arrangement[2] which transportation naturally takes on in the absence of diverse physical conditions.

More commonly, however, transportation and place-specialization in industry are closely associated with and determined by differences in the character of the earth's surface. For the purposes of the present inquiry we may think of all these natural differences as of two sorts: first, fixed local facilities for production, such as coal, iron and other mines, water power, fisheries, peculiar qualities of soil, etc.; second, natural facilities for transportation. Differences of the first sort are precedent to and independent of transportation, but affect it indirectly by influencing production. Those of the second sort are not only the chief factors in determining transportation but in doing so they create facilities for production. These propositions will be more fully elabo-

2. But not so much as would be advantageous. Compare Professor Jenks's monograph on "Road Legislation for the American State," p. 49 *et seq.* [in *Publications of the American Economic Association,* vol. iv.]. The allotment of land by sections interferes with the natural arrangement.

rated as we proceed. The point here made is that the economic distribution of persons and goods over the surface of any country is ultimately determined by natural conditions falling under these two classes.

In hilly regions a point convenient for getting water power from a stream very commonly fixes a mill site about which a village grows up. Here is a simple example of a natural facility for production making the nucleus about which population clusters under the operation of the principle of local division of labor. This simple example may be looked upon as the prototype of a large class of mining and manufacturing towns and cities. The existence of mines builds up towns and cities in regions otherwise wholly uninhabitable, and manufactures of a coarser sort, such as lumber mills, blast furnaces, etc., must commonly be placed near the source of raw material, as in the case of sawmills, or of fuel, as in the case of the iron industries.

These local facilities cannot be utilized without transportation, and they supply one of the chief spurs to its progress. From this point of view the efficiency of transportation is measured by the degree in which it enables natural resources to be exploited. The more perfect is transportation the more exclusively can people everywhere devote themselves to those pursuits for which their dwelling-place is suited. The territorial division of labor takes place and industry becomes interdependent and organic. How but for this could a large population in the southwest devote themselves exclusively to the raising of cattle, another large population in the northwest to growing wheat, another in Pennsylvania to the iron manufacture, and so on? To make only one thing means that nearly all the product must be sent abroad and most needs supplied from thence. We see in the condition of agriculture in many parts of the United States what a hindrance imperfect transportation is to economic development. The secondary or long distance transportation, the railroad, has outstripped the means of the local or primary movement, the country road. The last remains for the most part in a miserable condition, offering an insuperable obstacle to the bringing of agricultural products from any great distance and confining profitable farming to the strip of land nearest the railroad.

So in turn the existence of local facilities for production stimulates transportation. It was the movement of coal that caused the construction of tramways in England, that suggested and stimulated the inventions of Stephenson,[3] that furnished an early motive for the building of

3. Smiles, *Life of Stephenson.*

railways in the United States.[4] In general, mines, which are commonly situated among mountains, have been of the first importance in the development of land transportation. They have forced it out of its easier channels and compelled it to surmount the most formidable obstacles.

In attempting comparison between different countries and different times with reference to the development of industrial specialization, we find the question greatly modified and complicated by differences in the state of the industrial arts and in the industrial character of the people. We may, however, abstract some general principles concerning the relation between the development of transportation and that of the territorial division of labor. Thus, from the point of view of the utilization of natural forces, the local division of labor may be said to develop, under the influence of transportation, in three chief ways.

1. From a natural or primary specialization, that is, one so necessitated by natural conditions that it exists before the interchange of products, to a social or secondary specialization, that is, one that could not exist without interchange.

2. From a specialization upon light and costly commodities, that is, those comprising great value in small bulk, to one upon those that are heavier and cheaper.

3. From a specialization confined to durable commodities to one that includes also perishable commodities.

It is clear that these changes in production are the reflection of changes in transportation and are inseparable from the latter. The interchange of bulky and perishable commodities means quicker and cheaper movement.

That there is a natural specialization of products before trade arises is easily seen. Nature supplies gold, spices, furs and other things of great value which are unattainable in some places, and in others to be had almost without labor. Savage tribes produce what they can produce easiest. In the tropics they live upon cocoa-nuts, elsewhere upon game or milk. The earliest trade is simply an interchange of these familiar products, and production is at first stimulated without being changed in character. Thus Heeren[5] classifies the commodities of the primitive land commerce of the east as follows:

I. Precious metals and gems: gold, silver, precious stones, pearls, etc.

---

4. Ringwalt, *Transportation Systems in the United States*, p. 68 *et seq.*
5. *Researches, Asiatic Nations*, I, p. 40 *et seq.*

II. Articles of clothing: fine wool and cotton and their manufactures, silks, furs.

III. Spices, aromatic woods and gums.

Most of these things are obviously primary natural products. They are also such as comprise great value in small bulk and are not perishable through simple lapse of time. Modern commerce is widely different in all these respects. Only a minute portion of its commodities are at once natural, costly and durable. The great bulk of it consists of relatively cheap things: grain, iron and its manufactures, coal, cattle and meat, cheap cloths. Again, though it is still largely concerned with raw materials, the products of mines and of agriculture, these are seldom the obvious and indigenous products of a primitive industry. And, lastly, a large and increasing proportion of what is exchanged is perishable, as dressed meat, fruit and the like.

It seems only necessary to state these principles in order to secure their acceptance. How little, for example, of that specialization now existing among the pursuits of the people of the United States could have been maintained under a system of transportation like that caravan movement which sufficed for the splendid commerce of the primitive east. Ours could have none of that splendor. We have gold, to be sure, on one border of our land, but silks, gems, spices, unguents and the like are almost entirely lacking. Our heavy though useful products could not be moved at all; each neighborhood would have to produce what it consumed; agricultural tools could not be had, the men of the plains would have to live in *adobe* huts, food would everywhere be limited to a few indigenous products, great cities would be out of the question; in a word, the American continent could support nothing but a squalid, ignorant and hopeless peasantry.

Of the two sorts of diversity in natural conditions alleged a few pages back as chiefly determining the territorial distribution of population and wealth, namely, natural facilities for production and natural facilities for transportation, I have so far confined myself as closely as possible to the former. I have considered mines, water power, fertility of soil and the like, as fundamental causes in determining the growth and location of industries and of population, stimulating movement and in great part determining its character. Passing now to natural facilities for transportation we note, in the first place, that it is in many if not most cases these, and not facilities of the former class, that determine the location of manufacturing industries and of the population associated with them. Convenience of transportation becomes itself, in all advanced conditions of industry, the most important of local facilities for production. While it is true that the cruder manufacturing processes, such as the sawing of lumber, the smelting of ore and the coarser iron industries, must take place near the source of raw material; those of a finer sort, in which the cost of moving the raw materials is relatively less important, tend to seek the large centers of the collection, distribution and exchange of products. The vicinity of cities, wherever these may be located, will always be the chief seat of the finer manufactures on account of the conveniences that cities offer for selling and shipping goods.

Before going farther it will be well, for the sake of clearness, to indicate in a general way the character of the relation between the conveyance of goods and commercial exchange. I have just pointed out the connection of transportation with one part of the economic process, namely, agricultural and manufacturing industry; if I can now show its connection with the exchange of goods I shall have isolated it, as far as possible, from those inquiries with which it is most closely associated, and shall be in a position to formulate a theory of its own peculiar action in determining the local distribution of population and goods.

What, speaking generally, is the relation that transportation bears to the rest of those activities known as trade or commerce? Commerce is commonly understood to embrace transportation and exchange (purchase and sale), with incidental regard to the underlying conditions of production and consumption. Of these, transportation grows out of territorial conditions, purchase and sale out of the institution of property. As the need for the division of labor, conditioned by territorial relations, finds its solution in transportation, so the same need, conditioned by the institution of property, works itself out in exchange. The movement of goods cannot be organized without changes in their ownership any more than without means of transportation. The one is physical, the other symbolic.

Since, then, the two are so intimately bound together, how, it may be asked, is it possible to dissociate them, and what is gained by such dissociation? The reply is that all social processes are intimately bound up with others, and isolation of one can only be partial and provisional. This provisional isolation, however, is indispensable to analysis. In this case, by separating transportation from commerce and fixing attention upon territorial relations, we eliminate most of those numerous and complicated phenomena that make up exchange, and get a comparatively limited field that offers interesting questions peculiarly its own. These questions are chiefly those arising from a study of the economic process from the point of view of location. In the theory of the location of towns and cities, a question at which we are now arrived, exchange plays a subordinate part and may be regarded simply as the symbolic aspect of transportation. As far as place relations are concerned, transportation determines exchange and not *vice versa*.

Darwinism

5

The Process of Social Change

The phrases "natural selection," "the survival of the fittest" and "the struggle for existence," with others that come from the *Origin of Species* and the *Synthetic Philosophy,* are now applied to social phenomena and circulate very generally as descriptions of what goes on among mankind. Some people would question, however, whether they do not, as is alleged of our silver dollars, pass rather on the credit of their authors than on the value of any definite ideas commonly associated with them.

In the use of such phrases there does, indeed, appear to be a great deal of vagueness; and it is one object of this paper to do something toward clearing it up—to find out, if possible, whether these dubious tokens are in any way exchangeable for standard coin of the realm of thought and fact. With this end in view I purpose first to inquire how far natural selection of the primary, animal sort taught by Darwin is a process of social change; and then, if it appears that there is another process, I shall go on to consider its nature and operation. The inquiry falls conveniently into three divisions:

  I. Natural selection as a process of social change.
  II. Social change, proper.
  III. The influence of communication upon social change.

I

So far as concerns the different race elements in the population of the earth, the Darwinian idea of change by survival—the idea that what exists does so because it has prevailed at some time or other in a struggle for existence—is not at all a speculation, but the most verifiable thing in the world. There may be doubt about other species, but in the case of *homo* the process has gone on in the light of history and continues in full vigor at the present time. It would be difficult to find any large region where one race, nation or tribe is not increasing in

From "The Process of Social Change," *Political Science Quarterly* 7, no. 1 (March 1897): 63–81.

numbers at the expense of the diminution of some other. Mr. Galton finds that "there are probably hardly any spots on the earth that have not, within the last few thousand years, been tenanted by very different races";[1] and "that on the average at least three different races are to be found in every moderately sized district on the earth's surface." His impression of the races in South Africa "was one of a continual state of ferment and change, of the rapid development of some clan here and of the complete or almost complete suppression of another clan there." We are ourselves a part of this process. We are in the midst of a rapid and complicated movement of which the general direction is sufficiently clear, though the details are concealed. The European races are almost everywhere on the increase: within the present century they have nearly trebled in number, and with the Teutonic peoples in the lead, and the English at the head of these, have spread and multiplied over a great part of the earth.[2] In the United States we have seen the Indian go and the negro stay; while in our cities and our newer farming regions there is active competition among recent immigrants from all the European stocks, and between these and the descendants of immigrants of earlier date.

If the student turns, however, from the competition of races to inquire what is going on within any particular race, he does not find it so easy to learn what natural selection is doing: indeed, it is not easy to show that it is making any change that is of moment. Suppose, for example, that he were to inquire what alterations, aside from those due to intermixture with other races, the English stock has undergone within historic time. To understand the nature of this question one must remember that great changes may come to pass in the institutions, manners, morals, and even in the outward appearance of a people, which do not necessarily imply that any organic change has taken place in the stock, either through natural selection or otherwise. If an English couple settles in this country, the children will contract from our climate and society peculiarities of appearance and behavior that will mark them as Americans to the eyes of all the world; but these changes have little to do with natural selection, and it is uncertain

1. Galton, *Inquiries into Human Faculty*, p. 310 *et seq.*
2. According to Hübner's *Tables* the population of Europe in 1895 was about 366 millions. In 1801 it was 175 millions. Levasseur calculates the number of Europeans out of Europe to have been 9½ millions in 1800 and 91½ in 1890—*La Population Française*, vol. iii, chap. ix. Professor Brinton states that the white race two centuries ago numbered 100 millions, or about 10 per cent of the population of the earth; while at the present time the European branches alone number 500 millions, or one-third of the population of the earth—see his *Races and Peoples*, p. 298.

whether they can in any degree be transmitted by heredity. So, also, those transformations which make up the rise and fall of nations are chiefly, if not altogether, of the same quality. They take place far too rapidly to be due to natural selection or to any organic change in the race. Decadence seems to be a social deterioration that drags down the individual by subjecting him to unwholesome influences. Thus, there is no evidence that the Chinamen or Spaniards of to-day are congenitally much different from their ancestors in the proudest days of those nations: their degeneracy is apparently of the same character as that observed in the behavior of a group of boys who have fallen into bad ways.[3] It is a decline of tone, of *morale,* of institutions, not of natural capacity.

The decisive illustration of the possible divergence between natural selection and social change is the fact that institutions hostile to survival, like the monastic system, can spread and flourish for centuries in defiance of animal heredity.

The scientific test of organic difference would be to take new-born infants typical of the stocks to be compared and note what unlikenesses they developed when brought up under the same social influences. Rude comparisons of this sort are possible between contemporary peoples, but they are, of course, impracticable between different periods in the history of the same race. In the case of the Jews the matter has been studied as thoroughly as the nature of the inquiry permits, and it is thought doubtful whether that race has undergone any noteworthy change since the time of Moses.[4] As regards our own and kindred peoples—always leaving aside the mixture of races—I imagine that few anthropologists would venture to say anything positive. If they did, it is quite certain that there would be no agreement among them as to what the direction of change is. Many suppose, for example, that physical vigor is declining by disuse, by the growing preponderance of intellect as a factor in success, by the preservation

3. "The Spanish-American of pure white blood, whose ancestors have lived for three centuries in tropical America, the citizen of the United States who traces his genealogy to the passengers in the *Mayflower* or the *Welcome,* have departed extremely little from the standard of the Andalusian or the Englishman of to-day though the contrary is often asserted by those who have not personally studied the variants in the countries compared. Conditions of climate and food materially impress the individual, but not the race. The Greeks of Nubia are as dark as Nubians, but let their children return to Greece and the Nubian hue is lost. This is a general truth and holds good of all the slight impressions made upon pure races by unaccustomed environments."—Brinton, *Races and Peoples,* pp. 44, 45.

4. See papers by Neubauer and Jacobs in vol. xv of the *Journal of the Anthropological Institute.*

of weakly children and by the support through charity of pauperism and vice.[5] There is, however, no direct proof of a decline; and it is quite possible that the forces mentioned are more than counterbalanced by others which may be held to have an opposite tendency, such as better and more regular nourishment, the more general practice of systematic exercise, congenial marriages and the improvement of a great variety of degrading social conditions. Either side of this argument may be maintained by plausible *a priori* arguments, and in the present insufficiency of direct evidence there is no way to reach a definite conclusion.

It is even possible to question whether the thinking faculties are now stronger than they used to be. There has certainly been a great deal of mental work of various kinds among the Teutonic peoples since the revival of learning; but even if we suppose that the effect of such exercise can be inherited, we have still to consider that only a small fraction of the race has taken part in it. Moreover, when we see that the men who lead in letters, science and statesmanship often spring from a peasant class whose forefathers have not shared appreciably in the intellectual activities of the past, it is clear that ancestral culture is not essential in producing eminence of this sort. It is significant, too, that one of the most noteworthy intellectual influences now at work comes from the Russians, a people new to civilization. In short, if we could transplant a few thousand babies out of our remote ancestry and give them modern nurture and training, they might, for aught we know, turn out their share of Congressmen, novelists and electrical engineers, and be little distinguishable in any way from the rest of the population. The statue called "The Dying Gladiator" represents a possible ancestor of more than two thousand years ago; yet he appears to me quite modern and familiar—a little wild perhaps, as we might expect from his mode of life, but otherwise such a man as we might come across almost anywhere at the present time.

Natural selection, apart from the conflict of races, is apparently much more active in preserving than in changing types, for it discourages wide deviation in any direction. Out-and-out criminals and those sunk in self-destructive vices are not, as a class, prolific; but no more are the people of conspicuous intellectual or moral power. It is the intermediate and undistinguished multitude that keeps up the population.

Some entertain the notion that the most degraded classes are the most prolific; but I know of no support for this. Among the conditions

5. For an admirable discussion of the influence of charity upon survival, see Warner, *American Charities,* chap. v.

of a rapid natural increase are physical vigor and a fairly stable family life. In both of these respects the pauper and criminal classes are decidedly inferior to the rest of the population. On the other hand, many suppose that success and survival go together—that what we call competition is only a more or less mitigated form of the struggle for existence; and that as a rule and in the long run those who gain wealth, power, and other things for which men strive, are enabled to leave more children than others and so to perpetuate those characteristics to which they owe their success. It is often assumed that this is too clearly the case to require special investigation; but this assumption will appear rash to any one at all familiar with statistics, and seems to have arisen, not from the direct study of mankind, but by a hasty inference from the results of biology. Men of unusual success are not unusually prolific: so far as can be made out from statistics they are as a class below the average in this respect. Indeed, a very plausible argument, backed by figures *ad libitum*, might be prepared to show that the successful do not survive and are therefore the unfit. Certainly nature's standard of success—that is, survival—is quite distinct from the social standard; and to a great degree the two are opposed. To marry early and raise a large family is by no means favorable to the gratification of personal ambition. It seems, therefore, that conspicuous failure and conspicuous success are about equally unfavorable to survival, and that those paths which diverge very widely from the main-traveled road of ordinary humanity lead to extinction.

This conservatism in the conditions of survival is well illustrated by the case of educated women. They seem to be, on the whole, a very beneficent class of persons, and one whose progressive spirit it would be well to transmit in every possible manner; yet we cannot expect that the women who belong to it will leave as many children as those whose entire energy goes into reproduction. In fact, a large part of college women do not marry at all; and the remainder are likely to marry later and to have children at less frequent intervals than other women.[6]

It is, accordingly, not at all clear that natural selection, aside from the prevalence of races, acts definitely or rapidly as a cause of social change. No doubt the races of men, and especially those whose history is eventful, undergo more or less organic transformation: this must have been so in the past, since otherwise new types could not have

6. See the Report of the Massachusetts Labor Bureau for 1885 on "The Health Statistics of Female College Graduates"; also "The Marriage Rate of College Women," *Century*, October 1895.

originated; and it is not likely that the process has altogether ceased. This transformation, however, is probably slow, and its character and direction are difficult to make out: the whole matter, involving as it does the laws of heredity, requires and will no doubt receive the most thorough study. In the meantime, it is apparent that natural selection of this simple, animal sort is not the ordinary process of social change. It has little to do with the rise, spread and decay of architecture, music, painting or poetry, or of the great religious systems; it is not the process by which governments become milder, popular education advances and manners meliorate; nor is it that by which new views prevail about childhood and the status of women.

II

The process which generates opinions, moral standards and institutions, and which results in progress or decadence, is especially characteristic of human life, though it is thought to be operative in some measure among all the social animals. It rests upon the imitative, sympathetic and intellectual faculties, and is related to natural selection through the probability that these faculties have an evolutionary history in which natural selection plays a part.

It would not be difficult to show that the higher faculties of man are not, as some suppose, elements quite apart from and inconsistent with the struggle for existence, but are decisive factors in it while it endures, though tending to supplant it by rational and sympathetic coöperation. Imitation and sympathy, as well as intellect, are conditions of social power; and the evidence that they have arisen by the aid of natural selection is similar to, though much less tangible than, that which indicates that our bodily frame has thus arisen. It is not, however, important that I should discuss this question: it is sufficient to note the fact that our ascendency over the other creatures is associated with a flexibility of nature that comes from imitation and sympathy, and makes us apt for social change.

A man is not so much strong in himself as formed to make part of a strong whole. If reared from his birth by some wild creature and so cut off from those communicated arts and actions for which alone he is well fitted, he would make a poor struggle for existence, and might have to fall back upon his primitive skill in climbing trees. But in society he is strong; and the chief element of his strength is the fact that he is so far dominated by imitative and sympathetic faculties, that he adapts himself to an infinite variety of activities. He is, on the whole, a docile, conforming animal, and owes his power to his amenability.

The trend of psychological and sociological studies is distinctly toward the conclusion that the social factor in individual conduct is greater than has been perceived.[7] Every thought and every act guided by thought bears some relation to the social environment, past or present, and could not be the same if that were altogether different. A man is born with energies and tendencies, strong but vague, which, being incited and nourished by the world into which he comes, mingle indistinguishably with it to form a new organic whole, a character and a career. Imitativeness, which controls so many of our actions without our knowing it; the fear of disapproval, which leads to conformity, not only in dress and manners, but in the gravest parts of conduct; the hope of approbation, inciting aggressive spirits to perform daring deeds in the sight of mankind; hero-worship, patriotism, sympathy and love—all these give to society control over its members. The passion to be something in the minds and hearts of men is the very life of life, the fire which fuses individual energies into social power. Where our faculties touch this stream of human interest they glow at a white heat, like a piece of ore where it touches the streaming flame of the blowpipe; the rest of us remains cold, inactive and unnoticed.

This need of approval is often called weakness and is contrasted with the supposed strength of self-sufficiency; but in fact no man with any humanity in him is self-sufficient, and the love of approbation is weakness only when it leads to inconstant behavior. It is likely to be strongest in the finest organizations, and can hardly be extirpated: try to get rid of it is to act like a man immersed in water, who should try to thrust the water from him with his hand. The most that men can do—and this is all-important—is to choose their approvers, perhaps substituting remote or even imaginary persons for those at hand, reading great books, observing wise persons, and thus cultivating a sense of heroic opinion. Since all must be hero-worshippers, it is a great thing to have the right sort of hero.

Human nature is hard to change, but its most inveterate quality is a susceptibility to social influences. We need to distinguish sharply between nature and conduct: one is the stable basis for infinite variety in the other. Association may not change nature, but it usually controls conduct. It will hardly make an irascible man patient or a dull one

7. It is hardly necessary to support this statement by references: the studies in "imitation," by Tarde, Baldwin, and others, and Professor Giddings's theory of the "consciousness of kind" are familiar examples of the fact stated. The *Proceedings* of the National Conference of Charities and Corrections for 1896 contains (p. 399) a paper by the present writer on "'Nature versus Nuture' in the Making of Social Careers" which treats briefly one phase of the matter.

clever, but it may easily make one clever man an engineer and another an ingenious burglar. A career never comes by nature alone; the same nature will result in any one of a hundred careers, according to the influences that act upon it. We are bound to our fellows by heredity as to what is relatively permanent, and by influence as to what is plastic: human nature is transmitted by the one, institutions, conduct and opinion by the other.

It is this plasticity which makes each of us not so much strong in himself as fit to make part of a strong whole. Our thinking and feeling are not, like the animal instincts, predetermined to work for a single object, but are unspecialized, working according to principles of general utility toward ends set before us by the society in which we live. We are so happily contrived that humanity can progress without a change in human nature, through the peculiar constitution of the nature we already have. A due measure of conformity is, accordingly, one of the conditions of social progress. The conforming influences are often deplored, as by Emerson, where he says that "society is in a conspiracy against the independence of each of its members," and that "to be a man is to be a non-conformist." This is true, in a way, and helpful; but it is also true that conformity is a social discipline from which no one can or ought to be entirely free. It levels up as well as down, prevents crime and anarchy as well as hinders genius, and knits men together into a strong yet tractable whole. A party of explorers who are on a difficult march must keep together, even if they cannot agree upon the best route; and most men are necessarily so constituted that they have no inclination to leave the ranks.

Human evolution, then, like animal evolution, rests primarily upon power; but power rests upon coöperation, and coöperation involves social discipline and individual amenability. Mankind is strong through good understanding, through the timely abnegation of strife, through institutions that symbolize and confirm social unity—above all through a human nature that is not only intellectual but imitative, conforming, sympathetic and capable of congregate enthusiasms.

This imitative and sympathetic human nature, which is a means to social power, implies the process of social change. Working and worked upon through the marvelous mechanism of language, it is capable of fusing men together into a fluid whole, every part of which in some way feels and responds to the motion of every other part. In this fluid are propagated an infinite number of movements of thought and action, among which—by the law of chances, if for no better reason,—opportune variations from time to time occur. Their opportuneness being in some measure perceived, these innovations tend to be preserved and accumulated, rooting themselves in tradition and tendency, and getting themselves set forth to the mind and eye in laws, creeds and architecture. It is of such movements that historical change chiefly consists. The process is one of survival, in which the conscious selection of men is an important factor; but the consciousness is mostly limited to the immediate detail. It is only recently that the general trend of social movements is beginning to be in some degree a matter of knowledge and of choice. In describing the process of social change it is suggestive to liken it to a wave or a combination of waves; but, as commonly happens in attempting to set forth social facts as analogous to physical phenomena, this figure falls hopelessly short of the truth. A reasonably clear perception of the matter can come only by a study of the process of communication—a study which is the key to the translation of the facts of social change from the language of psychology to that of history. The two things that must always coöperate are human nature and the mechanism of communication. The first is a relatively permanent factor; but the second is highly variable, and is for that reason of peculiar interest and importance. Its variations have generally been in the direction of greater efficiency, and it is largely because of this fact that the history of the past two thousand years is a record of rapid and accelerating social change.

III

We know that man is a sympathetic, communicating animal; and I have urged that this is what makes him amenable, plastic, fit to be formed by a social environment. But what forms the environment? The evolution of environment is the most momentous change in history.

A man's social environment embraces all persons with whom he has intelligence or sympathy, all influences that reach him. If I read Aristotle, my environment extends back two thousand years; if I read the dispatches from Japan, it takes in the antipodes. That I can be influenced by the *Iliad*, the New Testament and other utterances of men distant from me in time and place, is due to the arts of writing, printing and transportation, just as the fact that I can receive a complex thought from my neighbor is due to the art of speech. In other words, the social influences act through a mechanism; and the character of their action depends upon the character of the mechanism. The existing system of communication determines the reach of the environment. Society is a matter of the incidence of men upon one another; and since this incidence is a matter of communication, the history of the latter is the foundation of all history. It is perhaps worth while to recall some of the more obvious facts of this history, and to make some suggestions as to what they mean.

The mechanism of communication includes, of course, gesture, speech, writing, printing, mails, telephones, telegraphs, photography, the technique of the arts and sciences—all the ways through which thought and feeling can pass from man to man.

Speech no doubt knit prehistoric men into groups and enabled them to emerge into history with a social nature and social institutions. But as an instrument of social organization speech has great defects; it lacks range in both time and place. It can go only where the man goes; and though it can pass from man to man, and so from generation to generation, it flows in a slender and wandering stream, limited in capacity, and diverted in direction by every mind through which it passes. What would the New Testament or the works of Plato now be if they had come down to us by this route?

For the precarious strand of oral tradition writing substitutes strong bonds, numerous and indestructible, reaching all times and countries where the art is practiced and binding history firmly together. It makes possible wide political sway, which cannot well be organized and maintained without recorded laws and precise instructions;[8] it permits the advance of science, which is a cumulative achievement that implies the hoarding of knowledge in dusty manuscripts; it is the condition of a diversified literature, for tradition, which cannot carry much, limits itself to what is most prized, chiefly stories: writing, in short, may without much exaggeration be said to underlie all social enlargement and individual specialization. It extends immeasurably the environment of all persons who can read and can get hold of the manuscripts; and it permits one to form his own environment by retaining what suits him from a variety of materials, and by opening communication with congenial minds in remote times and places. In so doing each individual, of course, becomes a center for the distribution of what he receives, and extends the environment of many others. Mankind thus attains coöperation, continuity and the capacity for rational and enduring progress.

The particular function of printing is to make communication general or democratic. So long as handwriting was the only means of record, books were costly, newspapers were not to be thought of and direct access to the stores of thought and feeling was the privilege of

---

8. I believe there is no instance of a people which has attained a definite, extended and stable political organization without the use of some form of writing. Compare Gibbon's observations in the *Decline and Fall,* vol. I, p. 354 (Milman-Smith edition).

a few. Under such conditions opportunity was like the early sun: it lit up a hilltop here and there, but left the plain in shadow. Printing, to put it otherwise, may not make the stream of knowledge deeper or improve the taste of the water, but it does open a path along the margin and give every one a cup from which to drink. With popular education, which is its natural complement, it forms the principal free institution, without which no other sort of freedom could long endure, and by the aid of which we may hope to gain more freedom than we have.

It is well worth while to reflect what these changes mean to the individual man, born with the aptitude for indefinite development through an imitative and sympathetic nature. Consider, for instance, a group of our ancestors of several thousand years ago, comparatively small, without the art of writing and with little knowledge of other groups. Primitive life is a field fertile in controversy and one not likely to be exhausted; but most students will admit the probability that our distant forefathers lived in small societies, were unlettered and had the vaguest notions about the rest of mankind. Such groups carried on with one another a true struggle for existence; but within each of them—that is, within the range of possible good understanding—there was an active social life. Mothers loved their children and men fought for their chiefs; the thoughts and acts of all were bound together by imitation, the need of approbation and the communicative motives in general. In this social medium were propagated such movements of change as its dimensions permitted. But think of the narrowness of those dimensions, of the paucity of models for imitation, of the extreme vagueness of knowledge regarding the great men of the past and of the total ignorance regarding those of other societies! A meagre environment limited the development of innate tendencies and capacities, and the comparative sameness of thought and action reflected the narrowness of the general life.

In such a state of things all the wider social relations must be either hostile or authoritative. Since communication is the precise measure of the possibility of social organization, of good understanding among men, relations that are beyond its range are not truly social, but mechanical. In justice to the past we must recognize that before the rise of printing and telegraphy it was impossible for the mass of people in any large state to have a free and conscious relation to the social whole. The basis for a social consciousness did not exist. People in general could not comprehend what was going on, and their actions were necessarily regulated by authority. The peasant, the common soldier, could not coöperate in the larger social movements except as a truck horse coöperates in movements of trade.

If two persons who cannot understand each other come in contact, three things are possible: they can separate, they can fight or one can enslave the other. In the same way, the social groups of the ancient world could ignore one another, wage war or be bound by coercion into a mechanical whole. As the first was usually impracticable, and as mechanical union proved stronger than none, it was the third course that commonly prevailed. This was especially the case after communication was advanced to such a point that the organization of extensive military despotisms became practicable. In antiquity a large free state could not be formed, and a small one could not maintain itself.

If we put together these things, this poverty of influences and this habit of war that could be replaced only by something in the way of servitude, we have gone far in explaining the known differences between our remote forefathers and ourselves. They may have been very unlike us, but it is not necessary to suppose that they were, in order to explain their leading unlike lives.

To the man of to-day society, tending now to become a coöperating whole through that extension of knowledge and sympathy which has come with the rise of communication, offers a selection among many environments. In the relation between himself and the rest of mankind he takes more and more an active part, accumulating the elements of a characteristic environment by the working of elective affinity. One may be an imitator—as indeed all must be—and yet unfold, through imitation, a character different from that of every one else. The breadth and diversity of life, dependent upon communication and daily widening before our eyes, tends, in short, to set man free by opening to his sympathetic and conforming nature a "proud choice of influences." He is not merely, as in primitive times, a member of a social group which tends to shape his thought and action; he is the point of intersection of many groups, each of which, though dispersed in time and place, has a real and definite influence upon him. Nowadays one is not less dependent upon social influences than formerly, but he is less dependent upon the particular ones that happen to be nearest him. Every book, every newspaper, every work of sculpture, painting or music to which one has access, every person or place brought within his reach by the facility of travel, is a shop which he may enter to examine the goods and buy if he will. A million environments solicit him; there is eager competition in place of monopoly.

It is upon this multiplicity of accessible influences, and not upon any radical change in human nature, that the present variety and comparative freedom of individual development chiefly rest. If one looks at the circle of his acquaintances he sees nothing of the sameness that prevails among savages; each man has distinctive opinions and modes of action, and so appears to stand by himself. This deceptive appearance is due to the fact that social relations are no longer controlled by mere contiguity. Through the arts of intercourse association is throwing off the gross and oppressive bonds of time and place, and substituting congenial relations of sympathy and choice. So, if a man seems to stand alone, it is mostly because he stands with those who are not visible; if he seems not to keep step with the procession, it is probably because, as Thoreau said, he hears a different drummer. We know little of the influences that formed his early imaginations, or of those persons whose approval he now desires and to whose examples and opinions he tries to conform his actions. They are often far distant—his parents and early friends, perhaps, or the leaders of his profession, or book-people—but the fact remains that character and conduct are nourished upon social influences.

A reading of autobiographies, or a perusal of those private records which people carry in their memories, would show that men are still imitators and hero-worshippers. This is particularly true of children, who spend much of their mental life in imagining scenes wherein by glorious actions they gain the applause of some persons they admire. And of course the modes of thinking and acting that originate in sympathy and admiration tend, like everything else we do, to become habit, and to persist amid circumstances very different from those in which they began, seeming then to come from self-sufficient personality.

The same conditions favor also the more conspicuous forms of individuality—that is, originality and genius. Originality is not something independent of surroundings, but rather a characteristic way of reacting upon them. Let a man be as original as you please, he can unfold and express his originality only through such influences and materials as are accessible, and the number and variety of these are matters of communication. "We are indeed born with faculties," said Goethe, who gave lifelong study to this matter, "but we owe our development to a thousand influences of the great world, from which we appropriate to ourselves what we can and what is suitable to us." In order to have genius it is essential that a remarkable child shall be born into the world; but an outfit of natural faculties, however remarkable, is only one of two sets of factors whose product is a career. A gifted child, like an acorn, has indeed the capacity of marvelous growth, but can come to nothing unless it finds fit nutriment. The idea of a necessary antagonism between individuality and association is an illusion.

The two are mutually dependent: they have always developed, and always must develop, side by side. As a rule, it is not too much association that cramps us, but the wrong kind.

Finally, it is not hard to see how this enlargement of intercourse has affected the processes of social change. Let us go back to the comparison with waves, which, after all, is better than none. As regards the transmission of influences, primitive societies may be likened to narrow strips of water. They extended more in time than in place, but even in the former direction were liable to be cut off by conquest or decay; they were connected with one another by the shallows and marshes of occasional intercourse and by quickly subsiding freshets of federation. Social change was necessarily local, like the waves on such small waters. Modern society, on the other hand, is more like the uninterrupted ocean, upon which the waves of change meet with no obstacles except one another, and roll as high and as far as the propagating impulse can carry them. Thus, to take a conspicuous instance, certain movements in art, letters and philosophy, originating we scarcely know how or where, but attaining great height among the Greeks, rolled on over the unconscious Middle Ages till they struck the contemporaries of Petrarch and thence were propagated in widening circles to the present time. The invention of writing opened the world to the competition of social institutions very much as maritime navigation opened it to the competition of races. The field was enlarged, and all movements proceeded on a great scale.[9]

This extension of the medium of change is accompanied by an equally remarkable differentiation within it, implied in what I have already said about the growth of individuality. There are as many social media as there are specialized groups of sympathetic and communicating individuals, and in choosing his environment a man chooses what groups he will belong to. Each of these groups or media is subject to movements more or less peculiar to itself; it has in some measure its own opinions, institutions and traditions. So, if one wishes to liken modern social movements to waves, he must conceive an indefinite number of wave-transmitting fluids, interpenetrating one another as the light-bearing ether interpenetrates the sound-bearing air; each of these transmitting most readily undulations originating in itself, yet feeling the influence of those originating in the others; each fluid by

9. There is no better illustration of this than the rise of vast religious systems based upon the recorded lives and maxims of their founders. It is quite possible that individuals of transcendent character appeared in prehistoric times; but the imitation of them could not be organized into extensive and enduring systems without the aid of authentic records.

itself, as well as the united whole, traversed continually by a multitude of waves having every imaginable difference in force, period and direction. Even when so stated the comparison is still inadequate in various ways, chiefly in that it does not suggest the active part that may be taken by individuals. It represents what would happen if each one were in equilibrium, with every congenial relation established; when in fact each of us is continually stirring about more or less in search of the congenial—resisting, refracting or augmenting the social impulse in a way peculiar to himself. Yet, so far as men have like natures that come into sympathy through communication, they really form a sort of a fluid in which impulses are propagated by simple suggestion or contact. If two persons of like feeling for form and color stand before a painting, they and the artist are one through the picture.

The freer development of individuals involves, of course, a freer development of the social order; inasmuch as relations of choice— relations that suit the feelings of men—tend to spread and to prevail over those of hostility or coercion. It is the tendency of communication to give human nature a fair chance, levelling before it the barriers of ignorance, blind hostility and constraint of place, and permitting man to organize his higher sympathetic and aesthetic impulses.

Within the past fifty years there have been developed new means of communication,—fast mails, telegraphs, telephones, photography and the marvels of the daily newspaper,—all tending to hasten and diversify the flow of thought and feeling and to multiply the possibilities of social relation. The working of these agencies is too important to be discussed hastily, and to discuss it fully would carry me too far; I shall therefore only point out that they make all influences quicker in transmission and more general in their incidence, accessible at a greater distance and to a larger proportion of the people. So far as concerns the general character of social change, the effect may be described as a more perfect liquefaction of the social medium. A thick, inelastic liquid, like tar or molasses, will transmit only comparatively large waves; but in water the large waves bear upon their surface countless wavelets and ripples of all sizes and directions. So if we were to compare the society of to-day with that of fifty years ago, we should find that great changes are somewhat facilitated, and that there is added to them a multitude of small changes which in former times could not have extended beyond the reach of personal contact. Light ripples now run far: the latest fashion in coats or books permeates the back counties and encircles the earth.

The process of change that I have described involves selection, and is perhaps as natural as anything else. Hence we may, if we choose, call it natural selection. It comes about through the competition of influences and the propagation of opportune innovations in thought and action. The selective principle, the arbiter of competition, is ever human nature—but human nature conditioned in its choices by the state of communication, which determines what influences are accessible, as well as by the constraining momentum of its own past.

II

THE FOUNDATIONS
OF COOLEY'S SOCIOLOGY
AND SOCIAL PSYCHOLOGY

The Plasticity of Human Nature

6

Heredity and Instinct in Human Life

Although the transmission of heredity through the germ-plasm is much the same process in man as in the other animals, there is a notable difference in the kind of traits that are found to exist at birth. This difference is in teachability or plasticity.

The mental outfit of the human child is above all things teachable and therefore, of course, indefinite, consisting not of tendencies to do particular things that life calls for, but of vague aptitudes or lines of teachability that are of no practical use until they are educated. The mental outfit of the animal, on the other hand, is relatively definite and fixed, giving rise to activities which are useful with little or no teaching.

This difference is fundamental to any understanding of the relation of man to the evolutionary process, or of the relation of human nature and human life to animal nature and animal life. We need to see it with all possible clearness and to follow out its implications.

Roughly speaking, then, the heredity of the other animals is a mechanism like that of a hand-organ: it is made to play a few tunes; you can play these tunes at once, with little or no training; and you can never play any others. The heredity of man, on the other hand, is a mechanism more like that of a piano: it is not made to play particular tunes; you can do nothing at all on it without training; but a trained player can draw from it an infinite variety of music.

A newly hatched chick is able to run about and to pick up small objects of a certain size and form which prove to be food, and to sustain its life. It scarcely needs education, and I am told by a breeder that the product of the incubator, having no link with the past of their race except the germ-plasm, gets along as well as those that have all a mother's care.

A baby, on the other hand, takes a year to learn to walk, and many, many more years to learn the activities by which he is eventually to get his living. He has, to be sure, a definite capacity to draw nourishment from his mother, but this is only a makeshift, an animal method

From "Heredity and Instinct in Human Life," *Survey* 49 (January 1923): 454–69.

to help him out until his more human powers have time to develop. In general, his wonderful hereditary capacities are as ineffectual as a piano when the player begins to practise. Definite function is wholly dependent upon education.

Thus the plastic, indeterminate character of human heredity involves a long and helpless infancy; and this, in turn, is the basis of the human family, since the primary and essential function of the family is the care of children. Those species of animals in which the young are adequately prepared for life by definite heredity have no family at all, while those which more or less resemble man as regards plastic heredity, resemble him also in having some rudiments, at least, of a family. Kittens, for instance, are cared for by the mother for several months and profit in some measure by her example and instruction.

More generally, this difference as regards plasticity means that the life-activities of the animal are comparatively uniform and fixed, while those of man are varied and changing. Human functions are so numerous and intricate that no fixed mechanism could provide for them; they are also subject to radical change, not only in the life of the individual but from one generation to another. The only possible hereditary basis for them is an outfit of indeterminate capacities which can be developed and guided by experience as the needs of life require.

I see a flycatcher sitting on a dead branch, where there are no leaves to interrupt his view. Presently he darts toward a passing insect, hovers about him a few seconds, catches him, or fails to do so, and returns to his perch. That is his way of getting a living: he has done it all his life and will go on doing it to the end. Millions of other flycatchers on millions of other dead branches are doing precisely the same. And this has been the life of the species for unknown thousands of years. They have, through the germ-plasm, a definite capacity for this—the keen eye, the swift, fluttering movement to follow the insect, the quick, sure action of the neck and bill to seize him—all effective with no instruction and very little practice.

Man has a natural hunger like the flycatcher and a natural mechanism of tasting, chewing, swallowing and digestion; but his way of getting the food varies widely at different times of his life, is not the same with different individuals and often changes completely from one generation to another. The great majority of us gain our food after we have left the parental nest through what we call a job and a job is any activity whatever that a complex and shifting society esteems sufficiently to pay us for. It is very likely nowadays to last only part of our lives and to be something our ancestors never heard of. Thus whatever is most distinctively human, our adaptability, our power of growth, our arts and sciences, our social institutions and progress, is bound up with the indeterminate character of human heredity.

Of course there is no sharp line in this matter of teachability between man and the other animals. The activities of the latter are not wholly predetermined and in so far as they are not there is a learning process based upon plastic heredity. The higher animals—horses, dogs, elephants for example—are notably teachable and may even participate in the changes of human society, as when dogs learn to draw carts, trail fugitives, guide the lost, or perform in a circus. And, on the other side, those activities of man which do not require much adaptation, such as the breathing, sucking and crying of infants, and even walking (which is learned without instruction when the legs become strong enough), are provided for by definite heredity.

The question of the place of instinct in human life involves the relation between human and animal heredity, and especially that distinction between fixed and plastic reactions to the environment that we have just discussed.

There is no agreement upon the definition of instinct, some confining it to definite modes of hereditary behavior, like the squirrel's burying a nut, others giving it a much wider and vaguer meaning. To inquire how this disagreement arose will throw light upon the whole matter.

Animals, as we have seen, have definite and effective modes of acting which they do not have to learn, and it was these that first attracted attention, by their contrast to human behavior, and were called instinct, as opposed to the more rational or acquired activities of man. Darwin says in his *Origin of Species:*

> I will not attempt any definition of instinct . . . but every one understands what is meant when it is said that instinct impels the cuckoo to migrate and to lay her eggs in other birds' nests. An action, which we ourselves require experience to enable us to perform, when performed by an animal, more especially by a very young one, without experience, and when performed by many individuals in the same way, without their knowing for what purpose it is performed, is usually said to be instinctive. But I could show that none of these characters are universal.

Men have few instinctive actions, in this original sense of the word. But when investigators began to study our behavior from the evolutionary point of view, they saw that if not instinctive in the strict sense it had yet grown out of instinctive behavior, was historically continuous with it, and, in short, that there was no sharp line to be drawn, in this matter, between human and animal. Moreover, although our outward actions had ceased to be determined by heredity, it seemed that we still had inward emotions and dispositions that were so determined and had an immense influence on our conduct. The question, then, was whether human behavior, guided in a general way by these hereditary emotions and dispositions, should be called instinctive or not.

Those who answer yes, would say that a man is acting instinctively when he is impelled in any degree by hunger, fear, rage or sexual attraction, even though his mode of expressing these impulses is quite new. Those who say no, would mean that such action is not instinctive because not definitely predetermined by a hereditary mechanism. Hence the disagreement as to the place of instinct in human life. If we are to give it a large place it must be used in the former sense, that is, to mean an inner rather than an outer process, it must be defined in terms of motive rather than of specific action.

Perhaps a reasonable middle course would be to avoid the word "instinct" as applied to most human behavior, which has nothing of the fixity of animal instinct, and speak instead of "instinctive emotion," since the emotional side of our activity clearly includes a hereditary element which seems to remain much the same under the most diverse manifestations.

If we do this we shall still find that there is little agreement as to just what instinctive emotions there are and how they work. The reason for this lack of agreement is that our experience bearing upon the question, although real and vivid, is yet elusive, hard to define and classify, subject to various interpretations. Thus the passion of love is the hackneyed topic of literature and conversation. Most of us have undergone it, have observed it in others, and are willing to impart what we know about it; yet who can say precisely what the essential phenomena are, or just what is inherited, and how this inheritance is awakened, modified, developed by experience? These are obscure questions, and perhaps always will be. There are similar questions with reference to fear, anger, grief, and the like. The student will find informing books that aim to elucidate these phases of life, analyzing and describing our modes of feeling and tracing their probable evolution from animal instinct, but these works differ immensely in their views, and none of them is conclusive. The operation of instinct in human life seems hardly capable of convincing elucidation.

It is fairly clear that we have at least half a dozen well-marked types of instinctive emotional disposition that are social in that they concern directly our attitude toward other persons. I might name, as perhaps the plainest, the dispositions to anger, to fear, to maternal love, to male and female sexual love and to the emotion of self-assertion or power. We may accept these as instinctive,

1. Because they appear to be universal in the human race, as shown by common observation, by introspection, by the evidence accumulated in literature, and by more or less scientific methods of study, such as those used by psychoanalysts. This universality would not of itself prove them instinctive: they might be due to universal social conditions. It adds greatly, however, to the cogency of other reasons.

2. Because they are associated with physical reactions or modes of expression which can hardly be other than instinctive, many of them being practically universal among the human race and some of them found also among the apes. The clenching of the fists and teeth in rage, and the uncovering of the teeth as if to bite are an example of what I mean. Darwin investigated these in his *Expression of the Emotions,* but, owing to his belief that the effects of habit are inherited, he did not discriminate as clearly as we could wish between what is hereditary and what is learned from others.

3. Because they correspond to and motivate certain enduring types of function found not only in man but in other animals; because, in short, they are so deeply rooted in animal evolution that it would be strange if they were not instinctive. Human anger, for example, motivates conflict with opposing persons or other agents, being similar in function to the anger, clearly instinctive, of all the fighting animals. In the same way fear motivates escape from danger, with us as with all animals who have dangers to escape from, and so on. These instinctive emotions predetermine, not specific actions, but, in a measure, the energy that flows into actions having a certain function with reference to our environment.[1]

Beyond such clearly ascertainable hereditary dispositions there are innumerable others, some of them, perhaps, equally clear, but most of them elusive, undefined and disputable. Moreover, all such dispositions including those mentioned are rapidly developed, transformed,

---

1. Apparently there must be, along with the hereditary emotional disposition, some hereditary nervous mechanism to connect the emotion with the various stimuli that awaken it. Some regard this as a difficulty, but if so it is one for the psychologist to solve. That generalized types of function, as personal conflict, do awaken specific emotions, as anger, and are also motivated by them, is a matter of direct observation.

and interwoven by social experience, giving rise to a multitude of complex passions and sentiments which no one has satisfactorily elucidated. Indeed, as these change very considerably with changes in the social life that moulds them, it is impossible that they should be definitely and finally described. Each age and country has its own more or less peculiar modes of feeling, as it has of thinking. There is no finality in this field.

Although instinctive emotion probably enters into everything we do, it enters in such a way that we can rarely or never explain human behavior by it alone. In human life it is not, in any considerable degree, a motive to specific behavior at all, but an impulse whose definite expression depends upon education and social situation. It does not act except through a complex, socially determined organism of thought and sentiment.

If, for example, we say "War is due to an instinct of pugnacity," we say something that includes so little of the truth and ignores so much that it is practically false. War is rooted in many instinctive tendencies, all of which have been transformed by education, tradition and organization, so that to study its sources is to study the whole process of society. This calls, above all things, for detailed historical and sociological analysis: there could hardly be anything more inimical to real knowledge or rational conduct regarding it than to ascribe it to pugnacity and let the question go at that.

Much the same may be said of the employment of a supposed gregarious instinct, or "instinct of the herd," to explain a multiplicity of phenomena, including mob-excitement, dread of isolation, conformity to fads and fashions, which require, like war, a detailed study of social antecedents. This is, as Professor Findlay remarks (in *An Introduction of Sociology*) "an easy, dogmatic way of explaining phenomena whose causes and effects are far more complicated than these authors would admit." Indeed I am not aware that there is any such evidence of the existence of a gregarious instinct as there is of an instinct of fear or anger: and many think the phenomena which it is used to explain may be accounted for by sympathy and suggestion, without calling in a special instinct. It seems to me to be the postulate of an individualistic psychology in search of some special motive to explain collective behavior. If you regard human nature as primarily social you need no such special motive.[2]

2. The notion that collective behavior is to be attributed to an "instinct of the herd" seems to owe its vogue in great part to Nietzsche who made much use of it, in a contemptuous sense, to animate his anti-democratic philosophy.

There is, indeed, a wide-spread disposition among psychologists, psychoanalysts, biologists, economists, writers on education, and others who are interested in instinct but would gladly avoid history or sociology, to short-circuit their current of causation, leading it directly from instinct to social events, without following it into those intricate convolutions of social process through which, in the real world, it actually flows and by which it is transformed.

How are we to think of reason in relation to instinct? This depends upon our view as to that question, already discussed, whether instinct means only fixed modes of behavior or whether it may include also instinctive emotion that expresses itself in plastic behavior. If we confine it to the former, then instinct and reason exclude each other, because it is the nature of reason to adapt conduct to varying conditions: but if we admit the latter, then reason and instinct may work together. Fixed instincts call for no general control: life presses a button and the hereditary mechanism does the rest. But teachable instincts imply a teacher. They must be guided, developed, coordinated, organized, so that they may work effectually; and this is the part of reason. Reason, in one aspect, is team-work in the mind; it is the mental organization required by the various and changing life of man. It takes the crude energy of the instinctive dispositions, as an officer takes his raw recruits, instructing and training them until they can work together for any end he may propose, and in any manner that the situation demands. If a man wants a wife it teaches him how, in the existing state of things, he may be able to woo and win her, and how support her when won, guiding him through a complicated course of behavior adapted to the present and yet impelled in part by hereditary emotion.

Reason, in this view, does not supplant instinct any more than the captain supplants the private soldiers; it is a principle of higher organization, controlling and transforming instinctive energies. Indeed, reason is itself an instinctive disposition, in a large use of the term, a disposition to compare, combine, and organize the activities of the mind. Animals have it in some measure, and it is unique in man only by the degree of its development: it might be compared to a common soldier emerging from the rank, taking the lead by virtue of peculiar ability and becoming in time the commanding officer.

And human history, in distinction from animal history, is a natural outcome of those traits of human psychology that we have discussed.

It is a process possible only to a species endowed with teachable instinctive dispositions, organized, partly by reason, into a plastic and growing social whole. This whole, responsive to the outer world in a thousand ways, and containing also diverse and potent energies within itself, is ever putting forth new forms of life which we describe as progress or decadence according as we think them better or worse than the old. These changes do not require any alteration in our hereditary powers. In fact there is little or no reason to think that the Teutonic stocks from which most of us are sprung are appreciably different now, so far as heredity is concerned, from what they were when Cæsar met and fought and described them. If we could substitute a thousand babies from that time for those in our own cradles, it would probably make no perceptible difference. They would grow up in our ways, driving automobiles instead of war chariots, reading the newspapers and, in general, playing the human game as it is played today quite like the rest of us.

And, finally, just what do we mean by human nature? The phrase is used vaguely, but there are at least three meanings that can be distinguished with some precision. And as we distinguish them we may be able, at the same time, to answer the perennial question. Does human nature change?

It may mean, first, the strictly hereditary nature of man, borne by the germ-plasm, the formless impulses and capacities that we infer to exist at birth, but of which we have little definite knowledge because they do not manifest themselves except as a factor in social development. This nature appears to charge very slowly, and we have no reason to think we are very different at birth from our ancestors of, say, a thousand years ago.

It may mean, second, a social nature developed in man by simple forms of intimate association or "primary groups," especially the family and neighborhood, which are found everywhere and everywhere work upon the individual in somewhat the same way. This nature consists chiefly of certain primary social sentiments and attitudes, such as consciousness of oneself in relation to others, love of approbation, resentment of censure, emulation, and a sense of social right and wrong formed by the standards of a group. This seems to me to correspond very closely to what is meant by "human nature" in ordinary speech. We mean something much more definite than hereditary disposition, which most of us know nothing about, and yet something fundamental and wide-spread if not universal in the life of man, found in ancient history and in the accounts of remote nations, as well as now and here. Thus, when we read that Joseph's brethren hated him and could not speak peaceably to him because they saw that their father loved him more than all the rest, we say, "Of course, that is human nature." This social nature is much more alterable than heredity, and if it is "pretty much the same the world over," as we commonly say, this is because the intimate groups in which it is formed are somewhat similar. If these are essentially changed, human nature will change with them.

There is a third sense of the phrase which is not unusual, especially in discussions which turn upon the merits or demerits of human nature. This is not easy to define but differs from the preceding in identifying it with somewhat specific types of behavior, such as pecuniary selfishness or generosity, belligerency or peacefulness, efficiency or inefficiency, conservatism or radicalism, and the like. In other words, it departs from the generality of the idea and brings in elements that come from particular situations and institutions. Human nature, in any such sense as this, is in the highest degree changeful, because the behavior to which it gives rise varies, morally and in every other way, with the influences that act upon it. It may be selfish, inefficient, quarrelsome, conservative now, and a few years hence or in another situation generous, peaceful, efficient, and progressive; all turns upon how it is evoked and organized. Perhaps the commonest fallacy we meet in this connection is that which assumes that human nature does not change, points out respects in which it has worked deplorably, and concludes that it will always work so. An unchanging human nature, it is said, has given us wars and economic greed; it always will. On the contrary, since these things disappear or are controlled under certain conditions we may conclude that human nature, in this sense, is subject to change.

But, in the more general sense, it is a nature whose primary trait is teachability, and so does not need to change in order to be an inexhaustible source of changing conduct and institutions. We can make it work in almost any way if we understand it, as a clever mechanic can mould to his will the universal laws of mass and motion.

Communication and Understanding

7

Sympathy or Understanding
as an Aspect of Society

The growth of personal ideas through intercourse implies a growing
power of sympathy, of entering into and sharing the minds of other
persons. To converse with another, through words, looks, or other
symbols, means to have more or less understanding or communion
with him, to get on common ground and partake of his ideas and
sentiments. If one uses sympathy in this connection—and it is perhaps
the most available word—one has to bear in mind that it denotes the
sharing of any mental state that can be communicated, and has not
the special implication of pity or other "tender emotion" that it very
commonly carries in ordinary speech.[1] This emotionally colorless us-

From "Sympathy or Understanding as an Aspect of Society," chapter 4 of *Human Nature and the Social Order* (1902; reprint New York: Schocken, 1964), 136–67.
    1. Sympathy in the sense of compassion is a specific emotion or sentiment, and has
nothing necessarily in common with sympathy in the sense of communion. It might be
thought, perhaps, that compassion was one form of the sharing of feeling; but this appears not to be the case. The sharing of painful feelings may precede and cause compassion, but is not the same with it. When I feel sorry for a man in disgrace, it is, no
doubt, in most cases, because I have imaginatively partaken of his humiliation; but my
compassion for him is not the thing that is shared, but is something additional, a comment on the shared feeling. I may imagine how a suffering man feels—sympathize with
him in that sense—and be moved not to pity but to disgust, contempt, or perhaps admiration. Our feeling makes all sorts of comments on the imagined feeling of others. Moreover it is not essential that there should be any real understanding in order that compassion may be felt. One may compassionate a worm squirming on a hook, or a fish, or
even a tree. As between persons pity, while often a helpful and healing emotion, leading
to kindly acts, is sometimes indicative of the absence of true sympathy. We all wish to
be understood, at least in what we regard as our better aspects, but few of us wish to
be pitied except in moments of weakness and discouragement. To accept pity is to confess that one falls below the healthy standard of vigor and self-help. While a real understanding of our deeper thought is rare and precious, pity is usually cheap, many people
finding an easy pleasure in indulging it, as one may in the indulgence of grief, resentment,
or almost any emotion. It is often felt by the person who is its object as a sort of an
insult, a back-handed thrust at self-respect, the unkindest cut of all. For instance, as
between richer and poorer classes in a free country a mutually respecting antagonism

age is, however, perfectly legitimate, and is, I think, more common in classical English literature than any other. Thus Shakespeare, who uses sympathy five times, if we may trust the *Shakespeare Phrase Book*, never means by it the particular emotion of compassion, but either the sharing of a mental state, as when he speaks of "sympathy in choice," or mere resemblance, as when Iago mentions the lack of "sympathy in years, manners, and beauties" between Othello and Desdemona. This latter sense is also one which must be excluded in our use of the word, since what is here meant is an active process of mental assimilation, not mere likeness.

In this chapter sympathy, in the sense of understanding or personal insight, will be considered chiefly with a view to showing something of its nature as a phase or member of the general life of mankind.

The content of it, the matter understood, is chiefly thought and sentiment, in distinction from mere sensation or crude emotion. I do not venture to say that these latter cannot be shared, but certainly they play a relatively small part in the communicative life. Thus although to get one's finger pinched is a common experience, it is impossible, to me at least, to recall the sensation when another person has his finger pinched. So when we say that we feel sympathy for a person who has a headache, we mean that we pity him, not that we share the headache. There is little true communication of physical pain, or anything of that simple sort. The reason appears to be that as ideas of this kind are due to mere physical contacts, or other simple stimuli, in the first instance, they are and remain detached and isolated in the mind, so that they are unlikely to be recalled except by some sensation of the sort originally associated with them. If they become objects of thought and conversation, as is likely to be the case when they are agreeable, they are by that very process refined into sentiments. Thus when the pleasures of the table are discussed the thing communicated is hardly the sensation of taste but something much subtler, although partly based upon that. Thought and sentiment are from the first parts or aspects of highly complex and imaginative personal ideas, and of course may be reached by anything which recalls any part of those ideas. They are aroused by personal intercourse because in their origin they are connected with personal symbols. The sharing of a sentiment

---

is much healthier than pity on the one hand and dependence on the other, and is, perhaps, the next best thing to fraternal feeling.

ordinarily comes to pass by our perceiving one of these symbols or traits of expression which has belonged with the sentiment in the past and now brings it back. And likewise with thought: it is communicated by words, and these are freighted with the net result of centuries of intercourse. Both spring from the general life of society and cannot be separated from that life, nor it from them.

It is not to be inferred that we must go through the same visible and tangible experiences as other people before we can sympathize with them. On the contrary, there is only an indirect and uncertain connection between one's sympathies and the obvious events—such as the death of friends, success or failure in business, travels, and the like—that one has gone through. Social experience is a matter of imaginative, not of material, contacts; and there are so many aids to the imagination that little can be judged as to one's experience by the merely external course of his life. An imaginative student of a few people and of books often has many times the range of comprehension that the most varied career can give to a duller mind; and a man of genius, like Shakespeare, may cover almost the whole range of human sentiment in his time, not by miracle, but by a marvellous vigor and refinement of imagination. The idea that seeing life means going from place to place and doing a great variety of obvious things is an illusion natural to dull minds.

One's range of sympathy is a measure of his personality, indicating how much or how little of a man he is. It is in no way a special faculty, but a function of the whole mind to which every special faculty contributes, so that what a person is and what he can understand or enter into through the life of others are very much the same thing. We often hear people described as sympathetic who have little mental power, but are of a sensitive, impressionable, quickly responsive type of mind. The sympathy of such a mind always has some defect corresponding to its lack of character and of constructive force. A strong, deep understanding of other people implies mental energy and stability; it is a work of persistent, cumulative imagination which may be associated with a comparative slowness of direct sensibility. On the other hand, we often see the union of a quick sensitiveness to immediate impressions with an inability to comprehend what has to be reached by reason or constructive imagination.

Sympathy is a requisite to social power. Only in so far as a man understands other people and thus enters into the life around him has he any effective existence; the less he has of this the more he is a mere animal, not truly in contact with human life. And if he is not in contact with it he can of course have no power over it. This is a principle of familiar application, and yet one that is often overlooked, practical men having, perhaps, a better grasp of it than theorists. It is well understood by men of the world that effectiveness depends at least as much upon address, *savoir-faire*, tact, and the like, involving sympathetic insight into the minds of other people, as upon any more particular faculties. There is nothing more practical than social imagination; to lack it is to lack everything. All classes of persons need it—the mechanic, the farmer, and the tradesman, as well as the lawyer, the clergyman, the railway president, the politician, the philanthropist, and the poet. Every year thousands of young men are preferred to other thousands and given positions of more responsibility largely because they are seen to have a power of personal insight which promises efficiency and growth. Without "caliber," which means chiefly a good imagination, there is no getting on much in the world. The strong men of our society, however much we may disapprove of the particular direction in which their sympathy is sometimes developed or the ends their power is made to serve, are very human men, not at all the abnormal creatures they are sometimes asserted to be. I have met a fair number of such men, and they have generally appeared, each in his own way, to be persons of a certain scope and breadth that marked them off from the majority.

A person of definite character and purpose who comprehends our way of thought is sure to exert power over us. He cannot altogether be resisted; because, if he understands us, he can make us understand him, through the word, the look, or other symbol, which both of us connect with the common sentiment or idea; and thus by communicating an impulse he can move the will. Sympathetic influence enters into our system of thought as a matter of course, and affects our conduct as surely as water affects the growth of a plant. The kindred spirit can turn on a system of lights, . . . and so transform the mental illumination. This is the nature of all authority and leadership . . .

Again, sympathy, in the broad sense in which it is here used, underlies also the moral rank of a man and goes to fix our estimate of his justice and goodness. The just, the good, or the right under any name is of course not a thing by itself, but is a finer product wrought up out of the various impulses that life affords, and colored by them. Hence no one can think and act in a way that strikes us as right unless he feels, in great part, the same impulses that we do. If he shares the feelings that seem to us to have the best claims, it naturally follows, if he is a person of stable character, that he does them justice in thought and action. To be upright, public-spirited, patriotic, charitable, generous, and just implies that a man has a broad personality which feels the urgency of sympathetic or imaginative motives that in narrower minds are weak or lacking. He has achieved the higher sentiments, the wider range of personal thought. And so far as we see in his conduct that he feels such motives and that they enter into his decisions, we are likely to call him good. What is it to do good, in the ordinary sense? Is it not to help people to enjoy and to work, to fulfil the healthy and happy tendencies of human nature; to give play to children, education to youth, a career to men, a household to women, and peace to old age? And it is sympathy that makes a man wish and need to do these things. One who is large enough to live the life of the race will feel the impulses of each class as his own, and do what he can to gratify them as naturally as he eats his dinner. The idea that goodness is something apart from ordinary human nature is pernicious; it is only an ampler expression of that nature.

On the other hand, all badness, injustice, or wrong is, in one of its aspects, a lack of sympathy. If a man's action is injurious to interests which other men value, and so impresses them as wrong, it must be because, at the moment of action, he does not feel those interests as they do. Accordingly the wrong-doer is either a person whose sympathies do not embrace the claims he wrongs, or one who lacks sufficient stability of character to express his sympathies in action. A liar, for instance, is either one who does not feel strongly the dishonor, injustice, and confusion of lying, or one who, feeling them at times, does not retain the feeling in decisive moments. And so a brutal person may be such either in a dull or chronic way, which does not know the gentler sentiments at any time, or in a sudden and passionate way which perhaps alternates with kindness.

Much the same may be said regarding mental health in general; its presence or absence may always be expressed in terms of sympathy. The test of sanity which every one instinctively applies is that of a certain tact or feeling of the social situation, which we expect of all right-minded people and which flows from sympathetic contact with other minds. One whose words and bearing give the impression that he stands apart and lacks intuition of what others are thinking is judged as more or less absent-minded, queer, dull, or even insane or imbecile, according to the character and permanence of the phenomenon. The essence of insanity, from the social point of view (and, it would seem, the only final test of it) is a confirmed lack of touch with other minds in matters upon which men in general are agreed; and imbecility might be defined as a general failure to compass the more complex sympathies.

A man's sympathies as a whole reflect the social order in which he lives, or rather they are a particular phase of it. Every group of which he is really a member, in which he has any vital share, must live in his sympathy; so that his mind is a microcosm of so much of society as he truly belongs to. Every social phenomenon, we need to remember, is simply a collective view of what we find distributively in particular persons—public opinion is a phase of the judgments of individuals; traditions and institutions live in the thought of particular men, social standards of right do not exist apart from private consciences, and so on. Accordingly, so far as a man has any vital part in the life of a time or a country, that life is imaged in those personal ideas or sympathies which are the impress of his intercourse.

So, whatever is peculiar to our own time implies a corresponding peculiarity in the sympathetic life of each one of us. Thus the age, at least in the more intellectually active parts of life, is strenuous, characterized by the multiplication of points of personal contact through enlarged and accelerated communication. The mental aspect of this is a more rapid and multitudinous flow of personal images, sentiments, and impulses. Accordingly there prevails among us an animation of thought that tends to lift men above sensuality; and there is also possible a choice of relations that opens to each mind a more varied and congenial development than the past afforded. On the other hand, these advantages are not without their cost; the intensity of life often becomes a strain, bringing to many persons an over-excitation which weakens or breaks down character; as we see in the increase of suicide and insanity, and in many similar phenomena. An effect very generally produced upon all except the strongest minds appears to be a sort of superficiality of imagination, a dissipation and attenuation of impulses, which watches the stream of personal imagery go by like a procession, but lacks the power to organize and direct it.

The different degrees of urgency in personal impressions are reflected in the behavior of different classes of people. Every one must have noticed that he finds more real openness of sympathy in the country than in the city—though perhaps there is more of a superficial readiness in the latter—and often more among plain, hand-working people than among professional and business men. The main reason for this, I take it, is that the social imagination is not so hard worked in the one case as in the other. In the mountains of North Carolina the hospitable inhabitants will take in any stranger and invite him to spend the night; but this is hardly possible upon Broadway; and the case is very much the same with the hospitality of the mind. If one sees few people and hears a new thing only once a week, he accumulates a fund of sociability and curiosity very favorable to eager intercourse; but if he is assailed all day and every day by calls upon feeling and thought in excess of his power to respond, he soon finds that he must put up some sort of a barrier. Sensitive people who live where life is insistent take on a sort of social shell whose function is to deal mechanically with ordinary relations and preserve the interior from destruction. They are likely to acquire a conventional smile and conventional phrases for polite intercourse, and a cold mask for curiosity, hostility, or solicitation. In fact, a vigorous power of resistance to the numerous influences that in no way make for the substantial development of his character, but rather tend to distract and demoralize him, is a primary need of one who lives in the more active portions of present society, and the loss of this power by strain is in countless instances the beginning of mental and moral decline. There are times of abounding energy when we exclaim with Schiller,

Seid willkommen, Millionen,
Diesen Kuss der ganzen Welt!

but it is hardly possible or desirable to maintain this attitude continuously. Universal sympathy is impracticable; what we need is better control and selection, avoiding both the narrowness of our class and the dissipation of promiscuous impressions. It is well for a man to open out and take in as much of life as he can organize into a consistent whole, but to go beyond that is not desirable. In a time of insistent suggestion, like the present, it is fully as important to many of us to know when and how to restrict the impulses of sympathy as it is to avoid narrowness. And this is in no way inconsistent, I think, with that modern democracy of sentiment—also connected with the enlargement of communication—which deprecates the limitation of sympathy by wealth or position. Sympathy must be selective, but the less it is controlled by conventional and external circumstances, such as wealth, and the more it penetrates to the essentials of character, the better. It is this liberation from convention, locality, and chance, I think, that the spirit of the time calls for.

8

The Significance of Communication

By Communication is here meant the mechanism through which human relations exist and develop—all the symbols of the mind, together with the means of conveying them through space and preserving them in time. It includes the expression of the face, attitude and gesture, the tones of the voice, words, writing, printing, railways, telegraphs, telephones, and whatever else may be the latest achievement in the conquest of space and time. All these taken together, in the intricacy of their actual combination, make up an organic whole corresponding to the organic whole of human thought; and everything in the way of mental growth has an external existence therein. The more closely we consider this mechanism the more intimate will appear its relation to the inner life of mankind, and nothing will more help us to understand the latter than such consideration.

There is no sharp line between the means of communication and the rest of the external world. In a sense all objects and actions are symbols of the mind, and nearly anything may be used as a sign—as I may signify the moon or a squirrel to a child by merely pointing at it, or by imitating with the voice the chatter of the one or drawing an outline of the other. But there is also, almost from the first, a conventional development of communication, springing out of spontaneous signs but soon losing evident connection with them, a system of standard symbols existing for the mere purpose of conveying thought; and it is this we have chiefly to consider.

Without communication the mind does not develop a true human nature, but remains in an abnormal and nondescript state neither human nor properly brutal. This is movingly illustrated by the case of Helen Keller, who, as all the world knows, was cut off at eighteen months

From "The Significance of Communication," and "Modern Communication: Enlargement and Animation," chapters 6 and 8, respectively, of *Social Organization: A Study of the Larger Mind* (1909; reprint New York: Schocken, 1963), 61–65, 80–90.

from the cheerful ways of men by the loss of sight and hearing; and did not renew the connection until she was nearly seven years old. Although her mind was not wholly isolated during this period, since she retained the use of a considerable number of signs learned during infancy, yet her impulses were crude and uncontrolled, and her thought so unconnected that she afterward remembered almost nothing that occurred before the awakening which took place toward the close of her seventh year.

The story of that awakening, as told by her teacher, gives as vivid a picture as we need have of the significance to the individual mind of the general fact and idea of communication. For weeks Miss Sullivan had been spelling words into her hand which Helen had repeated and associated with objects; but she had not yet grasped the idea of language in general, the fact that everything had a name, and that through names she could share her own experience with others, and learn theirs—the idea that there is *fellowship in thought*. This came quite suddenly.

> "This morning," writes her teacher, "while she was washing, she wanted to know the name for water. . . . I spelled w-a-t-e-r and thought no more about it until after breakfast. Then it occurred to me that with the help of this new word I might succeed in straightening out the mug-milk difficulty [a confusion of ideas previously discussed]. We went out into the pump-house and I made Helen hold her mug under the pump while I pumped. As the cold water gushed forth filling the mug I spelled w-a-t-e-r in Helen's free hand. The word coming so close upon the sensation of cold water rushing over her hand seemed to startle her. She dropped the mug and stood as one transfixed. A new light came into her face. She spelled water several times. Then she dropped on the ground and asked for its name, and pointed to the pump and the trellis, and suddenly turning round she asked for my name. I spelled 'teacher.' Just then the nurse brought Helen's little sister into the pump-house, and Helen spelled 'baby' and pointed to the nurse. All the way back to the house she was highly excited, and learned the name of every object she touched, so that in a few hours she had added thirty new words to her vocabulary."

> The following day Miss Sullivan writes, "Helen got up this morning like a radiant fairy. She has flitted from object to object, asking the name of everything and kissing me for very gladness." And four days later, "Everything must have a name now. . . . She drops the signs and pantomime she used before, so soon as she has words to supply their place, and the acquirement of a new word affords her the liveliest pleasure. And we notice that her face grows more expressive each day."[1]

1. Anne Sullivan, in *The Story of My Life*, by Helen Keller, pp. 316, 317.

This experience is a type of what happens more gradually to all of us: it is through communication that we get our higher development. The faces and conversation of our associates; books, letters, travel, arts, and the like, by awakening thought and feeling and guiding them in certain channels, supply the stimulus and framework for all our growth.

In the same way, if we take a larger view and consider the life of a social group, we see that communication, including its organization into literature, art, and institutions, is truly the outside or visible structure of thought, as much cause as effect of the inside or conscious life of men. All is one growth: the symbols, the traditions, the institutions are projected from the mind, to be sure, but in the very instant of their projection, and thereafter, they react upon it, and in a sense control it, stimulating, developing, and fixing certain thoughts at the expense of others to which no awakening suggestion comes. By the aid of this structure the individual is a member not only of a family, a class, and a state, but of a larger whole reaching back to prehistoric men whose thought has gone to build it up. In this whole he lives as in an element, drawing from it the materials of his growth and adding to it whatever constructive thought he may express.

Thus the system of communication is a tool, a progressive invention, whose improvements react upon mankind and alter the life of every individual and institution. A study of these improvements is one of the best ways by which to approach an understanding of the mental and social changes that are bound up with them; because it gives a tangible framework for our ideas—just as one who wished to grasp the organic character of industry and commerce might well begin with a study of the railway system and of the amount and kind of commodities it carries, proceeding thence to the more abstract transactions of finance.

And when we come to the modern era, especially, we can understand nothing rightly unless we perceive the manner in which the revolution in communication has made a new world for us. So in the pages that follow I shall aim to show what the growth of intercourse implies in the way of social development, inquiring particularly into the effect of recent changes.

Modern Communication: Enlargement and Animation

The changes that have taken place since the beginning of the nineteenth century are such as to constitute a new epoch in communication, and in the whole system of society. They deserve, therefore, careful consideration, not so much in their mechanical aspect, which is familiar to every one, as in their operation upon the larger mind.

If one were to analyze the mechanism of intercourse, he might, perhaps, distinguish four factors that mainly contribute to its efficiency, namely:

> Expressiveness, or the range of ideas and feelings it is competent to carry.
> Permanence of record, or the overcoming of time.
> Swiftness, or the overcoming of space.
> Diffusion, or access to all classes of men.

Now while gains have no doubt been made in expressiveness, as in the enlargement of our vocabulary to embrace the ideas of modern science; and even in permanence of record, for scientific and other special purposes; yet certainly the long steps of recent times have been made in the direction of swiftness and diffusion. For most purposes our speech is no better than in the age of Elizabeth, if so good; but what facility we have gained in the application of it! The cheapening of printing, permitting an inundation of popular books, magazines and newspapers, has been supplemented by the rise of the modern postal system and the conquest of distance by railroads, telegraphs and telephones. And along with these extensions of the spoken or written word have come new arts of reproduction, such as photography, photoengraving, phonography and the like—of greater social import than we realize—by which new kinds of impression from the visible or audible world may be fixed and disseminated.

It is not too much to say that these changes are the basis, from a mechanical standpoint, of nearly everything that is characteristic in the psychology of modern life. In a general way they mean the expansion of human nature, that is to say, of its power to express itself in social wholes. They make it possible for society to be organized more and more on the higher faculties of man, on intelligence and sympathy, rather than on authority, caste, and routine. They mean freedom, outlook, indefinite possibility. The public consciousness, instead of being confined as regards its more active phases to local groups, extends by even steps with that give-and-take of suggestions that the new intercourse makes possible, until wide nations, and finally the world itself, may be included in one lively mental whole.

The general character of this change is well expressed by the two words *enlargement* and *animation*. Social contacts are extended in space and quickened in time, and in the same degree the mental unity they imply becomes wider and more alert. The individual is broadened by coming into relation with a larger and more various life, and he is kept stirred up, sometimes to excess, by the multitude of changing suggestions which this life brings to him.

From whatever point of view we study modern society to compare it with the past or to forecast the future, we ought to keep at least a subconsciousness of this radical change in mechanism, without allowing for which nothing else can be understood.

In the United States, for instance, at the close of the eighteenth century, public consciousness of any active kind was confined to small localities. Travel was slow, uncomfortable and costly, and people undertaking a considerable journey often made their wills beforehand. The newspapers, appearing weekly in the larger towns, were entirely lacking in what we should call news; and the number of letters sent during a year in all the thirteen states was much less than that now handled by the New York office in a single day. People are far more alive today to what is going on in China, if it happens to interest them, than they were then to events a hundred miles away. The isolation of even large towns from the rest of the world, and the consequent introversion of men's minds upon local concerns, was something we can hardly conceive. In the country "the environment of the farm was the neighborhood; the environment of the village was the encircling farms and the local tradition; . . . few conventions assembled for discussion and common action; educational centres did not radiate the shock of a new intellectual life to every hamlet; federations and unions did not bind men, near and remote, into that fellowship that makes one composite type of many human sorts. It was an age of sects, intolerant from lack of acquaintance."[2]

The change to the present régime of railroads, telegraphs, daily pa-

2. W. L. Anderson, *The Country Town,* pp. 209, 210.

pers, telephones and the rest has involved a revolution in every phase of life; in commerce, in politics, in education, even in mere sociability and gossip—this revolution always consisting in an enlargement and quickening of the kind of life in question.

Probably there is nothing in this new mechanism quite so pervasive and characteristic as the daily newspaper, which is as vehemently praised as it is abused, and in both cases with good reason. What a strange practice it is, when you think of it, that a man should sit down to his breakfast table and, instead of conversing with his wife, and children, hold before his face a sort of screen on which is inscribed a world-wide gossip!

The essential function of the newspaper is, of course, to serve as a bulletin of important news and a medium for the interchange of ideas, through the printing of interviews, letters, speeches and editorial comment. In this way it is indispensable to the organization of the public mind.

The bulk of its matter, however, is best described by the phrase organized gossip. The sort of intercourse that people formerly carried on at cross-road stores or over the back fence, has now attained the dignity of print and an imposing system. That we absorb a flood of this does not necessarily mean that our minds are degenerate, but merely that we are gratifying an old appetite in a new way. Henry James speaks with a severity natural to literary sensibility of "the ubiquitous newspaper face, with its mere monstrosity and deformity of feature, and the vast open mouth, adjusted as to the chatter of Bedlam, that flings the flood-gates of vulgarity farther back [in America] than anywhere else on earth."[3] But after all is it any more vulgar than the older kind of gossip? No doubt it seems worse for venturing to share with literature the use of the printed word.

That the bulk of the contents of the newspaper is of the nature of gossip may be seen by noting three traits which together seem to make a fair definition of that word. It is copious, designed to occupy, without exerting, the mind. It consists mostly of personalities and appeals to superficial emotion. It is untrustworthy—except upon a few matters of moment which the public are likely to follow up and verify. These traits any one who is curious may substantiate by a study of his own morning journal.

3. H. James, "The Manners of American Women," *Harper's Bazaar,* May 1907.

There is a better and a worse side to this enlargement of gossip. On the former we may reckon the fact that it promotes a widespread sociability and sense of community; we know that people all over the country are laughing at the same jokes or thrilling with the same mild excitement over the foot-ball game, and we absorb a conviction that they are good fellows much like ourselves. It also tends powerfully, through the fear of publicity, to enforce a popular, somewhat vulgar, but sound and human standard of morality. On the other hand it fosters superficiality and commonplaces in every sphere of thought and feeling, and is, of course, the antithesis of literature and of all high or fine spiritual achievement. It stands for diffusion as opposed to distinction.

In politics communication makes possible public opinion, which, when organized, is democracy. The whole growth of this, and of the popular education and enlightenment that go with it, is immediately dependent upon the telegraph, the newspaper and the fast mail, for there can be no popular mind upon questions of the day, over wide areas, except as the people are promptly informed of such questions and are enabled to exchange views regarding them.

Our government, under the Constitution, was not originally a democracy, and was not intended to be so by the men that framed it. It was expected to be a representative republic, the people choosing men of character and wisdom, who would proceed to the capital, inform themselves there upon current questions, and deliberate and decide regarding them. That the people might think and act more directly was not foreseen. The Constitution is not democratic in spirit, and, as Mr. Bryce has noted,[4] might under different conditions have become the basis of an aristocratic system.

That any system could have held even the original thirteen states in firm union without the advent of modern communication is very doubtful. Political philosophy, from Plato to Montesquieu, had taught that free states must be small, and Frederick the Great is said to have ridiculed the idea of one extending from Maine to Georgia. "A large empire," says Montesquieu, "supposes a despotic authority in the per-

4. J. Bryce, *The American Commonwealth*, chap. 26.

son who governs. It is necessary that the quickness of the prince's reso-
lutions should supply the distance of the places they are sent to."[5]

Democracy has arisen here, as it seems to be arising everywhere
in the civilized world, not, chiefly, because of changes in the formal
constitution, but as the outcome of conditions which make it natural
for the people to have and to express a consciousness regarding questions of the day. It is said by those who know China that while that
country was at war with Japan the majority of the Chinese were unaware that a war was in progress. Such ignorance makes the sway of
public opinion impossible; and, conversely, it seems likely that no
state, having a vigorous people, can long escape that sway except by
repressing the interchange of thought. When the people have information and discussion they will have a will, and this must sooner or later
get hold of the institutions of society.

One is often impressed with the thought that there ought to be some
wider name for the modern movement than democracy, some name
which should more distinctly suggest the enlargement and quickening
of the general mind, of which the formal rule of the people is only one
among many manifestations. The current of new life that is sweeping
with augmenting force through the older structures of society, now
carrying them away, now leaving them outwardly undisturbed, has no
adequate name.

Popular education is an inseparable part of all this: the individual
must have at least those arts of reading and writing without which he
can hardly be a vital member of the new organism. And that further
development of education, rapidly becoming a conscious aim of modern society, which strives to give to every person a special training in
preparation for whatever function he may have aptitude for, is also a
phase of the freer and more flexible organization of mental energy.
The same enlargement runs through all life, including fashion and
other trivial or fugitive kinds of intercourse. And the widest phase of
all, upon whose momentousness I need not dwell, is that rise of an
international consciousness, in literature, in science and, finally, in politics, which holds out a trustworthy promise of the indefinite enlargement of justice and amity.

This unification of life by a freer course of thought is not only con-
temporaneous, overcoming space, but also historical, bringing the past
into the present, and making every notable achievement of the race a
possible factor in its current life—as when, by skilful reproduction the

---

5. Montesquieu, *The Spirit of the Laws,* book viii, chap. 19.

work of a mediæval painter is brought home to people dwelling five hundred years later on the other side of the globe. Our time is one of "large discourse, looking before and after."

There are remarkable possibilities in this diffusive vigor. Never, certainly, were great masses of men so rapidly rising to higher levels as now. There are the same facilities for disseminating improvement in mind and manners as in material devices; and the new communication has spread like morning light over the world, awakening, enlightening, enlarging, and filling with expectation. Human nature desires the good, when it once perceives it, and in all that is easily understood and imitated great headway is making.

Nor is there, as I shall try to show later, any good reason to think that the conditions are permanently unfavorable to the rise of special and select types of excellence. The same facility of communication which animates millions with the emulation of common models, also makes it easy for more discriminating minds to unite in small groups. The general fact is that human nature is set free; in time it will no doubt justify its freedom.

The enlargement affects not only thought but feeling, favoring the growth of a sense of common humanity, of moral unity, between nations, races and classes. Among members of a communicating whole feeling may not always be friendly, but it must be, in a sense, sympathetic, involving some consciousness of the other's point of view. Even the animosities of modern nations are of a human and imaginative sort, not the blind animal hostility of a more primitive age. They are resentments, and resentment, as Charles Lamb says, is of the family of love.

The relations between persons or communities that are without mutual understanding are necessarily on a low plane. There may be indifference, or a blind anger due to interference, or there may be a good-natured tolerance; but there is no consciousness of a common nature to warm up the kindly sentiments. A really human fellow-feeling was anciently confined within the tribe, men outside not being felt as members of a common whole. The alien was commonly treated as a more or less useful or dangerous animal—destroyed, despoiled or enslaved.

Even in these days we care little about people whose life is not brought home to us by some kind of sympathetic contact. We may read statistics of the miserable life of the Italians and Jews in New York and Chicago; of bad housing, sweatshops and tuberculosis; but we care little more about them than we do about the sufferers from the Black Death, unless their life is realized to us in some human way, either by personal contact, or by pictures and imaginative description.

And we are getting this at the present time. The resources of modern communication are used in stimulating and gratifying our interest in every phase of human life. Russians, Japanese, Filipinos, fishermen, miners, millionaires, criminals, tramps and opium-eaters are brought home to us. The press well understands that nothing human is alien to us if it is only made comprehensible.

With a mind enlarged and suppled by such training, the man of to-day inclines to look for a common nature everywhere, and to demand that the whole world shall be brought under the sway of common principles of kindness and justice. He wants to see international strife allayed—in such a way, however, as not to prevent the expansion of capable races and the survival of better types; he wishes the friction of classes reduced and each interest fairly treated—but without checking individuality and enterprise. There was never so general an eagerness that righteousness should prevail; the chief matter of dispute is upon the principles under which it may be established.

The work of communication in enlarging human nature is partly immediate, through facilitating contact, but even more it is indirect, through favoring the increase of intelligence, the decline of mechanical and arbitrary forms of organization, and the rise of a more humane type of society. History may be regarded as a record of the struggle of man to realize his aspirations through organization; and the new communication is an efficient tool for this purpose. Assuming that the human heart and conscience, restricted only by the difficulties of organization, is the arbiter of what institutions are to become, we may expect the facility of intercourse to be the starting-point of an era of moral progress.

9

The Roots of Social Knowledge

If we are to gain a large view of knowledge we should, it seems to me, consider it genetically by tracing it to its sources in human nature and human history. Knowledge is, after all, a phase of higher organic evolution, and has apparently been developed for the sake of its function in giving us adjustment to, and power over, the conditions under which we live. If these conditions present any fundamental division in kind we should expect that the capacities of the human mind and the knowledge based upon these capacities would show a corresponding division.

In fact, the conditions with which the mind has to deal, and has had to deal ever since life began to be human, divide themselves rather sharply into two kinds: the material, on the one hand, and the human or social, on the other. We have always needed to understand both things and persons, and the most primitive savage, though he may occasionally confuse them, is quite aware that they are different and must be understood in different ways.

This division lies as deep as anything in our experience, and it corresponds to a like division in our mental apparatus. For the external contacts we have our various senses, and also, in recent times, the extension and refinement of these through aptly named "instruments of precision" which have made the exact sciences possible. For the internal contacts we have a vast and obscure outfit of human susceptibilities, known as instincts, sentiments, emotions, drives, and the like, quite as firmly grounded in the evolutionary process as the senses, capable of extension and refinement in ways of their own, and giving rise to a kind of knowledge that we recognize as peculiarly human and social.

You will say, perhaps, that all knowledge, whether of things or of men, comes to us by the aid of the senses, and that the division I assert

From "The Roots of Social Knowledge," in *Sociological Theory and Social Research: Selected Papers of Charles Horton Cooley,* ed. Robert Cooley Angell (New York: Kelley, 1969), 289–309. This paper was read as the Presidential Address before the Michigan Academy of Science, Arts, and Letters on 31 March 1926, at Ann Arbor, and was first published in *American Journal of Sociology* 32, no. 1 (July 1926): 59–79.

is therefore imaginary. It is true that all knowledge calls for sense activity of some sort or degree, but the function of this activity in material or spatial knowledge, on the one hand, and in human or social knowledge, on the other, is quite different. In dealing with things sensation is the main source of the raw material which the mind works up into knowledge; in dealing with men it serves chiefly as a means of communication, as an inlet for symbols which awaken a complex inner life not primarily sensuous at all. In the one case it is our principal instrument; in the other only ancillary. When I meet a stranger and judge by his face, bearing, and voice that he is a kindly and cultured man, and by his words perceive, in a measure, the working of his mind, the sensuous images are like the starting mechanism of an automobile; they set at work processes more complicated and potent than themselves, of which, mainly, the resulting knowledge consists.

For our present purpose we may, then, distinguish two sorts of knowledge: one, the development of sense contacts into knowledge of things, including its refinement into mensurative science. This I call spatial or material knowledge. The second is developed from contact with the minds of other men, through communication, which sets going a process of thought and sentiment similar to theirs and enables us to understand them by sharing their states of mind. This I call personal or social knowledge. It might also be described as sympathetic, or, in its more active forms, as dramatic, since it is apt to consist of a visualization of behavior accompanied by imagination of corresponding mental processes.

There is nothing mysterious or unfamiliar about social knowledge, except as we may be unaccustomed to recognize and think about it. It is quite as early to appear in the child and in the race as is material knowledge, quite as useful in the everyday affairs of life, and quite as universally accepted as real by common sense. If there are men of science who do not see that it is something distinct in kind, but are inclined to regard it as spatial knowledge in an imperfect state, destined in time to be perfected by more delicate measurements, this is doubtless because they approach the matter with the *a priori* conceptions appropriate to physical research. In relation to social phenomena the merely spatial conception of knowledge indicates an abstract way of thinking that does not envisage the facts. It is not, in this field, in accord with common sense. All of us know that the essential things in our relation to other men are not subject to numerical measurement.

I trust it will not be supposed that I am advocating any metaphysical dualism between mind and matter. It is not necessary, for my present purpose, to take a side on that question, but I have myself no doubt that all the phenomena connected with social knowledge, including introspection, have physical concomitants in the brain and nervous system. In theory these physical facts are capable of physical measurement, but when we consider their minuteness and inaccessibility, the likelihood of their being measured in a spatial sense seems quite remote. We must get at them, in practice, through consciousness and through overt behavior.

Spatial knowledge, we know, has been extended and refined by processes of measurement, calculation, and inference, and has given rise to exact science. It is generally agreed that knowledge of this sort is verifiable and cumulative, making possible that ever growing structure of ascertained fact which is among the proudest of human achievements. It may be worth while to consider for a moment to what this peculiarly verifiable character is owing.

It is owing, I take it, to the fact that this sort of knowledge consists essentially in the measurement of one material thing in terms of another, man, with his senses and his reason, serving only as a mediator between them. If, then, a group of investigators can agree upon a technique of measurement they may go ahead, achieving results and passing them on from man to man and from generation to generation, without concerning themselves with the vagaries of human nature and social life. This technical agreement is found possible, and the accumulation of knowledge goes on. But we must, of course, discriminate between the immediate results of measurement and the body of hypothesis and theory which is constantly arising out of them. Science gives us fact out of which the intellect endeavors to build truth. And what we judge to be true, even in the spatial sciences, is largely a social matter dependent upon the general movement of thought. A group of scientific men, familiar with previous investigation in a given field and armed with a sound technique, is the best instrument we have for the pursuit of truth, and is one of the most remarkable products of our social system; yet it is, of course, far from infallible. All groups have a body of beliefs which are taken for granted merely because no one disputes them, and which often turn out to be illusions. Assent is induced by conforming influences not wholly different from those operating in religion or politics. In short, no group is a trustworthy critic of its own conclusions, and only the test of time and of exacting criticism from wholly different points of view can determine the value of its contribution. There have been many groups, made up of very intelligent men working devotedly and in full assurance of being on the right track, who are now seen to have been astray. And although scientific methods are no doubt improved, it would be fatuous to suppose that they are a guaranty against group error. Some of the teachings of science are permanent truth, but only time reveals which they are.

The practical success of spatial science in enabling us to predict, and even to control, the behavior of the material world about us has given it vast prestige and brought about a feeling that the more all our mental processes are like it the more perfect they will become. A conception of what social science ought to be has accordingly grown up and gained wide vogue which is based rather upon analogy than upon scrutiny of the conditions with which we have to deal. Let us return, then, to the sources of our knowledge of mankind, and consider for a moment the development of this sort of knowledge in a child. He comes into the human world already provided with a vast complex of innate capacity for life peculiar to the human race and embracing in its potential content those processes of social emotion, sentiment, and intelligence in which men find their chief interests and motives. All this is an outcome of evolution, highly practical, the very stuff that has made man the most puissant of animals, and it has, no doubt, the same physical reality as any other nervous or mental processes. Regarding the exact content of this inborn raw material of personal and social life there has been much discussion, into which, fortunately, we need not enter. Some say that it includes quite definitely organized mechanisms, similar to the instincts of the lower animals; others, that the inborn mechanisms of man are small and indeterminate, taking on organization only under the stimulus of a particular kind of life. However this may be, no one can doubt that we are born with an inchoate world of mental capacity, existing physically as a mass of brain and nerve complexes, which requires as the main condition of its growth an interchange of stimulation with similar complexes existing in other personal organisms.

The process by which a distinctively human or social mind and a corresponding type of knowledge grows up within us was first expounded at some length in 1895 by James Mark Baldwin, who called it "the dialectic of personal growth." It resembles a game of tennis in that no one can play it alone; you must have another on the opposite side of the net to return the ball. From earliest infancy our life is passed in eager response to incitements that reach us through the expressive behavior of other people, through facial expression, gesture, spoken words, writing, printing, painting, sculpture, the symbols of science, and the mechanic arts. Every response we make is a step in our education, teaching us to act, to think, and to feel a little more humanly. Our brain and nerve complexes develop in the sense of our social surroundings. And at the same time our consciousness takes account of this inward experience and proceeds to ascribe it to other people in similar conditions. Thus by a single process we increase our understanding of persons, of society, and of ourselves. When you play golf you not only acquire spatial knowledge in the shape of a certain muscular skill, but also social knowledge through learning the pride one feels when he makes a long drive, or the humiliation when he tops the ball and gets into the creek. As you see another man do these things you repeat, sympathetically, your own inner response on former occasions and ascribe it to him. A new reach of human experience is opened to you and you enlarge your understanding of men. And you extend your knowledge of domestic life, of letters, arts, and sciences in much the same way. Consider scientific work in the laboratory and in the field. Does it give only material knowledge of the behavior of *things* in test tubes, of the look and feel of strata, of the habits of fishes, or does it also teach you to understand chemists, geologists, and zoölogists as *men*, to participate in a phase of human life, share its ideals, and learn its social methods? And is not the latter knowledge quite as important to the man of science as the former? Able men in every field excel, as a rule, in human as well as technical knowledge, because both are the fruit of a richly developed mind, and both must also be cultivated as instruments of success.

If the distinctive trait of spatial knowledge is that it is mensurative, that of social knowledge is, perhaps, that it is dramatic. As the former may be resolved into distinctions among our sensations, and hence among the material objects that condition those sensations, so the latter is based ultimately on perceptions of the inter-communicating behavior of men, and experience of the processes of mind that go with it. What you know about a man consists, in part, of flashes of vision as to what he would do in particular situations, how he would look, speak and move; it is by such flashes that you judge whether he is brave or a coward, hasty or deliberate, honest or false, kind or cruel, and so on. It also consists of inner sentiments which you yourself feel in some degree when you think of him in these situations, ascribing them to him. It is these latter sympathetic elements which make the difference between our knowledge of a man and our knowledge of a horse or a dog. The latter is almost wholly external or behavioristic, although those who associate intimately with them may acquire some measure of true sympathy. We know animals mostly as a peculiarly lively kind of thing. On the other hand, although our knowledge of people is likewise behavioristic, it has no penetration, no distinctively human insight, unless it is sympathetic also.

There is, no doubt, a way of knowing people with whom we do

not sympathize which is essentially external or animal in character. An example of this is the practical but wholly behavioristic knowledge that men of much sexual experience sometimes have of women, or women of men—something that involves no true participation in thought and feeling. The more behavior in the other sex is instinctively sexual, the more our understanding of it is apt to be external rather than sympathetic. Or, to put it rather coarsely, a man sometimes understands a woman as he does a horse; not by sharing her psychic processes, but by watching what she does. There is, in fact, a complete series in our knowledge of persons, from the purely external, like our knowledge of babies, of idiots, of the wildly insane, up through all grades to the completely internal or sympathetic, as when, in reading a meditative writer like Marcus Aurelius, we know his consciousness and nothing else. For the most part, however, human knowledge is both behavioristic and sympathetic: the perception or imagination of the external trait is accompanied by sympathy with the feeling, sentiment, or idea that goes with it.

This is also the process by which we come to understand the meaning of a word, and through such understanding make ourselves at home in that vast realm of meanings to which words are the key. We may know words as mere behavior, as when a man speaks to us in a strange tongue, but in that case they do not admit us to the realm of meanings. To have human value the word and the inner experience that interprets it must go together.

In short, we learn to know human life outwardly and inwardly at the same time and by a single process continuous from infancy.

Adopting a convenient and popular term, I will call the individual human mind, including all these socially developed sentiments and understandings, the *mental-social complex.* I hope by the use of this colorless expression to escape from the traditional implications that obscure such terms as mind, consciousness, spirit, and soul.[1] About this, whatever we call it, the question of the nature and possibilities of social knowledge centers. It is our supreme gift; but for that very reason, because all the deep things of life are in it, it is the part of us about which we know least, and is least amenable to precise treatment. Can it be made available for science, or shall we try in some way to dodge it, or cancel it out, as the physical scientist does when he requires that the ideas about nature which come from it shall be verified by nature

1. In a similar way the "group mind," that is, a collective view of individual complexes communicating with, and influencing, one another, might be called the social-mental complex.

herself through physical measurement? The trouble with any such plan would seem to be that in human life the mental-social complex *is* nature. It is the very heart of what we seek to describe and make intelligible. It cannot be dodged without dodging life itself.

Suppose, for example, you secure, by a series of mental tests, detailed knowledge of what a certain person does in various situations. This may be of great value; I expect important results from such studies; but after all they cannot enable you to know the person as a living whole. The social man is something more than the sum of standardized acts, no matter how many or how well chosen. You can grasp him only by the understanding and synthetic power of your own mental complex, without which any knowledge you may gain from behavior tests must remain superficial and unintelligent. Is it not a somewhat equivocal use of terms when we talk of measuring intelligence or personality? What we measure is the performance of standardized operations. To pass from these to the organic whole of intelligence or personality is always a difficult and fallible work of the constructive imagination.

Many people, agreeing perhaps with what I have said about the ultimate difference in kind between spatial and social knowledge, will hold that just because of this difference anything like social science is impossible. While spatial knowledge is precise and communicable, and hence cumulative, the dramatic and intuitive perceptions that underlie social knowledge are so individual, so subjective, that we cannot expect that men will be able to agree upon them or to build them up into an increasing structure of ascertained truth.

This is, in fact, a formidable difficulty which enthusiasts for exact social science are apt to ignore. I may say at once that I do not look for any rapid growth of science that is profound, as regards its penetration into human life, and at the same time exact and indisputable. There is a difference in kind here which it would be fatuous to overlook.

Regarding subjectivity, I may say that all knowledge is subjective in one sense: in the sense, namely, that it is mental, not the external thing, but a construct of the mind. Even the simplest perceptions of form or extent, much more the exact perceptions of science, far from being mere physical data, are the outcome of an extended process of education, interpretation, and social evolution. Your so-called physical sciences are, after all, part of the social heritage and creatures of the mental-social complex. In so far, then, spatial knowledge and social knowledge are on the same footing.

The question of more or less subjectivity, as among different kinds of knowledge, I take to be one of more or less agreement in the elementary perceptions. If the phenomena can be observed and described in such a way as to command the assent of all intelligent men, without regard to theory or to bias of any sort, then the factual basis of knowledge acquires that independence of particular minds which we call objectivity. A yardstick is objective because it provides an undisputed method of reaching agreement as to certain spatial relations. Professor Einstein has shown, I believe, that this objectivity is not absolute, but it suffices for most purposes of spatial science. Strictly speaking, there are no yardsticks in social knowledge, no elementary perceptions of distinctively social facts that are so alike in all men, and can be so precisely communicated, that they supply an unquestionable means of description and measurement. I say distinctively social facts, because there are many facts commonly regarded as social which are also material events, like marriages, and as such can be precisely observed and enumerated. But the distinctively social phenomena connected with marriage are inward and mental, such as the affection and desire of the parties, pecuniary considerations, their plans for setting up a household, and so on. These also can be known and communicated, but not with such precise agreement among observers as to make decisive measurement possible.

You may say that while it is true that the mental-social phenomena cannot be observed directly with much precision, they express themselves in behavior, which is tangible and which we may hope eventually to record and measure with great exactness. Even our inmost thoughts and feelings take form in the symbols of communication, in gesture, voice, words, and the written symbols which are preserved unchanged for ages. All this is true and much to the point. I am a behaviorist as far as I think I can be without being a fanatic. But we must not forget, as behaviorists sometimes appear to do, that the symbol is nothing in itself, but only a convenient means of developing, imparting, and recording a meaning, and that meanings are a product of the mental-social complex and known to us only through consciousness. Reliance upon symbols, therefore, in no way releases us from the difficulty arising from the unmeasurable nature of our elementary social perceptions. We can record behavior and handle the record by statistics, but I see no way of avoiding the ultimate question, What does it mean?

And how about introspection? Does not the kind of perception which I inculcate involve this disreputable practice, and if so, is it not thereby hopelessly vitiated?

The word "introspection," as commonly used, suggests a philosopher exploring his inner consciousness in more or less complete abstraction from the ordinary functions of life. While this method may have its uses it is thought to have been more relied upon in the past than it deserves. Let us observe men under more normal conditions, and preferably, it is urged, through their actions rather than through their supposed thoughts.

But just what, after all, is introspection? It is not merely the philosophic introversion I have indicated, but takes various forms, some of which, in everyday use by all of us, are indispensable to any real knowledge of the minds of other men.

That whole process of the social growth of the mind which I have mentioned involves elements introspective in character. We come to know about other people and about ourselves by watching not only the interplay of action, but also that of thought and feeling. As we perceive and remember sensuous images of gesture, voice, and facial expression, so, at the same time, we record the movements of thought and feeling in our consciousness, ascribe similar movements to others, and so gain an insight into their minds. We are not, for the most part, reflectively aware of this, but we do it and the result is social knowledge. This process is stimulated and organized by language and—indirectly, through language—by the social heritage from the past. Under the leading of words we interpret our observation, both external and introspective, according to patterns that have been found helpful by our predecessors. When we have come to use understandingly such words as "kindly," "resolute," "proud," "humble," "angry," "fearful," "lonesome," "sad," and the like, words recalling motions of the mind as well as of the body, it shows that we have not only kept a record of our inner life, but have worked up the data into definite conceptions which we can pass on to others by aid of the common symbol.

Much of our social knowledge, especially that acquired from reading, involves a process more consciously introspective. One can hardly read a play or a novel intelligently, I should say, without recalling ideas and emotions from his own past for comparison with those of the people described. The hero, as we conceive him, is fashioned out of material from our own lives. Is it not rather absurd for scientific men to repudiate introspection? Does any one prepare a scientific report or article without first turning an inward eye upon the contents of his mind in order to see what he has to offer and how he can arrange and present it? In short, introspection, however abused by philosophers, is a normal and common process, without which we could know very little about life.

Introspection, if critical, is more objective than the usual practice of floating upon social currents without attempting to become aware of them. How can you be objective with regard to your motives unless you hold them off and look at them? I have in mind a recent book, a good book, too, in which the writer, who deprecates introspection, advances a series of opinions on social questions of the day so obviously those of his race, country, and social class that one can only smile at his naïveté. Surely a little introspection would not be out of place here: one's subjectivity needs to be understood, if only to avoid it.

It seems, then, that outside and inside in human life, consciousness and behavior, mutually complement and explain each other, and that the study of external behavior as a thing by itself must, in the human field, be as barren as mere introspection, and for much the same reason, namely, that it isolates one aspect of a natural process from another. Nature has joined these things together, and I do not think that we gain anything by putting them asunder. Records of behavior without introspective interpretation are like a library of books in a strange tongue. They came from minds, and mean nothing until they find their goal in other minds.

However, I see no reason for quarreling with those extreme behaviorists who hold that we should observe men merely from the outside, as we do other animals. Let them work on this theory, if they find it helpful, and show what they can do. Even if it is wrong it may give rise to a valuable technique, as wrong theories have done in the past. It is fair to judge behaviorists by their behavior. I suspect that they will be found in practice to make use of introspection when they need it, much like the rest of us.[2]

At the opposite pole, it would seem, from behaviorism we have the method, or rather various methods, of mental analysis through the probing of consciousness and memory. These all rest in great part upon sympathetic introspection, or the understanding of another's consciousness by the aid of your own, and give full play to the mental-social complex. They may be used in sociology as well as in psychiatry, and, in fact, do not differ in principle from the personal interviews widely employed in the study of social situations. Indeed, I take it that the psychoanalytic psychology owes its vogue to its boldness in disre-

2. I need hardly say that the scientific study of behavior has no necessary connection with the group of men who call themselves "behaviorists." Their extreme doctrine of the rejection of consciousness is best understood as a reaction against a former extreme, in psychology, of purely introspective study. Social studies have always been mainly behavioristic.

garding the rather narrowly spatial methods within which laboratory psychologists were confining themselves, and venturing, by the light of clinical interviews and introspective interpretation, to explore the weird caverns of the human mind. Men saw that the sequent revelations resembled what they knew of their own egos. The method is quite separable from the extravagant theories associated with it and will no doubt be largely used.

I have conceded that social observation is, on the whole, less precise and verifiable, and hence less surely cumulative, than spatial observation, not only because the conditions can seldom be reproduced by experiment, but because the perceptions themselves are less alike in different persons, and so less easy to agree upon. Experience shows, however, that these difficulties are by no means sufficient to prevent objective and co-operative study of social phenomena, and a cumulation of knowledge which, though not so tangible as in experimental science, is capable in time of yielding vast results.

The basis of common social perceptions, and hence of cumulation, is in the general similarity of mental-social complexes throughout the human race, and the much closer similarity among those formed by the common language and culture. We become aware of this similarity by watching the behavior of other men, including their language, and finding that this behavior can be interpreted successfully by ascribing to them thoughts and sentiments similar to our own. The idea that they are like us is practically true; it works. It was generated in the experience of our earliest childhood, and we have gone upon it all our lives. This fundamental agreement upon meanings can be made more precise by the careful use of language and other communicative signs, something as sense-perceptions are refined by the use of instruments of precision (though probably to nothing like the same degree), and thus allows a transmission and cumulation exact enough for practical use.

All history, all news, all social investigation, is a record of what men did—of such visible acts as are thought to be significant, and also of their symbolic acts, their speech, and their works of art. But what makes the record interesting is that through our likeness to them it becomes also a record of what they were, of their meanings, of their inner life, the semblance of which is awakened in us by the acts recorded.

I open Herodotus at random and find an account of how the Carthaginians, having captured many Phoceans from disabled ships, landed them and stoned them to death. But after this the sheep, oxen, or men who passed the spot were stricken with palsy. So they consulted the Delphic Oracle, who required them to institute a custom of honoring the dead Phoceans with funeral rites. Here is a record of behavior which we interpret by sympathy. We feel the cruelty of the Carthaginians, their wonder and alarm at the strange conduct of the stricken men and animals, their anxious resort to Delphi, their awed obedience to the oracle. Of the grounds for criticizing this narrative from the standpoint of a wider study of human ideas and human behavior I need not now speak. Like all social observation that comes down from the past, it must be interpreted in view of the difference in mental complexes between the men who made the records and us who read them. We must, as we say, get their background and point of view. But men are, after all, so much alike that an imagination trained by comparative study can usually make out fairly well what the records mean. The true reason why we must, in sociology, rely mainly upon contemporary rather than historical facts is the inadequacy of the record. History does not tell what we want to know, and we must look in the world about us for answers to questions which the men of old never thought of putting.

At any rate we actually have accumulations of social knowledge. Aristotle and many other early writers collected facts which are still held to be trustworthy, and interpreted them by generalizations which still command respect. In modern times the process has gone on developing in volume, diversity, and precision, and has given rise to technical groups of specially trained men. We have many kinds of history, we have social anthropology, political science, law, economics, sociology, comparative religion, comparative literature and art, and other departments, each with its own archives of recorded fact.

Indeed, as regards cumulation the study of mankind has a great advantage in that its subject matter is uniquely self-recording. Even the records of geology and paleontology do not compare in richness with those that man hands down about himself through language and the several arts. And the more he approaches and enters a civilized state, the more extensive these records become. The dinosaur may leave his skeleton and even his (or her) eggs, but man deposits a fossil mind. We know infinitely more about him than we do about any other animal, and the difficulty of accumulating knowledge, so far as primary facts are concerned, is quite imaginary. Dispute, as in other fields, is mainly about interpretation. The selection and explanation of facts has heretofore proved provisional; it has to be done over again with every change in the general current of thought. But is not this true of all science? At this moment the whole theoretical trunk of physics has been torn up by the roots and seems likely to be thrown upon the rubbish pile. A lasting structure of knowledge is hardly to be expected, except as regards the primary facts and their simpler relations, and this much we may expect in social science as well as in spatial.

It is high time that I referred to that body of knowledge and practice known as statistics. Statistics is an exact method, and it is enabled to be such precisely because it is not in itself social but mathematical. It does not directly *perceive* social facts, or any other kind of facts, but it takes standard units of some sort, which may be perceived social facts, and compiles, arranges, manipulates, and presents them in a way intended to make them yield illumination. The statistician operates between the primary observer, on the one hand, and, on the other, the theorist who demands light on certain hypotheses. Perhaps I may without offense liken him to a cook, who neither supplies the food nor consumes it, but is a specialist upon the intervening processes.

Evidently it would not be good sense to assume any antagonism between the exact methods of statistics and the more fallible procedure of sympathetic observation and interpretation. They are complementary and do not or should not overlap. The only opposition likely to arise is one due to the bias of the practitioner. A statistician, if he lacks breadth of mind, is apt to be so fond of his exact processes that he avoids and depreciates anything else, while the sympathetic observer is apt to be impatient of statistics. This difference of tastes would not do much harm if the functions were kept separate, but when a man who is fit for only one assumes both the result is unfortunate. Much statistical work, especially that based upon questionnaires or interviews, is vitiated by a lack of dramatic insight into the states of mind of the people who supply the information. A questionnaire is an instrument of social perception, and if its use is to have any scientific character, the first duty of the user is to dramatize the play of thought and feeling that takes place between the person that puts the question and the person that answers it. What was the actual state of mind of the latter, and what the human significance of his reply? Not every investigator has the insight and the conscience to perceive and report this real fact, commonly so different from the apparent fact, upon which the value of his work depends.

And so with the questions or problems used in mental tests. If they aim only to test the power to perform standardized operations they are objective, but, socially speaking, superficial; if they go beyond this and attempt to discover social or moral attitudes they are subjective, and of no value for science without sympathetic interpretation.

It is not the case that social science is becoming exact through the substitution of statistics for social sympathy and imagination. What is taking place is, rather, that the use of sympathy and imagination is becoming more competent, while statistics is being substituted for guesswork in the manipulation of data.

Another impression which I take to be erroneous is that statistics is revealing uniformities or regularities in social phenomena which indicate that these phenomena may in time prove to be subject to exact prediction in quite the same way as those of physics. It is true that statistics is revealing sequence, order, and a remarkable degree of predictability in certain social processes. By analysis of what has taken place during the past ten years, especially in the economic field, where the facts are largely material, it may be possible to forecast what will take place in the next five; and no one can say how far we may go in this direction. The whole basis of this, however, seems to be the prevalence of inertia and the rarity and slowness of the more originative processes. The greater part of human phenomena are so far routinized as to be more or less subject to calculation. Wherever men, under the impetus of habit and suggestion, are moving ahead in a mechanical manner, or where their intelligence is merely repeating what is essentially an old synthesis of motives—as, for example, in deciding whether to marry or not—exact methods are in place. The complex of human events can, to a great extent, be resolved into currents of tendency moving on definite lines at ascertainable speeds. If we can measure these lines and speeds it may be possible to predict their combined operation, much as the motion of a comet is predicted by calculating the resultant of the gravity, tangential momentum, and other forces acting upon it. The whole basis of prediction in such fields as that of the business cycle is the belief that the underlying motivation is essentially standardized or repetitive.

Probably no exact science could have foreseen the sudden rise of the automotive industry and the genius of Henry Ford, although now that this industry is developed and institutionized we may perhaps calculate with some precision what it will bring forth in the near future.

There is no good reason to think that such statistical methods can anticipate that which, after all, chiefly distinguishes human life from physical processes, namely, originative mental synthesis, whether by outstanding individuals or by groups. The kind of mechanistic theory which would exclude the unique function of human consciousness and will is not only highly speculative and unverifiable, but seems, as a speculation, to be losing ground. Recent philosophic writers (for example, our colleague Professor Sellars),[3] in so far as they accept mecha-

3. R. W. Sellars, *Evolutionary Naturalism*, *passim*.

nism or determinism, interpret them in such a way as to leave intact
our human power of reorganizing and redirecting life in a manner that
no exact science can hope to foresee.

There is indeed one way in which physical and social science may
be assimilated. We may find that atoms and electrons are not so uniform and reliable as has been believed, that the supposed physical laws
are only statistical, covering diversity in the phenomena somewhat as
social statistics cover the diversities of individual men. Indeed, we are
told by men apparently competent that "the present state of physics
lends no support whatever to the belief that there is a causality in
physical nature which is founded on rigorously exact laws."[4] In some
such way as this the gulf may be bridged, but never, I think, by reducing the human will to zero.

Having dealt so far with observation, either direct or mediated by
technique, I come now to the interpretive use of the data, to the attempt to build a structure of social truth. This is, in all sciences, a work
of the imagination, and a work which has always in the past proved
to be provisional and to require renewal to meet the general advance
of thought. I see no reason to expect anything else in the future.

At the present time all the sciences of life are, I suppose, controlled
by the idea of organic development. Darwin gave these studies their
orientation by making them studies of process rather than state, of
what is going on rather than what is, of a drama rather than a picture.
For many years, however, evolutionary ideas were applied to social
phenomena chiefly in an external and analogical way; they were imposed artificially, not allowed to grow naturally out of the social processes themselves. The result was a vast body of social theory and pro-
paganda, all claiming to be evolutionary and scientific, but none of it
the work of a technical group devoted primarily and disinterestedly
to the study of social facts. Even at the present time specialists in con-
tiguous evolutionary fields contribute profusely to social literature and
by no means hide their belief that they know more about what is important to society than do the so-called "sociologists." Whether they
do or not, it is a fact that some of these extraneous doctrines, like the
pseudo-Darwinism of Nietzsche or the hereditary determinism of the
more extreme followers of Galton, have had, and still have, a wide
influence.

I shall assume, however, that, after all, social phenomena are most
likely to be understood by those who make the study of them their
main business, and that the application of evolutionary ideas in this

---

4. Hermann Weyl, quoted by J. W. N. Sullivan, *Aspects of Science,* p. 158.

sphere is the task mainly of history, anthropology, ethnology, political science, economics, social psychology, sociology, and kindred disciplines. All of these studies have, in fact, a decidedly evolutionary trend, and several of them may be said to have been created by the evolutionary movement. All of them aim at the understanding of personal and social wholes in the actual process of living. All make increasing use of social psychology. They do not aim to resolve social phenomena into elements which are not social, but rather to investigate the simpler and more general social processes and use the knowledge thus gained in synthetic interpretation of larger social wholes. This may be done by the use of well-chosen samples, as in studies of individual persons, of typical local or institutional conditions, and the like.

In general, the insights of sociology, if I may take that subject as representative, are imaginative reconstructions of life whose truth depends upon the competence of the mind that makes them to embrace the chief factors of the process studied and reproduce or anticipate their operation. This requires native ability, factual knowledge, social culture, and training in a particular technique.

It is sometimes supposed that pre-Darwinian studies in history, literature, art, and social theory were essentially unscientific and futile; in fact, mere rubbish needing to be swept aside by the advancing forces of science. On the contrary, many of these studies were based on common sense, had a sound empirical basis, and are even now of more value than hurried, dogmatical, and mostly analogical efforts to supplant them by something having the appearance of natural science. Such efforts have given rise to a variety of pseudo-sciences, some of which are flourishing at the present time, but they have not broken the real continuity of contemporary social knowledge with the solid work of earlier generations. Sociology, at least, recognizes whole-heartedly the value of pre-evolutionary research, and expects that its students shall know something of the great currents of historical, literary, and artistic tradition; shall have, indeed, as broad a culture in the humanities as possible. This culture affords the only access to great stores of facts with which we cannot dispense. It also affords a perspective of the development of social interpretation. Most of the generalizations now being defined, explored, tested, and developed into systematic knowledge were foreshadowed by penetrating minds of the past. How much of modern social psychology is implicit in the maxims of La Rochefoucauld, what insight into social processes had Gibbon! Sainte-Beuve, who saw literature as an organic human whole, observing the individual writer and the current of literary tendency with equal understanding, was a real sociologist in the field of criticism. Goethe was one in an even larger sense. An honest and competent student will be deferent to the achievements of the past and will lend no countenance to those shallow spirits who see scientific method as a sort of trick of laboratories and schedules by which they may avoid the slow approaches of actual social knowledge.

As to prediction, I have already pointed out that in the more mechanized processes of the social system it may be remarkably exact. We have no ground, however, to expect any such exactness in foretelling the multitudinous fluctuations of human life in general. Prediction, in any science, requires that the mind embrace the process, as the physicist, in his formula, embraces the process of a falling body, and so, through participation, foresee the outcome. Even in natural science this can usually be done with precision only when the process is artificially simplified, as in the laboratory. The social processes of actual life can be embraced only by a mind working at large, participating through intellect and sympathy with many currents of human force, and bringing them to an imaginative synthesis. This can hardly be done with much precision, nor done at all except by infusing technical methods with a total and creative spirit.

The human mind participates in social processes in a way that it does not in any other processes. It is itself a sample, a phase, of those processes, and is capable, under favorable circumstances, of so far identifying itself with the general movement of a group as to achieve a remarkably just anticipation of what the group will do. Prediction of this sort is largely intuitive rather than intellectual; it is like that of the man with a genius for business as contrasted with that of the statistician; it is not sincere, but it is the very process by which many of the great generalizations of science have first been perceived.

Predictions of any sort, however, are most likely to be sound when they are made by those who have the most precise familiarity with the observable processes, and it is the increase of this familiarity on the part of social observers, along with their greater insight into principles, that should make them better guessers of what is to happen than they have been in the past.

What, then, is there new in contemporary social science, what, if anything, that promises a more rapid and secure accumulation of knowledge than in the past? Mainly, I should say, the following:

1. Liberation from outworn theological and metaphysical assumptions and reorganization on the basis of factual study and an evolutionary outlook.

2. The rise of a technical group of adequately trained scholars, with

those traditions and standards, that expert criticism and exacting group atmosphere, indispensable to all higher achievement.

3. The development, since 1860, and especially since 1900, of a network of factual theory, by which I mean theory springing from observation and capable of being verified or refuted by the closer study of fact. Such theory is to be distinguished from much of the older speculation, which was largely metaphysical, unverifiable, and for that reason of no use in stimulating research.

There is nothing startling in the present movement. It shows no break with the past, does not promise any phenomenal power of prediction, and is, in fact, chiefly occupied with the ascertainment of what is actually going on and with the development of technique. We are trying to describe and interpret human life in the same spirit that the life of animals and plants has been described and interpreted, but with due regard to the different character of the problem. The human material is peculiar not only in its enormous abundance and variety, but in requiring, to deal with it, a radically different theoretical and technical equipment.

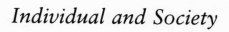

Individual and Society

10

Society and the Individual

"Society and the Individual" is really the subject of this whole book, and not merely of [this chapter]. It is my general aim to set forth, from various points of view, what the individual is, considered as a member of a social whole; while the special purpose of this chapter is only to offer a preliminary statement of the matter, as I conceive it, afterward to be unfolded at some length and variously illustrated.

If we accept the evolutionary point of view we are led to see the relation between society and the individual as an organic relation. That is, we see that the individual is not separable from the human whole, but a living member of it, deriving his life from the whole through social and hereditary transmission as truly as if men were literally one body. He cannot cut himself off; the strands of heredity and education are woven into all his being. And, on the other hand, the social whole is in some degree dependent upon each individual, because each contributes something to the common life that no one else can contribute. Thus we have, in a broad sense of the word, an "organism" or living whole made up of differentiated members, each of which has a special function.

This is true of society in that large sense which embraces all humanity, and also of any specific social group. A university, for example, is an organic whole, made up of students, teachers, officials, and others. Every member is more or less dependent upon every other, because all contribute to the common life. And note that it is precisely his individuality, his functional difference from the rest, that gives each member his peculiar importance. The professor of Paleontology has a part that no one else can play; and so, less obviously, perhaps, has every teacher and student. The organic view stresses both the unity of the whole and the peculiar value of the individual, explaining each by the other. What is a football team without a quarter-back? Almost as useless as a quarter-back without a team. A well-developed individual can exist only in and through a well-developed whole, and *vice versa*.

From "Society and the Individual," chapter 4 of *Human Nature and the Social Order* (1902; New York: Schocken, 1964), 35–50.

This seems a simple idea, and so it is, but it is so opposed to some of our most cherished habits of thought that we may well take time to look at it from various points of view.

A separate individual is an abstraction unknown to experience, and so likewise is society when regarded as something apart from individuals. The real thing is Human Life, which may be considered either in an individual aspect or in a social, that is to say a general, aspect; but is always, as a matter of fact, both individual and general. In other words, "society" and "individuals" do not denote separable phenomena, but are simply collective and distributive aspects of the same thing, the relation between them being like that between other expressions one of which denotes a group as a whole and the other the members of the group, such as the army and the soldiers, the class and the students, and so on. This holds true of any social aggregate, great or small; of a family, a city, a nation, a race; of mankind as a whole: no matter how extensive, complex, or enduring a group may be, no good reason can be given for regarding it as essentially different in this respect from the smallest, simplest, or most transient.

So far, then, as there is any difference between the two, it is rather in our point of view than in the object we are looking at: when we speak of society, or use any other collective term, we fix our minds upon some general view of the people concerned, while when we speak of individuals we disregard the general aspect and think of them as if they were separate. Thus "the Cabinet" may consist of President Lincoln, Secretary Stanton, Secretary Seward, and so on; but when I say "the Cabinet" I do not suggest the same idea as when I enumerate these gentlemen separately. Society, or any complex group, may, to ordinary observation, be a very different thing from all of its members viewed one by one—as a man who beheld General Grant's army from Missionary Ridge would have seen something other than he would by approaching every soldier in it. In the same way a picture is made up of so many square inches of painted canvas; but if you should look at these one at a time, covering the others, until you had seen them all, you would still not have seen the picture. There may, in all such cases, be a system or organization in the whole that is not apparent in the parts. In this sense, and in no other, is there a difference between society and the individuals of which it is composed; a difference not residing in the facts themselves but existing to the observer on account of the limits of his perception. A *complete* view of society would also be a complete view of all the individuals, and *vice versa;* there would be no difference between them.

And just as there is no society or group that is not a collective view of persons, so there is no individual who may not be regarded as a particular view of social groups. He has no separate existence; through both the hereditary and the social factors in his life a man is bound into the whole of which he is a member, and to consider him apart from it is quite as artificial as to consider society apart from individuals.

If this is true there is, of course, a fallacy in that not uncommon manner of speaking which sets the social and the individual over against each other as separate and antagonistic. The word "social" appears to be used in at least three fairly distinct senses, but in none of these does it mean something that can properly be regarded as opposite to individual or personal.

In its largest sense it denotes that which pertains to the collective aspect of humanity, to society in its widest and vaguest meaning. In this sense the individual and all his attributes are social, since they are all connected with the general life in one way or another, and are part of a collective development.

Again, social may mean what pertains to immediate intercourse, to the life of conversation and face-to-face sympathy—sociable, in short. This is something quite different, but no more antithetical to individual than the other; it is in these relations that individuality most obviously exists and expresses itself.

In a third sense the word means conducive to the collective welfare, and thus becomes nearly equivalent to moral, as when we say that crime or sensuality is unsocial or anti-social; but here again it cannot properly be made the antithesis of individual—since wrong is surely no more individual than right—but must be contrasted with immoral, brutal, selfish, or some other word with an ethical implication.

There are a number of expressions which are closely associated in common usage with this objectionable antithesis; such words, for instance, as individualism, socialism, particularism, collectivism.[1] These appear to be used with a good deal of vagueness, so that it is always in order to require that any one who employs them shall make it plain

---

1. Also free-will, determinism, egoism, and altruism, which involve, in my opinion, a kindred misconception.

in what sense they are to be taken. I wish to make no captious objections to particular forms of expression, and so far as these can be shown to have meanings that express the facts of life I have nothing to say against them. Of the current use of individualism and socialism in antithesis to each other, about the same may be said as of the words without the *ism*. I do not see that life presents two distinct and opposing tendencies that can properly be called individualism and socialism, any more than that there are two distinct and opposing entities, society and the individual, to embody these tendencies. The phenomena usually called individualistic are always socialistic in the sense that they are expressive of tendencies growing out of the general life, and, contrariwise, the so-called socialistic phenomena have always an obvious individual aspect. These and similar terms may be used, conveniently enough, to describe theories or programmes of the day, but whether they are suitable for purposes of careful study appears somewhat doubtful. If used, they ought, it seems to me, to receive more adequate definition than they have at present.

For example, all the principal epochs of European history might be, and most of them are, spoken of as individualistic on one ground or another, and without departing from current usage of the word. The decaying Roman Empire was individualistic if a decline of public spirit and an every-man-for-himself feeling and practice constitute individualism. So also was the following period of political confusion. The feudal system is often regarded as individualistic, because of the relative independence and isolation of small political units—quite a different use of the word from the preceding—and after this come the Revival of Learning, the Renaissance, and the Reformation, which are all commonly spoken of, on still other grounds, as assertions of individualism. Then we reach the seventeenth and eighteenth centuries, sceptical, transitional, and, again, individualistic; and so to our own time, which many hold to be the most individualistic of all. One feels like asking whether a word which means so many things as this means anything whatever.

There is always some confusion of terms in speaking of opposition between an individual and society in general, even when the writer's meaning is obvious enough: it would be more accurate to say either that one individual is opposing many, or that one part of society is opposing other parts; and thus avoid confusing the two aspects of life in the same expression. When Emerson says that society is in a conspiracy against the independence of each of its members, we are to understand that any peculiar tendency represented by one person finds itself

more or less at variance with the general current of tendencies organized in other persons. It is no more individual, nor any less social, in
a large sense, than other tendencies represented by more persons. A
thousand persons are just as truly individuals as one, and the man who
seems to stand alone draws his being from the general stream of life
just as truly and inevitably as if he were one of a thousand. Innovation
is just as social as conformity, genius as mediocrity. These distinctions
are not between what is individual and what is social, but between
what is usual or established and what is exceptional or novel. In other
words, wherever you find life as society there you will find life as individuality, and *vice versa*.

I think, then, that the antithesis, society *versus* the individual, is
false and hollow whenever used as a general or philosophical statement of human relations. Whatever idea may be in the minds of those
who set these words and their derivatives over against each other, the
notion conveyed is that of two separable entities or forces; and certainly such a notion is untrue to fact.

Most people not only think of individuals and society as more or
less separate and antithetical, but they look upon the former as antecedent to the latter. That persons make society would be generally
admitted as a matter of course; but that society makes persons would
strike many as a startling notion, though I know of no good reason
for looking upon the distributive aspect of life as more primary or
causative than the collective aspect. The reason for the common impression appears to be that we think most naturally and easily of the
individual phase of life, simply because it is a tangible one, the phase
under which men appear to the senses, while the actuality of groups,
of nations, of mankind at large, is realized only by the active and instructed imagination. We ordinarily regard society, so far as we conceive it at all, in a vaguely material aspect, as an aggregate of physical
bodies, not as the vital whole which it is; and so, of course, we do not
see that it may be as original or causative as anything else. Indeed,
many look upon "society" and other general terms as somewhat mysti-
cal, and are inclined to doubt whether there is any reality back of them.

This naïve individualism of thought—which, however, does not
truly see the individual any more than it does society—is reinforced
by traditions in which all of us are brought up, and is so hard to shake
off that it may be worth while to point out a little more definitely some
of the prevalent ways of conceiving life which are permeated by it, and
which any one who agrees with what has just been said may regard
as fallacious. My purpose in doing this is only to make clearer [this]

standpoint . . . , and I do not propose any thorough discussion of the
views mentioned.

First, then, we have *mere individualism*. In this the distributive aspect
is almost exclusively regarded, collective phases being looked upon as
quite secondary and incidental. Each person is held to be a separate
agent, and all social phenomena are thought of as originating in the
action of such agents. The individual is the source, the independent,
the only human source, of events. Although this way of looking at
things has been much discredited by the evolutionary science and philosophy of recent years, it is by no means abandoned, even in theory,
and practically it enters as a premise, in one shape or another, into
most of the current thought of the day. It springs naturally from the
established way of thinking, congenial, as I have remarked, to the ordinary material view of things and corroborated by theological and other
traditions.

Next is *double causation,* or a partition of power between society
and the individual, thought of as separate causes. This notion, in one
shape or another, is the one ordinarily met with in social and ethical
discussion. It is no advance, philosophically, upon the preceding.
There is the same premise of the individual as a separate, unrelated
agent; but over against him is set a vaguely conceived general or collective interest and force. It seems that people are so accustomed to thinking of themselves as uncaused causes, special creators on a small scale,
that when the existence of general phenomena is forced upon their
notice they are likely to regard these as something additional, separate,
and more or less antithetical. Our two forces contend with varying
fortunes, the thinker sometimes sympathizing with one, sometimes
with the other, and being an individualist or a socialist accordingly.
The doctrines usually understood in connection with these terms differ, as regards their conception of the nature of life, only in taking
opposite sides of the same questionable antithesis. The socialist holds
it desirable that the general or collective force should win; the individualist has a contrary opinion. Neither offers any change of ground, any
reconciling and renewing breadth of view. So far as breadth of view
is concerned a man might quite as well be an individualist as a socialist
or collectivist, the two being identical in philosophy though antagonistic in programme. If one is inclined to neither party he may take refuge
in the expectation that the controversy, resting, as he may hold that

it does, on a false conception of life, will presently take its proper place among the forgotten *débris* of speculation.

Thirdly we have *primitive individualism*. This expression has been used to describe the view that sociality follows individuality in time, is a later and additional product of development. This view is a variety of the preceding, and is, perhaps, formed by a mingling of individualistic preconceptions with a somewhat crude evolutionary philosophy. Individuality is usually conceived as lower in moral rank as well as precedent in time. Man *was* a mere individual, mankind a mere aggregation of such, but he had gradually become socialized, he is progressively merging into a social whole. Morally speaking, the individual is the bad, the social the good, and we must push on the work of putting down the former and bringing in the latter.

Of course the view which I regard as sound, is that individuality is neither prior in time nor lower in moral rank than sociality; but that the two have always existed side by side as complementary aspects of the same thing, and that the line of progress is from a lower to a higher type of both, not from the one to the other. If the word social is applied only to the higher forms of mental life it should, as already suggested, be opposed not to individual, but to animal, sensual, or some other word implying mental or moral inferiority. If we go back to a time when the state of our remote ancestors was such that we are not willing to call it social, then it must have been equally undeserving to be described as individual or personal; that is to say, they must have been just as inferior to us when viewed separately as when viewed collectively. To question this is to question the vital unity of human life.

The life of the human species, like that of other species, must always have been both general and particular, must always have had its collective and distributive aspects. The plane of this life has gradually risen, involving, of course, both the aspects mentioned. Now, as ever, they develop as one, and may be observed united in the highest activities of the highest minds. Shakespeare, for instance, is in one point of view a unique and transcendent individual; in another he is a splendid expression of the general life of mankind: the difference is not in him but in the way we choose to look at him.

Finally, there is *the social faculty view*. This expression might be used to indicate those conceptions which regard the social as including only a part, often a rather definite part, of the individual. Human nature is thus divided into individualistic or non-social tendencies or faculties, and those that are social. Thus, certain emotions, as love, are social; others, as fear or anger, are unsocial or individualistic. Some writers have even treated the intelligence as an individualistic faculty, and have found sociality only in some sorts of emotion or sentiment.

This idea of instincts or faculties that are peculiarly social is well enough if we use this word in the sense of pertaining to conversation or immediate fellow feeling. Affection is certainly more social in this sense than fear. But if it is meant that these instincts or faculties are in themselves morally higher than others, or that they alone pertain to the collective life, the view is, I think, very questionable. At any rate the opinion I hold, and expect to explain more fully in the further course of this book, is that man's psychical outfit is not divisible into the social and the non-social; but that he is all social in a large sense, is all a part of the common human life, and that his social or moral progress consists less in the aggrandizement of particular faculties or instincts and the suppression of others, than in the discipline of all with reference to a progressive organization of life which we know in thought as conscience.

Some instincts or tendencies may grow in relative importance, may have an increasing function, while the opposite may be true of others. Such relative growth and diminution of parts seems to be a general feature of evolution, and there is no reason why it should be absent from our mental development. But here as well as elsewhere most parts, if not all, are or have been functional with reference to a life collective as well as distributive; there is no sharp separation of faculties, and progress takes place rather by gradual adaptation of old organs to new functions than by disuse and decay.

To make it quite clear what the organic view involves, so far as regards theory, I will take several questions, such as I have found that people ask when discussing the relation of society and the individual, and will suggest how, as it seems to me, they may be answered.

1. Is not society, after all, made up of individuals, and of nothing else?

I should say, Yes. It is plain, every-day humanity, not a mysterious something else.

2. Is society anything more than the sum of the individuals?

In a sense, Yes. There is an organization, a life-process, in any social whole that you cannot see in the individuals separately. To study them one by one and attempt to understand society by putting them together will lead you astray. It is "individualism" in a bad sense of the word. Whole sciences, like political economy; great institutions, like the church, have gone wrong at this point. You must see your groups, your social processes, as the living wholes that they are.

3. Is the individual a product of society?

Yes, in the sense that everything human about him has a history in the social past. If we consider the two sources from which he draws his life, heredity and communication, we see that what he gets through the germ-plasm has a social history in that it has had to adapt itself to past society in order to survive: the traits we are born with are such as have undergone a social test in the lives of our ancestors. And what he gets from communication—language, education, and the like—comes directly from society. Even physical influences, like food and climate, rarely reach us except as modified and adapted by social conditions.

4. Can we separate the individual from society?

Only in an external sense. If you go off alone into the wilderness you take with you a mind formed in society, and you continue social intercourse in your memory and imagination, or by the aid of books. This, and this only, keeps humanity alive in you, and just in so far as you lose the power of intercourse your mind decays. Long solitude, as in the case of sheep-herders on the Western plains, or prisoners in solitary confinement, often produces imbecility. This is especially likely to happen with the uneducated, whose memories are not well stored with material for imaginative intercourse.

At times in the history of Christianity, and of other religions also, hermits have gone to dwell in desert places, but they have usually kept up some communication with one another and with the world outside, certain of them, like St. Jerome, having been famous letter-writers. Each of them, in fact, belonged to a social system from which he drew ideals and moral support. We may suspect that St. Simeon Stylites, who dwelt for years on top of a pillar, was not unaware that his austerity was visible to others.

A castaway who should be unable to retain his imaginative hold upon human society might conceivably live the life of an intelligent animal, exercising his mind upon the natural conditions about him, but his distinctively human faculties would certainly be lost, or in abeyance.

5. Is the individual in any sense free, or is he a mere piece of society?

Yes, he is free, as I conceive the matter, but it is an organic freedom, which he works out in co-operation with others, not a freedom to do things independently of society. It is team-work. He has freedom to function in his own way, like the quarter-back, but, in one way or another, he has to play the game as life brings him into it.

The evolutionary point of view encourages us to believe that life is a creative process, that we are really building up something new and worth while, and that the human will is a part of the creative energy that does this. Every individual has his unique share in the work, which no one but himself can discern and perform. Although his life flows into him from the hereditary and social past, his being as a whole is new, a fresh organization of life. Never any one before had the same powers and opportunities that you have, and you are free to use them in your own way.

It is, after all, only common sense to say that we exercise our freedom through co-operation with others. If you join a social group—let us say a dramatic club—you expect that it will increase your freedom, give your individual powers new stimulus and opportunity for expression. And why should not the same principle apply to society at large? It is through a social development that mankind has emerged from animal bondage into that organic freedom, wonderful though far from complete, that we now enjoy.

11

Social and Individual Aspects of Mind

Mind is an organic whole made up of coöperating individualities, in somewhat the same way that the music of an orchestra is made up of divergent but related sounds. No one would think it necessary or reasonable to divide the music into two kinds, that made by the whole and that of particular instruments, and no more are there two kinds of mind, the social mind and the individual mind. When we study the social mind we merely fix our attention on larger aspects and relations rather than on the narrower ones of ordinary psychology.

The view that all mind acts together in a vital whole from which the individual is never really separate flows naturally from our growing knowledge of heredity and suggestion, which makes it increasingly clear that every thought we have is linked with the thought of our ancestors and associates, and through them with that of society at large. It is also the only view consistent with the general standpoint of modern science, which admits nothing isolate in nature.

The unity of the social mind consists not in agreement but in organization, in the fact of reciprocal influence or causation among its parts, by virtue of which everything that takes place in it is connected with everything else, and so is an outcome of the whole. Whether, like the orchestra, it gives forth harmony may be a matter of dispute, but that its sound, pleasing or otherwise, is the expression of a vital coöperation, cannot well be denied. Certainly everything that I say or think is influenced by what others have said or thought, and, in one way or another, sends out an influence of its own in turn.

This differentiated unity of mental or social life, present in the simplest intercourse but capable of infinite growth and adaptation, is what I mean in this work by social organization. It would be useless, I think, to attempt a more elaborate definition. We have only to open our eyes to *see* organization; and if we cannot do that no definition will help us.

From "Social and Individual Aspects of Mind," chapter 1 of *Social Organization: A Study of the Larger Mind* (1909; reprint New York: Schocken, 1963), 3–12.

In the social mind we may distinguish—very roughly of course—conscious and unconscious relations, the unconscious being those of which we are not aware, which for some reason escape our notice. A great part of the influences at work upon us are of this character: our language, our mechanical arts, our government and other institutions, we derive chiefly from people to whom we are but indirectly and unconsciously related. The larger movements of society—the progress and decadence of nations, institutions and races—have seldom been a matter of consciousness until they were past. And although the growth of social consciousness is perhaps the greatest fact of history, it has still but a narrow and fallible grasp of human life.

Social consciousness, or awareness of society, is inseparable from self-consciousness, because we can hardly think of ourselves excepting with reference to a social group of some sort, or of the group except with reference to ourselves. The two things go together, and what we are really aware of is a more or less complex personal or social whole, of which now the particular, now the general, aspect is emphasized.

In general, then, most of our reflective consciousness, of our wide-awake state of mind, is social consciousness, because a sense of our relation to other persons, or of other persons to one another, can hardly fail to be a part of it. Self and society are twin-born, we know one as immediately as we know the other, and the notion of a separate and independent ego is an illusion.

This view, which seems to me quite simple and in accord with common-sense, is not the one most commonly held, for psychologists and even sociologists are still much infected with the idea that self-consciousness is in some way primary, and antecedent to social consciousness, which must be derived by some recondite process of combination or elimination. I venture, therefore, to give some further exposition of it, based in part on first-hand observation of the growth of social ideas in children.

Descartes is, I suppose, the best-known exponent of the traditional view regarding the primacy of self-consciousness. Seeking an unquestionable basis for philosophy, he thought that he found it in the proposition "I think, therefore I am" *(cogito, ergo sum)*. This seemed to him inevitable, though all else might be illusion. "I observed," he says, "that, whilst I thus wished to think that all was false, it was absolutely necessary that I, who thus thought, should be somewhat; and as I observed that this truth, *I think, hence I am,* was so certain and of such evidence that no ground of doubt, however extravagant, could be alleged by the sceptics capable of shaking it, I concluded that I might, without scruple, accept it as the first principle of the philosophy of which I was in search."[1]

From our point of view this reasoning is unsatisfactory in two essential respects. In the first place it seems to imply that "I"-consciousness is a part of all consciousness, when, in fact, it belongs only to a rather advanced stage of development. In the second it is one-sided or "individualistic" in asserting the personal or "I" aspect to the exclusion of the social or "we" aspect, which is equally original with it.

Introspection is essential to psychological or social insight, but the introspection of Descartes was, in this instance, a limited, almost abnormal, sort of introspection—that of a self-absorbed philosopher doing his best to isolate himself from other people and from all simple and natural conditions of life. The mind into which he looked was in a highly technical state, not likely to give him a just view of human consciousness in general.

Introspection is of a larger sort in our day. There is a world of things in the mind worth looking at, and the modern psychologist, instead of fixing his attention wholly on an extreme form of speculative self-consciousness, puts his mind through an infinite variety of experiences, intellectual and emotional, simple and complex, normal and abnormal, sociable and private, recording in each case what he sees in it. He does this by subjecting it to suggestions or incitements of various kinds, which awaken the activities he desires to study.

In particular he does it largely by what may be called *sympathetic introspection,* putting himself into intimate contact with various sorts of persons and allowing them to awake in himself a life similar to their own, which he afterwards, to the best of his ability, recalls and describes. In this way he is more or less able to understand—always by introspection—children, idiots, criminals, rich and poor, conservative and radical—any phase of human nature not wholly alien to his own.

This I conceive to be the principal method of the social psychologist.

One thing which this broader introspection reveals is that the "I"-consciousness does not explicitly appear until the child is, say, about

1. Descartes, *Discourse on Method,* part iv.

two years old, and that when it does appear it comes in inseparable conjunction with the consciousness of other persons and of those relations which make up a social group. It is in fact simply one phase of a body of personal thought which is self-consciousness in one aspect and social consciousness in another.

The mental experience of a new-born child is probably a mere stream of impressions, which may be regarded as being individual, in being differentiated from any other stream, or as social, in being an undoubted product of inheritance and suggestion from human life at large; but is not aware either of itself or of society.

Very soon, however, the mind begins to discriminate personal impressions and to become both naively self-conscious and naively conscious of society; that is, the child is aware, in an unreflective way, of a group and of his own special relation to it. He does not say "I" nor does he name his mother, his sister or his nurse, but he has images and feelings out of which these ideas will grow. Later comes the more reflective consciousness which names both himself and other people, and brings a fuller perception of the relations which constitute the unity of this small world.[2]

And so on to the most elaborate phases of self-consciousness and social consciousness, to the metaphysician pondering the Ego, or the sociologist meditating on the Social Organism. Self and society go together, as phases of a common whole. I am aware of the social groups in which I live as immediately and authentically as I am aware of myself; and Descartes might have said "We think," *cogitamus,* on as good grounds as he said *cogito.*

But, it may be said, this very consciousness that you are considering is after all located in a particular person, and so are all similar consciousness, so that what we see, if we take an objective view of the matter, is merely an aggregate of individuals, however social those individuals may be. Common-sense, most people think, assures us that the separate person is the primary fact of life.

If so, is it not because common-sense has been trained by custom

2. There is much interest and significance in the matter of children's first learning the use of "I" and other self-words—just how they learn them and what they mean by them. Some discussion of the matter, based on observation of two children, will be found in my book *Human Nature and the Social Order;* and more recently I have published a paper in the *Psychological Review,* vol. 15 (November 1908) called "A Study of the Early Use of Self-Words by a Child." "I" seems to mean primarily the assertion of will in a social medium of which the child is conscious and of which his "I" is an inseparable part. It is thus a social idea and, as stated in the text, arises by differentiation of a vague body of personal thought which is self-consciousness in one phase and social consciousness in another. It has no necessary reference to the body.

to look at one aspect of things and not another? Common-sense, moderately informed, assures us that the individual has his being only as part of a whole. What does not come by heredity comes by communication and intercourse; and the more closely we look the more apparent it is that separateness is an illusion of the eye and community the inner truth. "Social organism," using the term in no abstruse sense but merely to mean a vital unity in human life, is a fact as obvious to enlightened common-sense as individuality.

I do not question that the individual is a differentiated centre of psychical life, having a world of his own into which no other individual can fully enter; living in a stream of thought in which there is nothing quite like that in any other stream, neither his "I," nor his "you," nor his "we," nor even any material object; all, probably, as they exist for him, have something unique about them. But this uniqueness is no more apparent and verifiable than the fact—not at all inconsistent with it—that he is in the fullest sense member of a whole, appearing such not only to scientific observation but also to his own untrained consciousness.

There is then no mystery about social consciousness. The view that there is something recondite about it and that it must be dug for with metaphysics and drawn forth from the depths of speculation, springs from a failure to grasp adequately the social nature of all higher consciousness. What we need in this connection is only a better seeing and understanding of rather ordinary and familiar facts.

We may view social consciousness either in a particular mind or as a coöperative activity of many minds. The social ideas that I have are closely connected with those that other people have, and act and react upon them to form a whole. This gives us public consciousness, or to use a more familiar term, public opinion, in the broad sense of a group state of mind which is more or less distinctly aware of itself. By this last phrase I mean such a mutual understanding of one another's points of view on the part of the individuals or groups concerned as naturally results from discussion. There are all degrees of this awareness in the various individuals. Generally speaking, it never embraces the whole in all its complexity, but almost always some of the relations that enter into the whole. The more intimate the communication of a group the more complete, the more thoroughly knit together into a living whole, is its public consciousness.

In a congenial family life, for example, there may be a public consciousness which brings all the important thoughts and feelings of the members into such a living and coöperative whole. In the mind of each member, also, this same thing exists as a social consciousness embracing a vivid sense of the personal traits and modes of thought and feeling of the other members. And, finally, quite inseparable from all this, is each one's consciousness of himself, which is largely a direct reflection of the ideas about himself he attributes to the others, and is directly or indirectly altogether a product of social life. Thus all consciousness hangs together, and the distinctions are chiefly based on point of view.

The unity of public opinion, like all vital unity, is one not of agreement but of organization, of interaction and mutual influence. It is true that a certain underlying likeness of nature is necessary in order that minds may influence one another and so coöperate in forming a vital whole, but identity, even in the simplest process, is unnecessary and probably impossible. The consciousness of the American House of Representatives, for example, is by no means limited to the common views, if there are any, shared by its members, but embraces the whole consciousness of every member so far as this deals with the activity of the House. It would be a poor conception of the whole which left out the opposition, or even one dissentient individual. That all minds are different is a condition, not an obstacle, to the unity that consists in a differentiated and coöperative life.

Here is another illustration of what is meant by individual and collective aspects of social consciousness. Some of us possess a good many books relating to social questions of the day. Each of these books, considered by itself, is the expression of a particular social consciousness; the author has cleared up his ideas as well as he can and printed them. But a library of such books expresses social consciousness in a larger sense; it speaks for the epoch. And certainly no one who reads the books will doubt that they form a whole, whatever their differences. The radical and the reactionist are clearly part of the same general situation.

There are, then, at least three aspects of consciousness which we may usefully distinguish: self-consciousness, or what I think of myself; social consciousness (in its individual aspect), or what I think of other people; and public consciousness, or a collective view of the foregoing as organized in a communicating group. And all three are phases of a single whole.

12

Particularism versus the Organic View

We meet in social discussion a way of thinking opposed to the conception of organic process as I have tried to expound it, which I will call intellectual particularism.[1] It consists in holding some one phase of the process to be the source of all the others, so that they may be treated as subsidiary to it.

A form of particularism that until recently was quite general is one that regards the personal wills of individual men, supplemented, perhaps, by the similar will of a personal God, as the originative factor in life from which all else comes. Everything took place, it was assumed, because some one willed it so, and for the will there was no explanation or antecedent history: it was the beginning, the creative act. When this view prevailed there could be no science of human affairs, because there was no notion of system or continuity in them; life was kept going by a series of arbitrary impulses. As opposed to this we have the organic idea that will is as much effect as cause, that it always has a history, and is no more than one phase of a great whole.

In contrast to particularistic views of this sort we have others which find the originative impulse in external conditions of life, such as climate, soil, flora, and fauna; and regard intellectual and social activities merely as the result of the physiological needs of men seeking gratification under these conditions.

A doctrine of the latter character having wide acceptance at the present time is "economic determinism," which looks upon the production of wealth and the competition for it as the process of which everything else is the result. The teaching of Marxian socialism upon this point is well known, and some economists who are not socialists nevertheless hold that all important social questions grow out of the economic struggle, and that all social institutions, including those of education, art, and religion, should be judged according as they con-

From "Particularism versus the Organic View," chapter 5 of *Social Process* (1918; reprint Carbondale and Edwardsville: Southern Illinois University Press, 1966), 43–51.
    1. The word means, in general, devotion to a small part as against the whole, and is most commonly used in historical writing to describe excessive attachment to localities or factions as against nations or other larger unities.

tribute to success in this struggle. This is, indeed, a view natural to economists, who are accustomed to look at life from this window, though most of them have enough larger philosophy to avoid any extreme form of it.[2]

The fallacy of all such ideas lies in supposing that life is built up from some one point, instead of being an organic whole which is developing as a whole now and, so far as we know, always has done so in the past. Nothing is fixed or independent, everything is plastic and takes influence as well as gives it. No factor of life can exist for men except as it is merged in the organic system and becomes an effect as much as a cause of the total development. If you insist that there is a centre from which the influence comes, all flowing in one direction, you fly in the face of fact. What observation shows is a universal interaction, in which no factor appears antecedent to the rest.

Any particularistic explanation of things, I should say, must be based on the idea that most institutions, most phases of life, are passive, receive force but do not impart it, are mere constructions and not transitive processes. But where will you find such passive institutions or phases? Are not all alive, all factors in the course of history as we know it? It seems to me that if you think concretely, in terms of experience, such an explanation cannot be definitely conceived.

I hold that the organic view is not a merely abstract theory about the nature of life and of society, but is concrete and verifiable, giving a more adequate general description than other theories of what we actually see, and appealing to fact as the test of its value. It does not attempt to say how things began, but claims that their actual working, in the present and in the historical past, corresponds to the organic conception.

Let any one fix his mind upon some one factor or group of factors which may appear at first to be original, and see if, upon reflection, it does not prove to be an outgrowth of the organic whole of history. Thus many start their explanation of modern life with the industrial

2. American sociologists are, with a few exceptions, opponents of particularism and upholders of the organic view. Among recent writers of which this is notably true I may mention C. A. Ellwood, in his *Introduction to Social Psychology* and other works, E. C. Hayes, in his *Introduction to the Study of Sociology* and his papers on methodology, Maurice Parmelee, in his works on poverty and criminology, L. M. Bristol, in his *Social Adaptation,* Blackmar and Gillin, in their *Outlines of Sociology,* and A. J. Todd, in his *Theories of Social Progress.*

revolution in England. But what made the industrial revolution? Was
it brought into the world by an act of special creation, or was it a
natural sequence of the preceding political, social, intellectual, and industrial development? Evidently the latter: it is a historical fact, like
another, to be explained as the outcome of a total process, just as much
an effect of the mental and social conditions of the past as it came to
be a cause of those of the future. I think this will always prove to be
the case when we inquire into the antecedents of any factor in life.
There *is* no beginning; we know nothing about beginnings; there is
always continuity with the past, and not with any one element only
of the past, but with the whole interacting organism of man.

If universal interaction is a fact, it follows that social life is a whole
which can be understood only by studying its total working, not by
fixing attention upon one activity and attempting to infer the rest. The
latter method implies an idea similar to that of special creation, an
idea that there is a starting-place, a break of continuity, a cause that
is not also an effect.

Such visible and tangible things as climate, fuel, soils, fruits, grains,
wild or domestic animals, and the like have for many a more substantial appearance than ideas or institutions, and they are disposed to lean
upon these, or upon some human activity immediately connected with
them, as a solid support for their philosophy of life. But after all such
things exist *for us* only as they have interacted with our traditional
organism of life and become a part of it. Climate, as it actually touches
us, may be said to be a social institution, of which clothes, shelter,
artificial heat, and irrigation are obvious aspects. And so with our economic "environment." What are deposits of iron and coal, or fertility
of soil, or navigable waters, or plants and animals capable of domesti-
cation, except in conjunction with the traditional arts and customs
through which these are utilized? To a people with one inheritance of
ideas a coal-field means nothing at all, to a people with another it
means a special development of industry. Such conditions owe their
importance, like anything else, to the way they work in with the process already going on.

Another reason for the popularity of material or economic determinism is the industrial character of our time, and of many of our
more urgent problems, which has caused our minds to be preoccupied
with this class of ideas. A society like ours produces such theories just

as a militarist society produces theories that make war the dominating process.

It is easy to show that the "*mores* of maintenance," the way a people gets its living, exercise an immense influence upon all their ideas and institutions.[3] But what are the "*mores* of maintenance"? Surely not something external to their history and imposed upon them by their material surroundings, as seems often to be assumed in this connection, but simply their whole mental and social organism, functioning for self-support through its interaction with these surroundings. They are as much the effect as they can possibly be the cause of psychical phenomena, and to argue economic determinism from their importance begs the whole question. Material factors are essential in the organic whole of life, but certainly no more so than the spiritual factors, the ideas, and institutions of the group.

Professor W. G. Sumner, probably by way of protest against a merely ideal view of history, said: "We have not made America; America has made us." Evidently we might turn this around, and it would be just as plausible. "We" have made of America something very different from what the American Indians made of it, or from what the Spaniards would probably have made of it if it had fallen to them. "America" (the United States) is the total outcome of all the complex spiritual and material factors—the former chiefly derived from European sources—which have gone into its development.

To treat the human mind as the primary factor in life, gradually unfolding its innate tendencies under the moulding power of conditions, is no less and no more plausible than to begin with the material. Why should originative impulse be ascribed to things rather than to mind? I see no warrant in observed fact for giving preference to either.

It is the aim of the organic view to "see life whole," or at least as largely as our limitations permit. However, it by no means discredits the study of society from particular standpoints, such as the economic, the political, the military, the religious. This is profitable because the whole is so vast that to get any grasp of it we need to approach it now from one point of view, now from another, fixing our attention upon each phase in turn, and then synthesizing it all as best we can.

Moreover, every phenomenon stands in more immediate relation

3. Compare the views of Professor A. G. Keller, as expressed in his Societal *Evolution,* p. 141 *ff.*

to some parts of the process than to others, making it necessary that these parts should be especially studied in order to understand this phenomenon. Hence it may be quite legitimate, with reference to a given problem, to regard certain factors as of peculiar importance. I would not deny that poverty, for example, is to be considered chiefly in connection with the economic system; while I regard the attempt to explain literature, art, or religion mainly from this standpoint as fantastic. But when we are seeking a large view we should endeavor to embrace the whole process. No study of a special chain of causes is more than an incident in that perception of a reciprocating whole which I take to be our great aim.

If we think in this way we shall approach the comprehension of a period of history, or of any social situation, very much as we approach a work of organic art, like a Gothic cathedral. We view the cathedral from many points, and at our leisure, now the front and now the apse, now taking in the whole from a distance, now lingering near at hand over the details, living with it, if we can, for months, until gradually there arises a conception of it which is confined to no one aspect, but is, so far as the limits of our mind permit, the image of the whole in all its unity and richness.

We must distinguish between the real particularist, who will not allow that any other view but his own is tenable, and the specialist, who merely develops a distinctive line of thought without imagining that it is all-sufficing. The latter is a man you can work with, while the former tries to rule the rest of us off the field. Of course he does not succeed, and the invariable outcome is that men tire of him and retain only such special illumination as his ardor may have cast; so that he contributes his bit much like the specialist. Still, it would diminish the chagrin that awaits him, and the confusion of his disciples, if he would recognize that the life-process is an evolving whole of mutually interacting parts, any one of which is effect as well as cause.

It should be the outcome of the organic view that we embrace specialty with ardor, and yet recognize that it is partial and tentative, needing from time to time to be reabsorbed and reborn of the whole. The Babel of conflicting particularisms resembles the condition of religious doctrine a century ago, when every one took it for granted that there could be but one true form of belief, and there were dozens of antagonistic systems claiming to be this form. The organic conception, in any sphere, requires that we pursue our differences in the sense of a larger unity.

I take it that what the particularist mainly needs is a philosophy and general culture which shall enable him to see his own point of view in something like its true relation to the whole of thought. It is hard to believe, for example, that an economist who also reads Plato or Emerson comprehendingly could adhere to economic determinism.

There are several rather evident reasons for the prevalence of particularism. One is the convenience of a fixed starting-point for thinking. Our minds find it much easier to move by a lineal method, in one-two-three order, than to take in action and reaction, operating at many points, in a single view. In fact, it is necessary to begin somewhere, and when we have begun somewhere we soon come to feel that that *is* the beginning, for everybody, and not merely an arbitrary selection of our own.

Very like this is what I may call the *illusion of centrality,* the fact that if you are familiar with any one factor of life it presents itself to you as a centre from which influence radiates in all directions, somewhat in the same way that the trees in an orchard will appear to radiate from any point where you happen to stand. Indeed it really is such a centre; the illusion arises from not seeing that every other factor is a centre also. The individual is a very real and active thing, but so is the group or general tendency; it is true that you can see life from the standpoint of imitation (several writers have centred upon this) but so you can from the standpoint of competition or organization. The economic process is as vital as anything can be, and there is nothing in life that does not change when it changes; but the same is true of the ideal processes; geography is important, but not more so than the technical institutions through which we react upon it; and so on.

Another root of particularism is the impulse of self-assertion. After we have worked over an idea a while we identify ourselves with it, and are impelled to make it as big as possible—to ourselves as well as to others. There are few books on sociology, or any other subject, in which this influence does not appear at least as clearly as anything which the author intended to express. It is not possible or desirable to avoid these ambitions, but they ought to be disciplined by a total view.

I have little hope of converting hardened particularists by argument; but it would seem that the spectacle of other particularists maintaining by similar reasoning views quite opposite to their own must, in time, have some effect upon them.

III

THE SELF, SOCIAL ORDER, AND SOCIAL CHANGE

The Looking-Glass Self

13

The Social Self—the Meaning of "I"

It is well to say at the outset that by the word "self" in this discussion is meant simply that which is designated in common speech by the pronouns of the first person singular, "I," "me," "my," "mine," and "myself." "Self" and "ego" are used by metaphysicians and moralists in many other senses, more or less remote from the "I" of daily speech and thought, and with these I wish to have as little to do as possible. What is here discussed is what psychologists call the empirical self, the self that can be apprehended or verified by ordinary observation. I qualify it by the word social not as implying the existence of a self that is not social—for I think that the "I" of common language always has more or less distinct reference to other people as well as the speaker—but because I wish to emphasize and dwell upon the social aspect of it.

Although the topic of the self is regarded as an abstruse one this abstruseness belongs chiefly, perhaps, to the metaphysical discussion of the "pure ego"—whatever that may be—while the empirical self should not be very much more difficult to get hold of than other facts of the mind. At any rate, it may be assumed that the pronouns of the first person have a substantial, important, and not very recondite meaning, otherwise they would not be in constant and intelligible use by simple people and young children the world over. And since they have such a meaning why should it not be observed and reflected upon like any other matter of fact? As to the underlying mystery, it is no doubt real, important, and a very fit subject of discussion by those who are competent, but I do not see that it is a *peculiar* mystery. I mean that it seems to be simply a phase of the general mystery of life, not pertaining to "I" more than to any other personal or social fact; so that here as elsewhere those who are not attempting to penetrate the mystery may simply ignore it. If this is a just view of the matter, "I" is merely a fact like any other.

From "The Social Self—the Meaning of 'I,'" chapter 5 of *Human Nature and the Social Order* (1902; reprint New York Schocken, 1964), 168–210.

The distinctive thing in the idea for which the pronouns of the first
person are names is apparently a characteristic kind of feeling which
may be called the my-feeling or sense of appropriation. Almost any
sort of ideas may be associated with this feeling, and so come to be
named "I" or "mine," but the feeling, and that alone it would seem,
is the determining factor in the matter. As Professor James says in his
admirable discussion of the self, the words "me" and "self" designate
"all the things which have the power to produce in a stream of consciousness excitement of a certain peculiar sort."[1] This view is very
fully set forth by Professor Hiram M. Stanley, whose work, *The Evolutionary Psychology of Feeling*, has an extremely suggestive chapter on
self-feeling.

I do not mean that the feeling aspect of the self is necessarily more
important than any other, but that it is the immediate and decisive
sign and proof of what "I" is; there is no appeal from it; if we go
behind it it must be to study its history and conditions, not to question
its authority. But, of course, this study of history and conditions may
be quite as profitable as the direct contemplation of self-feeling. What
I would wish to do is to present each aspect in its proper light.

The emotion or feeling of self may be regarded as instinctive, and
was doubtless evolved in connection with its important function in
stimulating and unifying the special activities of individuals.[2] It is thus
very profoundly rooted in the history of the human race and apparently indispensable to any plan of life at all similar to ours. It seems
to exist in a vague though vigorous form at the birth of each individual,
and, like other instinctive ideas or germs of ideas, to be defined and
developed by experience, becoming associated, or rather incorporated,
with muscular, visual, and other sensations; with perceptions, apper-
ceptions, and conceptions of every degree of complexity and of infinite
variety of content; and, especially, with personal ideas. Meantime the
feeling itself does not remain unaltered, but undergoes differentiation

---

1. "The words *me*, then, and *self*, so far as they arouse feeling and connote emotional worth, are *objective* designations meaning *all the things* which have the power
to produce in a stream of consciousness excitement of a certain peculiar sort" (William
James, *Psychology*, i, p. 319). A little earlier he says. "In its widest possible sense, however, a man's self is the sum total of all he *can* call his, not only his body and his psychic
powers, but his clothes and his house, his wife and children, his ancestors and friends,
his reputation and works, his lands and horses and yacht and bank-account. All these
things give him the same emotions" (*Idem*, p. 291).

So Wundt says of "Ich": "Es ist ein *Gefühl*, nicht eine Vorstellung, wie es häufig
genannt wird" (*Grundriss der Psychologie*, 4 Auflage, S. 265).

2. It is, perhaps, to be thought of as a more general instinct, of which anger, etc.,
are differentiated forms, rather than as standing by itself.

and refinement just as does any other sort of crude innate feeling. Thus, while retaining under every phase its characteristic tone or flavor, it breaks up into innumerable self-sentiments. And concrete self-feeling, as it exists in mature persons, is a whole made up of these various sentiments, along with a good deal of primitive emotion not thus broken up. It partakes fully of the general development of the mind, but never loses that peculiar gusto of appropriation that causes us to name a thought with a first-personal pronoun. The other contents of the self-idea are of little use, apparently, in defining it, because they are so extremely various. It would be no more futile, it seems to me, to attempt to define fear by enumerating the things that people are afraid of, than to attempt to define "I" by enumerating the objects with which the word is associated. Very much as fear means primarily a state of feeling, or its expression, and not darkness, fire, lions, snakes, or other things that excite it, so "I" means primarily self-feeling, or its expression, and not body, clothes, treasures, ambition, honors, and the like, with which this feeling may be connected. In either case it is possible and useful to go behind the feeling and inquire what ideas arouse it and why they do so, but this is in a sense a secondary investigation.

Since "I" is known to our experience primarily as a feeling, or as a feeling-ingredient in our ideas, it cannot be described or defined without suggesting that feeling. We are sometimes likely to fall into a formal and empty way of talking regarding questions of emotion, by attempting to define that which is in its nature primary and indefinable. A formal definition of self-feeling, or indeed of any sort of feeling, must be as hollow as a formal definition of the taste of salt, or the color red; we can expect to know what it is only by experiencing it. There can be no final test of the self except the way we feel; it is that toward which we have the "my" attitude. But as this feeling is quite as familiar to us and as easy to recall as the taste of salt or the color red, there should be no difficulty in understanding what is meant by it. One need only imagine some attack on his "me," say ridicule of his dress or an attempt to take away his property or his child, or his good name by slander, and self-feeling immediately appears. Indeed, he need only pronounce, with strong emphasis, one of the self-words, like "I" or "my," and self-feeling will be recalled by association. Another good way is to enter by sympathy into some self-assertive state of mind depicted in literature; as, for instance, into that of Coriolanus when, having been sneered at as a "boy of tears," he cries out:

> Boy! . . .
> If you have writ your annals true, 'tis there,
> That, like an eagle in a dovecote, I

Fluttered your Volscians in Corioli;
Alone I did it.—Boy!

Here is a self indeed, which no one can fail to feel, though he might
be unable to describe it. What a ferocious scream of the outraged ego
is that "I" at the end of the second line!

So much is written on this topic that ignores self-feeling and thus
deprives "self" of all vivid and palpable meaning, that I feel it permissi-
ble to add a few more passages in which this feeling is forcibly expressed. Thus in Lowell's poem, "A Glance Behind the Curtain,"
Cromwell says:

"I, perchance,
Am one raised up by the Almighty arm
To witness some great truth to all the world."

And his Columbus, on the bow of his vessel, soliloquizes:

"Here am I, with no friend but the sad sea,
The beating heart of this great enterprise,
Which, without me, would stiffen in swift death."

And so the "I am the way" which we read in the New Testament is
surely the expression of a sentiment not very different from these. In
the following we have a more plaintive sentiment of self:

Philoctetes.—And know'st thou not, O boy, whom thou dost see?
Neoptolemus.—How can I know a man I ne'er beheld?
Philoctetes.—And didst thou never hear my name, nor fame Of
these my ills, in which I pined away?
Neoptolemus.—Know that I nothing know of what thou ask'st.
Philoctetes.—O crushed with many woes, and of the Gods Hated
am I, of whom, in this my woe, No rumor travelled homeward,
nor went forth Through any clime of Hellas.[3]

We all have thoughts of the same sort as these, and yet it is possible
to talk so coldly or mystically about the self that one begins to forget
that there is, really, any such thing.

But perhaps the best way to realize the naïve meaning of "I" is to
listen to the talk of children playing together, especially if they do not
agree very well. They use the first person with none of the conventional
self-repression of their elders, but with much emphasis and variety of
inflection, so that its emotional animus is unmistakable.

Self-feeling of a reflective and agreeable sort, an appropriative zest

3. Plumptre's Sophocles, p. 352.

of contemplation, is strongly suggested by the word "gloating." To gloat, in this sense, is as much as to think "mine, mine, mine," with a pleasant warmth of feeling. Thus a boy gloats over something he has made with his scroll-saw, over the bird he has brought down with his gun, or over his collection of stamps or eggs; a girl gloats over her new clothes, and over the approving words or looks of others; a farmer over his fields and his stock; a business man over his trade and his bank-account; a mother over her child; the poet over a successful quatrain; the self-righteous man over the state of his soul; and in like manner every one gloats over the prosperity of any cherished idea.

I would not be understood as saying that self-feeling is clearly marked off in experience from other kinds of feeling; but it is, perhaps, as definite in this regard as anger, fear, grief, and the like. To quote Professor James, "The emotions themselves of self-satisfaction and abasement are of a unique sort, each as worthy to be classed as a primitive emotional species as are, for example, rage or pain."[4] It is true here, as wherever mental facts are distinguished, that there are no fences, but that one thing merges by degrees into another. Yet if "I" did not denote an idea much the same in all minds and fairly distinguishable from other ideas, it could not be used freely and universally as a means of communication.

As many people have the impression that the verifiable self, the object that we name with "I," is usually the material body, it may be well to say that this impression is an illusion, easily dispelled by any one who will undertake a simple examination of facts. It is true that when we philosophize a little about "I" and look around for a tangible object to which to attach it, we soon fix upon the material body as the most available *locus;* but when we use the word naively, as in ordinary speech, it is not very common to think of the body in connection with it; not nearly so common as it is to think of other things. There is no difficulty in testing this statement, since the word "I" is one of the commonest in conversation and literature, so that nothing is more practicable than to study its meaning at any length that may be desired. One need only listen to ordinary speech until the word has occurred, say, a hundred times, noting its connections, or observe its use in a similar number of cases by the characters in a novel. Ordinarily it will be found that in not more than ten cases in a hundred does "I" have

4. William James, *Psychology,* i, p. 307.

reference to the body of the person speaking. It refers chiefly to opinions, purposes, desires, claims, and the like, concerning matters that
involve no thought of the body. *I* think or feel so and so; *I* wish or
intend so and so; *I* want this or that; are typical uses, the self-feeling
being associated with the view, purpose, or object mentioned. It should
also be remembered that "my" and "mine" are as much the names of
the self as "I," and these, of course, commonly refer to miscellaneous
possessions.

I had the curiosity to attempt a rough classification of the first hundred "I's" and "me's" in *Hamlet,* with the following results. The pronoun was used in connection with perception, as "I hear," "I see,"
fourteen times; with thought, sentiment, intention, etc., thirty-two
times; with wish, as "I pray you," six times; as speaking—"I'll speak
to it"—sixteen times; as spoken to, twelve times; in connection with
action, involving perhaps some vague notion of the body, as "I came
to Denmark," nine times; vague or doubtful, ten times; as equivalent
to bodily appearance—"No more like my father than I to Hercules"—
once. Some of the classifications are arbitrary, and another observer
would doubtless get a different result; but he could not fail, I think,
to conclude that Shakespeare's characters are seldom thinking of their
bodies when they say "I" or "me." And in this respect they appear to
be representative of mankind in general.

As already suggested, instinctive self-feeling is doubtless connected in
evolution with its important function in stimulating and unifying the
special activities of individuals. It appears to be associated chiefly with
ideas of the exercise of power, of being a cause, ideas that emphasize
the antithesis between the mind and the rest of the world. The first
definite thoughts that a child associates with self-feeling are probably
those of his earliest endeavors to control visible objects—his limbs,
his playthings, his bottle, and the like. Then he attempts to control the
actions of the persons about him, and so his circle of power and of
self-feeling widens without interruption to the most complex objects
of mature ambition. Although he does not say "I" or "my" during the
first year or two, yet he expresses so clearly by his actions the feeling
that adults associate with these words that we cannot deny him a self
even in the first weeks.

The correlation of self-feeling with purposeful activity is easily seen
by observing the course of any productive enterprise. If a boy sets
about making a boat, and has any success, his interest in the matter

waxes, he gloats over it, the keel and stem are dear to his heart, and its ribs are more to him than those of his own frame. He is eager to call in his friends and acquaintances, saying to them, "See what I am doing! Is it not remarkable?" feeling elated when it is praised, and resentful or humiliated when fault is found with it. But so soon as he finishes it and turns to something else, his self-feeling begins to fade away from it, and in a few weeks at most he will have become comparatively indifferent. We all know that much the same course of feeling accompanies the achievements of adults. It is impossible to produce a picture, a poem, an essay, a difficult bit of masonry, or any other work of art or craft, without having self-feeling regarding it, amounting usually to considerable excitement and desire for some sort of appreciation; but this rapidly diminishes with the activity itself, and often lapses into indifference after it ceases.

It may perhaps be objected that the sense of self, instead of being limited to times of activity and definite purpose, is often most conspicuous when the mind is unoccupied or undecided, and that the idle and ineffectual are commonly the most sensitive in their self-esteem. This, however, may be regarded as an instance of the principle that all instincts are likely to assume troublesome forms when denied wholesome expression. The need to exert power, when thwarted in the open fields of life, is the more likely to assert itself in trifles.

The social self is simply any idea, or system of ideas, drawn from the communicative life, that the mind cherishes as its own. Self-feeling has its chief scope *within* the general life, not outside of it; the special endeavor or tendency of which it is the emotional aspect finds its principal field of exercise in a world of personal forces, reflected in the mind by a world of personal impressions.

As connected with the thought of other persons the self idea is always a consciousness of the peculiar or differentiated aspect of one's life, because that is the aspect that has to be sustained by purpose and endeavor, and its more aggressive forms tend to attach themselves to whatever one finds to be at once congenial to one's own tendencies and at variance with those of others with whom one is in mental contact. It is here that they are most needed to serve their function of stimulating characteristic activity, of fostering those personal variations which the general plan of life seems to require. Heaven, says Shakespeare, doth divide

The state of man in divers functions
Setting endeavor in continual motion

and self-feeling is one of the means by which this diversity is achieved.

Agreeably to this view we find that the aggressive self manifests itself most conspicuously in an appropriativeness of objects of common desire, corresponding to the individual's need of power over such objects to secure his own peculiar development, and to the danger of opposition from others who also need them. And this extends from material objects to lay hold, in the same spirit, of the attentions and affections of other people, of all sorts of plans and ambitions, including the noblest special purposes the mind can entertain, and indeed of any conceivable idea which may come to seem a part of one's life and in need of assertion against some one else. The attempt to limit the word self and its derivatives to the lower aims of personality is quite arbitrary; at variance with common sense as expressed by the emphatic use of "I" in connection with the sense of duty and other high motives, and unphilosophical as ignoring the function of the self as the organ of specialized endeavor of higher as well as lower kinds.

That the "I" of common speech has a meaning which includes some sort of reference to other persons is involved in the very fact that the word and the ideas it stands for are phenomena of language and the communicative life. It is doubtful whether it is possible to use language at all without thinking more or less distinctly of some one else, and certainly the things to which we give names and which have a large place in reflective thought are almost always those which are impressed upon us by our contact with other people. Where there is no communication there can be no nomenclature and no developed thought. What we call "me," "mine," or "myself" is, then, not something separate from the general life, but the most interesting part of it, a part whose interest arises from the very fact that it is both general and individual. That is, we care for it just because it is that phase of the mind that is living and striving in the common life, trying to impress itself upon the minds of others. "I" is a militant social tendency, working to hold and enlarge its place in the general current of tendencies. So far as it can it waxes, as all life does. To think of it as apart from society is a palpable absurdity of which no one could be guilty who really *saw* it as a fact of life.

Der Mensch erkennt sich nur im Menschen, nur
Das Leben lehret jedem was er sei.[5]

5. "Only in man does man know himself, life alone teaches each one what he is" (Goethe, *Tasso,* act 2, sc. 3).

If a thing has no relation to others of which one is conscious he is unlikely to think of it at all, and if he does think of it he cannot, it seems to me, regard it as emphatically *his*. The appropriative sense is always the shadow, as it were, of the common life, and when we have it we have a sense of the latter in connection with it. Thus, if we think of a secluded part of the woods as "ours," it is because we think, also, that others do not go there. As regards the body I doubt if we have a vivid my-feeling about any part of it which is not thought of, however vaguely, as having some actual or possible reference to some one else. Intense self-consciousness regarding it arises along with instincts or experiences which connect it with the thought of others. Internal organs, like the liver, are not thought of as peculiarly ours unless we are trying to communicate something regarding them, as, for instance, when they are giving us trouble and we are trying to get sympathy.

"I," then, is not all of the mind, but a peculiarly central, vigorous, and well-knit portion of it, not separate from the rest but gradually merging into it, and yet having a certain practical distinctness, so that a man generally shows clearly enough by his language and behavior what his "I" is as distinguished from thoughts he does not appropriate. It may be thought of, as already suggested, under the analogy of a central colored area on a lighted wall. It might also, and perhaps more justly, be compared to the nucleus of a living cell, not altogether separate from the surrounding matter, out of which indeed it is formed, but more active and definitely organized.

The reference to other persons involved in the sense of self may be distinct and particular, as when a boy is ashamed to have his mother catch him at something she has forbidden, or it may be vague and general, as when one is ashamed to do something which only his conscience, expressing his sense of social responsibility, detects and disapproves; but it is always there. There is no sense of "I," as in pride or shame, without its correlative sense of you, or he, or they. Even the miser gloating over his hidden gold can feel the "mine" only as he is aware of the world of men over whom he has secret power; and the case is very similar with all kinds of hid treasure. Many painters, sculptors, and writers have loved to withhold their work from the world, fondling it in seclusion until they were quite done with it; but the delight in this, as in all secrets, depends upon a sense of the value of what is concealed.

I remarked above that we think of the body as "I" when it comes to have social function or significance, as when we say "I am looking well to-day," or "I am taller than you are." We bring it into the social world, for the time being, and for that reason put our self-consciousness into it. Now it is curious, though natural, that in precisely the same way we may call any inanimate object "I" with which we are identifying our will and purpose. This is notable in games, like golf or croquet, where the ball is the embodiment of the player's fortunes. You will hear a man say, "I am in the long grass down by the third tee," or "I am in position for the middle arch." So a boy flying a kite will say "I am higher than you," or one shooting at a mark will declare that he is just below the bullseye.

In a very large and interesting class of cases the social reference takes the form of a somewhat definite imagination of how one's self—that is any idea he appropriates—appears in a particular mind, and the kind of self-feeling one has is determined by the attitude toward this attributed to that other mind. A social self of this sort might be called the reflected or looking-glass self:

> Each to each a looking-glass
> Reflects the other that doth pass.

As we see our face, figure, and dress in the glass, and are interested in them because they are ours, and pleased or otherwise with them according as they do or do not answer to what we should like them to be; so in imagination we perceive in another's mind some thought of our appearance, manners, aims, deeds, character, friends, and so on, and are variously affected by it.

A self-idea of this sort seems to have three principal elements: the imagination of our appearance to the other person; the imagination of his judgment of that appearance; and some sort of self-feeling, such as pride or mortification. The comparision with a looking-glass hardly suggests the second element, the imagined judgment, which is quite essential. The thing that moves us to pride or shame is not the mere mechanical reflection of ourselves, but an imputed sentiment, the imagined effect of this reflection upon another's mind. This is evident from the fact that the character and weight of that other, in whose mind we see ourselves, makes all the difference with our feeling. We are ashamed to seem evasive in the presence of a straightforward man, cowardly in the presence of a brave one, gross in the eyes of a refined one, and so on. We always imagine, and in imagining share, the judg-

ments of the other mind. A man will boast to one person of an action—
say some sharp transaction in trade—which he would be ashamed to
own to another.

It should be evident that the ideas that are associated with self-feeling
and form the intellectual content of the self cannot be covered by any
simple description, as by saying that the body has such a part in it,
friends such a part, plans so much, etc., but will vary indefinitely with
particular temperaments and environments. The tendency of the self,
like every aspect of personality, is expressive of far-reaching hereditary
and social factors, and is not to be understood or predicted except
in connection with the general life. Although special, it is in no way
separate—speciality and separateness are not only different but contradictory, since the former implies connection with a whole. The object of self-feeling is affected by the general course of history, by the
particular development of nations, classes, and professions, and other
conditions of this sort.

The truth of this is perhaps most decisively shown in the fact that
even those ideas that are most generally associated or colored with the
"my" feeling, such as one's idea of his visible person, of his name, his
family, his intimate friends, his property, and so on, are not universally
so associated, but may be separated from the self by peculiar social
conditions. Thus the ascetics, who have played so large a part in the
history of Christianity and of other religions and philosophies, endeavored not without success to divorce their appropriative thought from
all material surroundings, and especially from their physical persons,
which they sought to look upon as accidental and degrading circumstances of the soul's earthly sojourn. In thus estranging themselves
from their bodies, from property and comfort, from domestic affections—whether of wife or child, mother, brother or sister—and
from other common objects of ambition, they certainly gave a singular
direction to self-feeling, but they did not destroy it: there can be no
doubt that the instinct, which seems imperishable so long as mental
vigor endures, found other ideas to which to attach itself; and the
strange and uncouth forms which ambition took in those centuries
when the solitary, filthy, idle, and sense-tormenting anchorite was a
widely accepted ideal of human life, are a matter of instructive study
and reflection. Even in the highest exponents of the ascetic ideal, like
St. Jerome, it is easy to see that the discipline, far from effacing the

self, only concentrated its energy in lofty and unusual channels. The self-idea may be that of some great moral reform, of a religious creed, of the destiny of one's soul after death, or even a cherished conception of the deity. Thus devout writers, like George Herbert and Thomas à Kempis, often address *my* God, not at all conventionally as I conceive the matter, but with an intimate sense of appropriation. And it has been observed that the demand for the continued and separate existence of the individual soul after death is an expression of self-feeling, as by J. A. Symonds, who thinks that it is connected with the intense egotism and personality of the European races, and asserts that the millions of Buddhism shrink from it with horror.[6]

Habit and familiarity are not of themselves sufficient to cause an idea to be appropriated into the self. Many habits and familiar objects that have been forced upon us by circumstances rather than chosen for their congeniality remain external and possibly repulsive to the self; and, on the other hand, a novel but very congenial element in experience, like the idea of a new toy, or, if you please, Romeo's idea of Juliet, is often appropriated almost immediately, and becomes, for the time at least, the very heart of the self. Habit has the same fixing and consolidating action in the growth of the self that it has elsewhere, but is not its distinctive characteristic.

As suggested in the previous chapter, self-feeling may be regarded as in a sense the antithesis, or better perhaps, the complement, of that disinterested and contemplative love that tends to obliterate the sense of a divergent individuality. Love of this sort has no sense of bounds, but is what we feel when we are expanding and assimilating new and indeterminate experience, while self-feeling accompanies the appropriating, delimiting, and defending of a certain part of experience; the one impels us to receive life, the other to individuate it. The self, from this point of view, might be regarded as a sort of citadel of the mind, fortified without and containing selected treasures within, while love is an undivided share in the rest of the universe. In a healthy mind each contributes to the growth of the other: what we love intensely or for a long time we are likely to bring within the citadel, and to assert

6. Symonds, *John Addington Symonds*, ed. H. F. Brown, vol. ii, p. 120.

as part of ourself. On the other hand, it is only on the basis of a substantial self that a person is capable of progressive sympathy or love.

The sickness of either is to lack the support of the other. There is no health in a mind except as it keeps expanding, taking in fresh life, feeling love and enthusiasm; and so long as it does this its self-feeling is likely to be modest and generous; since these sentiments accompany that sense of the large and the superior which love implies. But if love closes, the self contracts and hardens: the mind having nothing else to occupy its attention and give it that change and renewal it requires, busies itself more and more with self-feeling, which takes on narrow and disgusting forms, like avarice, arrogance, and fatuity. It is necessary that we should have self-feeling about a matter during its conception and execution; but when it is accomplished or has failed the self ought to break loose and escape, renewing its skin like the snake, as Thoreau says. No matter what a man does, he is not fully sane or human unless there is a spirit of freedom in him, a soul unconfined by purpose and larger than the practicable world. And this is really what those mean who inculcate the suppression of the self; they mean that its rigidity must be broken up by growth and renewal, that it must be more or less decisively "born again." A healthy self must be both vigorous and plastic, a nucleus of solid, well-knit private purpose and feeling, guided and nourished by sympathy.

The view that "self" and the pronouns of the first person are names which the race has learned to apply to an instinctive attitude of mind, and which each child in turn learns to apply in a similar way, was impressed upon me by observing my child M. at the time when she was learning to use these pronouns. When she was two years and two weeks old I was surprised to discover that she had a clear notion of the first and second persons when used possessively. When asked, "Where is your nose?" she would put her hand upon it and say "my." She also understood that when some one else said "my" and touched an object, it meant something opposite to what was meant when she touched the same object and used the same word. Now, any one who will exercise his imagination upon the question how this matter must appear to a mind having no means of knowing anything about "I" and "my" except what it learns by hearing them used, will see that it should be very puzzling. Unlike other words, the personal pronouns have, apparently, no uniform meaning, but convey different and even opposite ideas when employed by different persons. It seems remarkable that children should master the problem before they arrive at considerable power of abstract reasoning. How should a little girl of two, not particularly reflective, have discovered that "my" was not the sign of a definite object like other words, but meant something different with each person who used it? And, still more surprising, how should she have achieved the correct use of it with reference to herself which, it would seem, *could not be copied from any one else,* simply because no one else used it to describe what belonged to her? The meaning of words is learned by associating them with other phenomena. But how is it possible to learn the meaning of one which, as used by others, is never associated with the same phenomenon as when properly used by one's self? Watching her use of the first person. I was at once struck with the fact that she employed it almost wholly in a possessive sense, and that, too, when in an aggressive, self-as-sertive mood. It was extremely common to see R. tugging at one end of a plaything and M. at the other, screaming, "My, my." "Me" was sometimes nearly equivalent to "my," and was also employed to call attention to herself when she wanted something done for her. Another common use of "my" was to demand something she did not have at all. Thus if R. had something the like of which she wanted, say a cart, she would exclaim, "Where's *my* cart?"

It seemed to me that she might have learned the use of these pronouns about as follows. The self-feeling had always been there. From the first week she had wanted things and cried and fought for them. She had also become familiar by observation and opposition with similar appropriative activities on the part of R. Thus she not only had the feeling herself, but by associating it with its visible expression had probably divined it, sympathized with it, resented it, in others. Grasping, tugging, and screaming would be associated with the feeling in her own case and would recall the feeling when observed in others. They would constitute a language, precedent to the use of first-personal pronouns, to express the self-idea. All was ready, then, for the word to name this experience. She now observed that R., when contentiously appropriating something, frequently exclaimed, *"my," "mine," "give it to me," "I* want it," and the like. Nothing more natural, then, than that she should adopt these words as names for a frequent and vivid experience with which she was already familiar in her own case and had learned to attribute to others. Accordingly it appeared to me, as I recorded in my notes at the time, that "'my' and 'mine' are simply names for concrete images of appropriativeness," embracing both the appropriative feeling and its manifestation. If this is true the child does not at first work out the I-and-you idea in an abstract form. The first-personal pronoun is a sign of a concrete thing after all, but that thing is not primarily the child's body, or his muscular sensations as such, but the phenomenon of aggressive appropriation, practised by himself, witnessed in others, and incited and interpreted by a hereditary instinct. This seems to get over the difficulty above mentioned, namely, the seeming lack of a common content between the meaning of "my" when used by another and when used by one's self. This common content is found in the appropriative feeling and the visible and audible signs of that feeling. An element of difference and strife comes in, of course, in the opposite actions or purposes which the "my" of another and one's own "my" are likely to stand for. When another person says "mine" regarding something which I claim, I sympathize with him enough to understand what he means, but it is a hostile sympathy, overpowered by another and more vivid "mine" connected with the idea of drawing the object my way.

In other words, the meaning of "I" and "mine" is learned in the same way that the meanings of hope, regret, chagrin, disgust, and thousands of other words of emotion and sentiment are learned: that is, by having the feeling, imputing it to others in connection with some kind of expression, and hearing the word along with it. As to its communication and growth the self-idea is in no way peculiar that I see, but essentially like other ideas. In its more complex forms, such as are expressed by "I" in conversation and literature, it is a social sentiment, or type of sentiments, defined and developed by intercourse, in the manner suggested . . . previous[ly.][7]

R., though a more reflective child than M., was much slower in understanding these pronouns, and in his thirty-fifth month had not yet straightened them out, sometimes calling his father "me." I imagine that this was partly because he was placid and uncontentious in his earliest years, manifesting little social self-feeling, but chiefly occupied with impersonal experiment and reflection; and partly because he saw little of other children by antithesis to whom his self could be awakened. M., on the other hand, coming later, had R.'s opposition on which to whet her naturally keen appropriativeness. And her society had a marked effect in developing self-feeling in R., who found self-assertion necessary to preserve his playthings, or anything else capable of appropriation. He learned the use of "my," however, when he was about three years old, before M. was born. He doubtless acquired it in

7. Compare my "Study of the Early Use of Self-Words by a Child," in the *Psychological Review*, vol. 15 (November 1908), p. 339.

his dealing with his parents. Thus he would perhaps notice his mother claiming the scissors as *mine* and seizing upon them, and would be moved sympathetically to claim something in the same way—connecting the word with the act and the feeling rather than the object. But as I had not the problem clearly in mind at that time I made no satisfactory observations.

I imagine, then, that as a rule the child associates "I" and "me" at first only with those ideas regarding which his appropriative feeling is aroused and defined by opposition. He appropriates his nose, eye, or foot in very much the same way as a plaything—by antithesis to other noses, eyes, and feet, which he cannot control. It is not uncommon to tease little children by proposing to take away one of these organs, and they behave precisely as if the "mine" threatened were a separable object—which it might be for all they know. And, as I have suggested, even in adult life, "I," "me," and "mine" are applied with a strong sense of their meaning only to things distinguished as peculiar to us by some sort of opposition or contrast. They always imply social life and relation to other persons. That which is most distinctively mine is very private, it is true, but it is that part of the private which I am cherishing in antithesis to the rest of the world, not the separate but the special. The aggressive self is essentially a militant phase of the mind, having for its apparent function the energizing of peculiar activities, and, although the militancy may not go on in an obvious, external manner, it always exists as a mental attitude.

In some of the best-known discussions of the development of the sense of self in children the chief emphasis has been placed upon the speculative or quasi-metaphysical ideas concerning "I" which children sometimes formulate as a result either of questions from their elders, or of the independent development of a speculative instinct. The most obvious result of these inquiries is to show that a child, when he reflects upon the self in this manner, usually locates "I" in the body. Interesting and important as this juvenile metaphysics is, as one phase of mental development, it should certainly not be taken as an adequate expression of the childish sense of self, and probably President G. Stanley Hall, who has collected valuable material of this kind, does not so take it.[8] This analysis of the "I," asking one's self just where it is located, whether particular limbs are embraced in it, and the like, is somewhat remote from the ordinary, naïve use of the word, with children as with

8. Compare G. Stanley Hall, "Some Aspects of the Early Sense of Self," *American Journal of Psychology*, vol. 9, p. 351.

grown people. In my own children I only once observed anything of this sort, and that was in the case of R., when he was struggling to achieve the correct use of his pronouns; and a futile, and as I now think mistaken, attempt was made to help him by pointing out the association of the word with his body. On the other hand, every child who has learned to talk uses "I," "me," "mine," and the like hundreds of times a day, with great emphasis, in the simple, naïve way that the race has used them for thousands of years. In this usage they refer to claims upon playthings, to assertions of one's peculiar will or purpose, as "*I* don't want to do it that way," "*I* am going to draw a kitty," and so on, rarely to any part of the body. And when a part of the body is meant it is usually by way of claiming approval for it, as "Don't I look nice?" so that the object of chief interest is after all another person's attitude. The speculative "I," though a true "I," is not the "I" of common speech and workaday usefulness, but almost as remote from ordinary thought as the ego of metaphysicians, of which, indeed, it is an immature example.

That children, when in this philosophizing state of mind, usually refer "I" to the physical body, is easily explained by the fact that their materialism, natural to all crude speculation, needs to locate the self somewhere, and the body, the one tangible thing over which they have continuous power, seems the most available home for it.

The process by which self-feeling of the looking-glass sort develops in children may be followed without much difficulty. Studying the movements of others as closely as they do they soon see a connection between their own acts and changes in those movements; that is, they perceive their own influence or power over persons. The child appropriates the visible actions of his parent or nurse, over which he finds he has some control, in quite the same way as he appropriates one of his own members or a plaything, and he will try to do things with this new possession, just as he will with his hand or his rattle. A girl six months old will attempt in the most evident and deliberate manner to attract attention to herself, to set going by her actions some of those movements of other persons that she has appropriated. She has tasted the joy of being a cause, of exerting social power, and wishes more of it. She will tug at her mother's skirts, wriggle, gurgle, stretch out her arms, etc., all the time watching for the hoped-for effect. These performances often give the child, even at this age, an appearance of what is called affectation, that is, she seems to be unduly preoccupied with what other people think of her. Affectation, at any age, exists when the passion to influence others seems to overbalance the established character and give it an obvious twist or pose. It is instructive to find that even Darwin was, in his childhood, capable of departing from truth for the sake of making an impression. "For instance," he says in his autobiography, "I once gathered much valuable fruit from my father's trees and hid it in the shrubbery, and then ran in breathless haste to spread the news that I had discovered a hoard of stolen fruit."[9]

The young performer soon learns to be different things to different people, showing that he begins to apprehend personality and to foresee its operation. If the mother or nurse is more tender than just she will almost certainly be "worked" by systematic weeping. It is a matter of common observation that children often behave worse with their mother than with other and less sympathetic people. Of the new persons that a child sees it is evident that some make a strong impression and awaken a desire to interest and please them, while others are indifferent or repugnant. Sometimes the reason can be perceived or guessed, sometimes not; but the fact of selective interest, admiration, prestige, is obvious before the end of the second year. By that time a child already cares much for the reflection of himself upon one personality and little for that upon another. Moreover, he soon claims intimate and tractable persons as *mine,* classes them among his other possessions, and maintains his ownership against all comers. M., at three years of age, vigorously resented R.'s claim upon their mother. The latter was "*my* mamma," whenever the point was raised.

Strong joy and grief depend upon the treatment this rudimentary social self receives. In the case of M. I noticed as early as the fourth month a "hurt" way of crying which seemed to indicate a sense of personal slight. It was quite different from the cry of pain or that of anger, but seemed about the same as the cry of fright. The slightest tone of reproof would produce it. On the other hand, if people took notice and laughed and encouraged, she was hilarious. At about fifteen months old she had become "a perfect little actress," seeming to live largely in imaginations of her effect upon other people. She constantly and obviously laid traps for attention, and looked abashed or wept at any signs of disapproval or indifference. At times it would seem as if

9. Charles Darwin, *Life and Letters of Charles Darwin,* ed. F. Darwin, p. 27.

she could not get over these repulses, but would cry long in a grieved way, refusing to be comforted. If she hit upon any little trick that made people laugh she would be sure to repeat it, laughing loudly and affectedly in imitation. She had quite a repertory of these small performances, which she would display to a sympathetic audience, or even try upon strangers. I have seen her at sixteen months, when R. refused to give her the scissors, sit down and make-believe cry, putting up her under lip and snuffling, meanwhile looking up now and then to see what effect she was producing.[10]

In such phenomena we have plainly enough, it seems to me, the germ of personal ambition of every sort. Imagination co-operating with instinctive self-feeling has already created a social "I," and this has become a principal object of interest and endeavor.

Progress from this point is chiefly in the way of a greater definiteness, fulness, and inwardness in the imagination of the other's state of mind. A little child thinks of and tries to elicit certain visible or audible phenomena, and does not go back of them; but what a grown-up person desires to produce in others is an internal, invisible condition which his own richer experience enables him to imagine, and of which expression is only the sign. Even adults, however, make no separation between what other people think and the visible expression of that thought. They imagine the whole thing at once, and their idea differs from that of a child chiefly in the comparative richness and complexity of the elements that accompany and interpret the visible or audible sign. There is also a progress from the naïve to the subtle in socially self-assertive action. A child obviously and simply, at first, does things for effect. Later there is an endeavor to suppress the appearance of doing so; affection, indifference, contempt, etc., are simulated to hide the real wish to affect the self-image. It is perceived that an obvious seeking after good opinion is weak and disagreeable.

I doubt whether there are any regular stages in the development of social self-feeling and expression common to the majority of children. The sentiments of self develop by imperceptible gradations out of the crude appropriative instinct of new-born babes, and their manifestations vary indefinitely in different cases. Many children show "self-consciousness" conspicuously from the first half-year; others have little appearance of it at any age. Still others pass through periods of affectation whose length and time of occurrence would probably be found

10. This sort of thing is very familiar to observers of children. See, for instance, Miss Shinn's *Notes on the Development of a Child*, p. 153.

to be exceedingly various. In childhood, as at all times of life, absorption in some idea other than that of the social self tends to drive "self-consciousness" out.

Nearly every one, however, whose turn of mind is at all imaginative goes through a season of passionate self-feeling during adolescence, when, according to current belief, the social impulses are stimulated in connection with the rapid development of the functions of sex. This is a time of hero-worship, of high resolve, of impassioned revery, of vague but fierce ambition, of strenuous imitation that seems affected, of *gêne* in the presence of the other sex or of superior persons, and so on.

Many autobiographies describe the social self-feeling of youth which, in the case of strenuous, susceptible natures, prevented by weak health or uncongenial surroundings from gaining the sort of success proper to that age, often attains extreme intensity. This is quite generally the case with the youth of men of genius, whose exceptional endowment and tendencies usually isolate them more or less from the ordinary life about them. In the autobiography of John Addington Symonds we have an account of the feelings of an ambitious boy suffering from ill-health, plainness of feature—peculiarly mortifying to his strong aesthetic instincts—and mental backwardness. "I almost resented the attentions paid me as my father's son, . . . I regarded them as acts of charitable condescension. Thus I passed into an attitude of haughty shyness which had nothing respectable in it except a sort of self-reliant, world-defiant pride, a resolution to effectuate myself, and to win what I wanted by my exertions. . . . I vowed to raise myself somehow or other to eminence of some sort. . . . I felt no desire for wealth, no mere wish to cut a figure in society. But I thirsted with intolerable thirst for eminence, for recognition as a personality. . . . The main thing which sustained me was a sense of self—imperious, antagonistic, unmalleable. . . . My external self in these many ways was being perpetually snubbed, and crushed, and mortified. Yet the inner self hardened after a dumb, blind fashion. I kept repeating, 'Wait, wait. I will, I shall, I must.' " At Oxford he overhears a conversation in which his abilities are depreciated and it is predicted that he will not get his "first." "The sting of it remained in me; and though I cared little enough for first classes, I then and there resolved that I would win the best first of my year. This kind of grit in me has to be notified.

Nothing aroused it so much as a seeming slight, exciting my rebellious manhood." Again he exclaims, "I look round me and find nothing in which I excel. . . . I fret because I do not realize ambition, because I have no active work, and cannot win a position of importance like other men."[11]

This sort of thing is familiar in literature, and very likely in our own experience. It seems worth while to recall it and to point out that this primal need of self-effectuation, to adopt Mr. Symonds's phrase, is the essence of ambition, and always has for its object the production of some effect upon the minds of other people. We feel in the quotations above the indomitable surging up of the individualizing, militant force of which self-feeling seems to be the organ.

11. Symonds, *John Addington Symonds,* ed. H. F. Brown, vol. i, pp. 63, 70, 74, 120, 125, 348.

Social Order and Democracy

14

Primary Groups

By primary groups I mean those characterized by intimate face-to-face association and coöperation. They are primary in several senses, but chiefly in that they are fundamental in forming the social nature and ideals of the individual. The result of intimate association, psychologically, is a certain fusion of individualities in a common whole, so that one's very self, for many purposes at least, is the common life and purpose of the group. Perhaps the simplest way of describing this wholeness is by saying that it is a "we"; it involves the sort of sympathy and mutual identification for which "we" is the natural expression. One lives in the feeling of the whole and finds the chief aims of his will in that feeling.

It is not to be supposed that the unity of the primary group is one of mere harmony and love. It is always a differentiated and usually a competitive unity, admitting of self-assertion and various appropriative passions; but these passions are socialized by sympathy, and come, or tend to come, under the discipline of a common spirit. The individual will be ambitious, but the chief object of his ambition will be some desired place in the thought of the others, and he will feel allegiance to common standards of service and fair play. So the boy will dispute with his fellows a place on the team, but above such disputes will place the common glory of his class and school.

The most important spheres of this intimate association and coöperation—though by no means the only ones—are the family, the play-group of children, and the neighborhood or community group of elders. These are practically universal, belonging to all times and all stages of development; and are accordingly a chief basis of what is universal in human nature and human ideals. The best comparative studies of the family, such as those of Westermarck (*The History of*

From "Primary Groups," chapter 3 of *Social Organization: A Study of the Larger Mind* (1909; reprint New York: Schocken, 1963), 23–31.

Human Marriage) or Howard (*A History of Matrimonial Institutions*), show it to us as not only a universal institution, but as more alike the world over than the exaggeration of exceptional customs by an earlier school had led us to suppose. Nor can any one doubt the general prevalence of play-groups among children or of informal assemblies of various kinds among their elders. Such association is clearly the nursery of human nature in the world about us, and there is no apparent reason to suppose that the case has anywhere or at any time been essentially different.

As regards play, I might, were it not a matter of common observation, multiply illustrations of the universality and spontaneity of the group discussion and coöperation to which it gives rise. The general fact is that children, especially boys after about their twelfth year, live in fellowships in which their sympathy, ambition and honor are engaged even more, often, than they are in the family. Most of us can recall examples of the endurance by boys of injustice and even cruelty, rather than appeal from their fellows to parents or teachers—as, for instance, in the hazing so prevalent at schools, and so difficult, for this very reason, to repress. And how elaborate the discussion, how cogent the public opinion, how hot the ambitions in these fellowships.

Nor is this facility of juvenile association, as is sometimes supposed, a trait peculiar to English and American boys; since experience among our immigrant population seems to show that the offspring of the more restrictive civilizations of the continent of Europe form self-governing play-groups with almost equal readiness. Thus Miss Jane Addams, after pointing out that the "gang" is almost universal, speaks of the interminable discussion which every detail of the gang's activity receives, remarking that "in these social folk-motes, so to speak, the young citizen learns to act upon his own determination."[1]

Of the neighborhood group it may be said, in general, that from the time men formed permanent settlements upon the land, down, at least, to the rise of modern industrial cities, it has played a main part in the primary, heart-to-heart life of the people. Among our Teutonic forefathers the village community was apparently the chief sphere of sympathy and mutual aid for the commons all through the "dark" and middle ages, and for many purposes it remains so in rural districts at the present day. In some countries we still find it with all its ancient vitality, notably in Russia, where the mir, or self-governing village group, is the main theatre of life, along with the family, for perhaps fifty millions of peasants.

1. Jane Addams, *Newer Ideals of Peace*, p. 177.

In our own life the intimacy of the neighborhood has been broken up by the growth of an intricate mesh of wider contacts which leaves us strangers to people who live in the same house. And even in the country the same principle is at work, though less obviously, diminishing our economic and spiritual community with our neighbors. How far this change is a healthy development, and how far a disease, is perhaps still uncertain.

Besides these almost universal kinds of primary association, there are many others whose form depends upon the particular state of civilization; the only essential thing, as I have said, being a certain intimacy and fusion of personalities. In our own society, being little bound by place, people easily form clubs, fraternal societies and the like, based on congeniality, which may give rise to real intimacy. Many such relations are formed at school and college, and among men and women brought together in the first instance by their occupations—as workmen in the same trade, or the like. Where there is a little common interest and activity, kindness grows like weeds by the roadside.

But the fact that the family and neighborhood groups are ascendant in the open and plastic time of childhood makes them even now incomparably more influential than all the rest.

Primary groups are primary in the sense that they give the individual his earliest and completest experience of social unity, and also in the sense that they do not change in the same degree as more elaborate relations, but form a comparatively permanent source out of which the latter are ever springing. Of course they are not independent of the larger society, but to some extent reflect its spirit; as the German family and the German school bear somewhat distinctly the print of German militarism. But this, after all, is like the tide setting back into creeks, and does not commonly go very far. Among the German, and still more among the Russian, peasantry are found habits of free coöperation and discussion almost uninfluenced by the character of the state; and it is a familiar and well-supported view that the village commune, self-governing as regards local affairs and habituated to discussion, is a very widespread institution in settled communities, and the continuator of a similar autonomy previously existing in the clan. "It is man who makes monarchies and establishes republics, but the commune seems to come directly from the hand of God."[2]

2. De Tocqueville, *Democracy in America,* vol. i, chap. 5.

In our own cities the crowded tenements and the general economic and social confusion have sorely wounded the family and the neighborhood, but it is remarkable, in view of these conditions, what vitality they show; and there is nothing upon which the conscience of the time is more determined than upon restoring them to health.

These groups, then, are springs of life, not only for the individual but for social institutions. They are only in part moulded by special traditions, and, in larger degree, express a universal nature. The religion or government of other civilizations may seem alien to us, but the children or the family group wear the common life, and with them we can always make ourselves at home.

By human nature, I suppose, we may understand those sentiments and impulses that are human in being superior to those of lower animals, and also in the sense that they belong to mankind at large, and not to any particular race or time. It means, particularly, sympathy and the innumerable sentiments into which sympathy enters, such as love, resentment, ambition, vanity, hero-worship, and the feeling of social right and wrong.[3]

Human nature in this sense is justly regarded as a comparatively permanent element in society. Always and everywhere men seek honor and dread ridicule, defer to public opinion, cherish their goods and their children, and admire courage, generosity, and success. It is always safe to assume that people are and have been human.

It is true, no doubt, that there are differences of race capacity, so great that a large part of mankind are possibly incapable of any high kind of social organization. But these differences, like those among individuals of the same race, are subtle, depending upon some obscure intellectual deficiency, some want of vigor, or slackness of moral fibre, and do not involve unlikeness in the generic impulses of human nature. In these all races are very much alike. The more insight one gets into the life of savages, even those that are reckoned the lowest, the more human, the more like ourselves, they appear. Take for instance the natives of Central Australia, as described by Spencer and Gillen,[4] tribes having no definite government or worship and scarcely able to count

3. These matters are expounded at some length in the writer's *Human Nature and the Social Order.*

4. Spencer and Gillen, *The Native Tribes of Central Australia.* Compare also Darwin's views and examples given in chapter 7 of his *Descent of Man.*

to five. They are generous to one another, emulous of virtue as they understand it, kind to their children and to the aged, and by no means harsh to women. Their faces as shown in the photographs are wholly human and many of them attractive.

And when we come to a comparison between different stages in the development of the same race, between ourselves, for instance, and the Teutonic tribes of the time of Cæsar, the difference is neither in human nature nor in capacity, but in organization, in the range and complexity of relations, in the diverse expression of powers and passions essentially much the same.

There is no better proof of this generic likeness of human nature than in the ease and joy with which the modern man makes himself at home in literature depicting the most remote and varied phases of life—in Homer, in the Nibelung tales, in the Hebrew Scriptures, in the legends of the American Indians, in stories of frontier life, of soldiers and sailors, of criminals and tramps, and so on. The more penetratingly any phase of human life is studied the more an essential likeness to ourselves is revealed.

To return to primary groups: the view here maintained is that human nature is not something existing separately in the individual, but a *group-nature or primary phase of society,* a relatively simple and general condition of the social mind. It is something more, on the one hand, than the mere instinct that is born in us—though that enters into it—and something less, on the other, than the more elaborate development of ideas and sentiments that makes up institutions. It is the nature which is developed and expressed in those simple, face-to-face groups that are somewhat alike in all societies; groups of the family, the playground, and the neighborhood. In the essential similarity of these is to be found the basis, in experience, for similar ideas and sentiments in the human mind. In these, everywhere, human nature comes into existence. Man does not have it at birth; he cannot acquire it except through fellowship, and it decays in isolation.

If this view does not recommend itself to common-sense I do not know that elaboration will be of much avail. It simply means the application at this point of the idea that society and individuals are inseparable phases of a common whole, so that wherever we find an individual fact we may look for a social fact to go with it. If there is a universal nature in persons there must be something universal in association to correspond to it.

What else can human nature be than a trait of primary groups? Surely not an attribute of the separate individual—supposing there were any such thing—since its typical characteristics, such as affection, ambition, vanity, and resentment, are inconceivable apart from society. If it belongs, then, to man in association, what kind or degree of association is required to develop it? Evidently nothing elaborate, because elaborate phases of society are transient and diverse, while human nature is comparatively stable and universal. In short the family and neighborhood life is essential to its genesis and nothing more is.

Here as everywhere in the study of society we must learn to see mankind in psychical wholes, rather than in artificial separation. We must see and feel the communal life of family and local groups as immediate facts, not as combinations of something else. And perhaps we shall do this best by recalling our own experience and extending it through sympathetic observation. What, in our life, is the family and the fellowship; what do we know of the we-feeling? Thought of this kind may help us to get a concrete perception of that primary group-nature of which everything social is the outgrowth.

15

The Theory of Public Opinion

Public opinion is no mere aggregate of separate individual judgments, but an organization, a coöperative product of communication and reciprocal influence. It may be as different from the sum of what the individuals could have thought out in separation as a ship built by a hundred men is from a hundred boats each built by one man.

A group "makes up its mind" in very much the same manner that the individual makes up his. The latter must give time and attention to the question, search his consciousness for pertinent ideas and sentiments, and work them together into a whole, before he knows what his real thought about it is. In the case of a nation the same thing must take place, only on a larger scale. Each individual must make up his mind as before, but in doing so he has to deal not only with what was already in his thought or memory, but with fresh ideas that flow in from others whose minds are also aroused. Every one who has any fact, or thought, or feeling, which he thinks is unknown, or insufficiently regarded, tries to impart it; and thus not only one mind but all minds are searched for pertinent material, which is poured into the general stream of thought for each one to use as he can. In this manner the minds in a communicating group become a single organic whole. Their unity is not one of identity, but of life and action, a crystallization of diverse but related ideas.

It is not at all necessary that there should be agreement; the essential thing is a certain ripeness and stability of thought resulting from attention and discussion. There may be quite as much difference of opinion as there was before, but the differences now existing are comparatively intelligent and lasting. People know what they really think about the matter, and what other people think. Measures, platforms, candidates, creeds and other symbols have been produced which serve to express

From "The Theory of Public Opinion," chapter 12 of *Social Organization: A Study of the Larger Mind* (1909; reprint New York: Schocken, 1963), 121–34.

and assist coöperation and to define opposition. There has come to be a relatively complete organization of thought, to which each individual or group contributes in its own peculiar way.

Take, for instance, the state of opinion in the United States regarding slavery at the outbreak of the civil war. No general agreement had been reached; but the popular mind had become organized with reference to the matter, which had been turned over and regarded from all points of view, by all parts of the community, until a certain ripeness regarding it had been reached; revealing in this case a radical conflict of thought between the North and the South, and much local diversity in both sections.

One who would understand public opinion should distinguish clearly between a true or mature opinion and a popular impression. The former requires earnest attention and discussion for a considerable time, and when reached is significant, even if mistaken. It rarely exists regarding matters of temporary interest, and current talk or print is a most uncertain index of it. A popular impression, on the other hand, is facile, shallow, transient, with that fickleness and fatuity that used to be ascribed to the popular mind in general. It is analogous to the unconsidered views and utterances of an individual, and the more one studies it the less seriously he will take it. It may happen that ninety-nine men in a hundred hold opinions to-day contrary to those they will hold a month hence—partly because they have not yet searched their own minds, partly because the few who have really significant and well-grounded ideas have not had time to impress them upon the rest.

It is not unreasonable, then, to combine a very slight regard for most of what passes as public opinion with much confidence in the soundness of an aroused, mature, organic social judgment.

There is a widespread, but as I believe as fallacious, idea that the public thought or action must in some way express the working of an average or commonplace mind, must be some kind of a mean between the higher and lower intelligences making up the group. It would be more correct to say that it is representative, meaning by this that the preponderant *feeling* of the group seeks definite and effectual expression through individuals specially competent to give it such expression. Take for instance the activities of one of our colleges in inter-collegiate athletics or debates. What belongs to the group at large is a vague desire to participate and excel in such competitions; but in realizing itself this desire seeks as its agents the best athletes or debaters that are to be found. A little common-sense and observation will show that the expression of a group is nearly always superior, for the purpose in hand, to the average capacity of its members.

I do not mean morally superior, but simply more effective, in a direction determined by the prevalent feeling. If a mob is in question, the brutal nature, for the time-being ascendant, may act through the most brutal men in the group; and in like manner a money-making enterprise is apt to put forward the shrewdest agents it can find, without regard for any moral qualities except fidelity to itself.

But if the life of the group is deliberate and sympathetic, its expression may be morally high, on a level not merely of the average member, but of the most competent, of the best. The average theory as applied to public consciousness is wholly out of place. The public mind may be on a lower plane than that of the individual thinking in separation, or it may be on a higher, but is almost sure to be on a different plane; and no inkling of its probable character can be had by taking a mean. One mind in the right, whether on statesmanship, science, morals, or what not, may raise all other minds to its own point of view—because of the general capacity for recognition and deference—just as through our aptitude for sudden rage or fear one mind in the wrong may debase all the rest.

This is the way in which right social judgments are reached in matters so beyond commonplace capacity as science, philosophy, and much of literature and art. All good critics tell us that the judgment of mankind, in the long run, is sure and sound. The world makes no mistake as to Plato, though, as Emerson said, there are never enough understanding readers alive to pay for an edition of his works. This, to be sure, is a judgment of the few; and so, in a sense, are all finer judgments. The point is that the many have the sense to adopt them.

And let us note that those collective judgments in literature, art and science which have exalted Plato and Dante and Leonardo and Michelangelo and Beethoven and Newton and Darwin, are democratic judgments, in the sense that every man has been free to take a part in proportion to his capacity, precisely as the citizen of a democracy is free to take a part in politics. Wealth and station have occasionally tried to dictate in these matters, but have failed.

It is natural for an organism to use its appropriate organ, and it would be as reasonable to say that the capacity of the body for seeing is found by taking an average of the visual power of the hand, nose, liver, etc., along with that of the eye, as that the capacity of a group for a special purpose is that of its average member. If a group does not function through its most competent instruments, it is simply because of imperfect organization.

It is strange that people who apply the average theory to democracy do not see that if it were sound it must apply to all the social phenomena of history, which is a record of the works of the collective mind. Since the main difference between democracy and ancient or mediæval systems is merely that the former is less restricted by time, space and caste, is essentially an appeal to free human power as against what is merely mechanical or conventional; by what magic is this appeal to deprive us of our ancient privilege of acting through our efficient individuals?

One who ponders these things will see that the principles of collective expression are the same now as ever, and that the special difficulties of our time arise partly from confusion, due to the pace of change, and partly from the greater demands which a free system makes upon human capacity. The question is, whether, in practice, democracy is capable of the effective expression to which no very serious theoretical obstacle can be discerned. It is a matter of doing a rather simple thing on a vaster and more complicated scale than in the past.

Public opinion is no uniform thing, as we are apt to assume, but has its multifarious differentiations. We may roughly distinguish a general opinion, in which almost everybody in the community has a part, and an infinite diversity of special or class opinions—of the family, the club, the school-room, the party, the union, and so on.

And there is an equal diversity in the kind of thought with which the public mind may be concerned: the content may be of almost any sort. Thus there are group ideals, like the American ideal of indissoluble unity among the states, the French ideal of national glory, or the ideals of honor and good-breeding cherished in many families; and there are group beliefs, regarding religion, trade, agriculture, marriage, education and the like. Upon all matters in which the mind has, in the past, taken a lively interest there are latent inclinations and prepossessions, and when these are aroused and organized by discussion they combine with other elements to form public opinion. Mr. Higginson, recounting his experience in the Massachusetts legislature, speaks of "certain vast and inscrutable undercurrents of prejudice . . . which could never be comprehended by academic minds, or even city-bred minds," but which were usually irresistible. They related to the rights of towns, the public school system, the law of settlement, roads, navigable streams, breadth of wheels, close time of fishing, etc. "Every good debater in the House, and every one of its recognized legal authorities, might be on one side, and yet the smallest contest with one of these latent prejudices would land them in a minority."[1]

This diversity merely reflects the complexity of organization, current opinion and discussion being a pervasive activity, essential to growth, that takes place throughout the system at large and in each particular member. General opinion existing alone, without special types of thought as in the various departments of science and art, would indicate a low type of structure, more like a mob than a rational society. It is upon these special types, and the individuals that speak for them, that we rely for the guidance of general opinion (as, for instance, we rely upon economists to teach us what to think about the currency), and the absence of mature speciality involves weakness and flatness of general achievement. This fault is often charged to democracy, but it should rather be said that democracy is substituting a free type of speciality, based upon choice, for the old type based upon caste, and that whatever deficiency exists in this regard is due chiefly to the confused conditions that accompany transition.

General public opinion has less scope than is commonly imagined. It is true that with the new communication, the whole people, if they are enough interested, may form public judgments even upon transient questions. But it is not possible, nor indeed desirable, that they should be enough interested in many questions to form such judgments. A likeness of spirit and principle is essential to moral unity, but as regards details differentiation is and should be the rule. The work of the world is mostly of a special character, and it is quite as important that a man should mind his own business—that is, his own particular kind of

1. Higginson, "On the Outskirts of Public Life," *Atlantic Monthly,* February 1898.

general service—as that he should have public spirit. Perhaps we may say that the main thing is to mind his private business in a public spirit—always remembering that men who are in a position to do so should make it their private business to attend to public affairs. It is not indolence and routine, altogether, but also an inevitable conflict of claims, that makes men slow to exert their minds upon general questions, and underlies the political maxim that you cannot arouse public opinion upon more than one matter at a time. It is better that the public, like the general-in-chief of an army, should be relieved of details and free to concentrate its thought on essential choices.

I have only a limited belief in the efficacy of the referendum and similar devices for increased participation of the people at large in the details of legislation. In so far as these facilitate the formation and expression of public will upon matters to which the public is prepared to give earnest and continuous attention, they are serviceable; but if many questions are submitted, or those of a technical character, the people become confused or indifferent, and the real power falls into the hands of the few who manage the machinery.

The questions which can profitably be decided by this direct and general judgment of the public are chiefly those of organic change or readjustment, such, for instance, as the contemporary question of what part the government is to take in relation to the consolidation of industries. These the people must decide, since no lesser power will be submitted to, but routine activities, in society as in individuals, are carried on without arousing a general consciousness. The people are also, as I shall shortly point out, peculiarly fit to make choice among conspicuous personalities.

Specialists of all sorts—masons, soldiers, chemists, lawyers, bankers, even statesmen and public officials—are ruled for the most part by the opinion of their special group, and have little immediate dependence upon the general public, which will not concern itself with them so long as their work is not palpably inefficient or in some way distasteful.

Yet special phases of thought are not really independent, but are to be looked upon as the work of the public mind acting with a less general consciousness—partly automatic like the action of the legs in walking. They are still responsible to the general state of opinion; and it is usually a general need of the special product, as shoes, banks, education, medical aid and so on, that gives the special group its pecuniary support and social standing. Moreover, the general interest in a particular group is likely to become awakened and critical when the function is disturbed, as with the building trades or the coal-mine operators in case of a strike; or when it becomes peculiarly important, as with the army in time of war. Then is the day of reckoning when the specialist has to render an account of the talents entrusted to him.

The separateness of the special group is also limited by personality, by the fact that the men who perform the specialty do not in other matters think apart from the rest of the society, but, in so far as it is a moral whole, share its general spirit and are the same men who, all taken together, are the seat of public opinion. How far the different departments of a man's mind, corresponding to general and special opinion, may be ruled by different principles, is a matter of interest from the fact that every one of us is the theatre of a conflict of moral standards arising in this way. It is evident by general observation and confession that we usually accept without much criticism the principles we become accustomed to in each sphere of activity, whether consistent with one another or not. Yet this is not rational, and there is and must ever be a striving of conscience to redress such conflicts, which are really divisions in society itself, and tend toward anarchy. It is an easy but weak defence of low principles of conduct, in business, in politics, in war, in paying taxes, to say that a special standard prevails in this sphere, and that our behavior is justified by custom. We cannot wholly escape from the customary, but conscience should require of ourselves and others an honest effort to raise its standard, even at much sacrifice of lower aims. Such efforts are the only source of betterment, and without them society must deteriorate.

In other words, it is the chief and perhaps the only method of moral and intellectual progress that the thought and sentiment pertaining to the various activities should mingle in the mind, and that whatever is higher or more rational in each should raise the standard of the others. If one finds that as a business man he tends to be greedy and narrow, he should call into that sphere his sentiments as a patriot, a member of a family and a student, and he may enrich these latter provinces by the system and shrewdness he learns in business. The keeping of closed compartments is a principle of stagnation and decay.

The rule of public opinion, then, means for the most part a latent authority which the public will exercise when sufficiently dissatisfied with the specialist who is in immediate charge of a particular function. It cannot extend to the immediate participation of the group as a whole in the details of public business.

This principle holds good in the conduct of government as well as elsewhere, experience showing that the politics of an intricate state is always a specialty, closer to the public interest, perhaps, than most specialties, but ordinarily controlled by those who, for whatever reason, put their main energy into it. Professional politicians, in this sense, are sure to win as against the amateur; and if politics is badly managed the chief remedy is to raise the level of the profession.

De Tocqueville says that "the people reign in the American political world as the Deity does in the universe. They are the cause and the aim of all things; everything comes from them and is absorbed by them."[2] And we may add that, also like the Deity, they do things through agents in whom the supposed attributes of their master are much obscured.

There are some who say we have no democracy, because much is done, in government as elsewhere, in neglect or defiance of general sentiment. But the same is true under any form of sovereignty; indeed, much more true under monarchy or oligarchy than under our form. The rule of the people is surely more real and pervasive than that of Louis XIV or Henry VIII. No sovereign possesses completely its instruments, but democracy perhaps does so more nearly than any other.

When an important function, such as government, or trade or education, is not performed to the satisfaction of watchful consciences, the remedy is somewhat as follows. A rather general moral sentiment regarding the matter must be aroused by publishing the facts and exposing their inconsistency with underlying standards of right. This sentiment will effect little so long as it is merely general, but if vigorous it rapidly begets organs through which to work. It is the nature of such a sentiment to stimulate particular individuals or groups to organize and effectuate it. The press has a motive to exploit and increase it by vivid exposition of the state of affairs; enthusiasm, seeking for an outlet, finds it in this direction; ambition and even pecuniary interest are enlisted to gratify the demand. Effective leadership thus arises, and organization, which thrives in the warmth of public attention, is not long wanting. Civic leagues and the like—supposing that it is a matter of politics—unite with trusted leaders and the independent press to

2. De Tocqueville, *Democracy in America*, vol. i, chap. 4.

guide the voter in choosing between honesty and corruption. The moral standard of the professional group begins to rise: a few offenders are punished, many are alarmed, and things which every one has been doing or conniving at are felt as wrong. In a vigorous democracy like that of the United States, this process is ever going on, on a great scale and in innumerable minor groups: the public mind, like a careful farmer, moves about its domain, hoeing weeds, mending fences and otherwise setting things to rights, undeterred by the fact that the work will not stay done.

Such regeneration implies the existence of a real, though perhaps latent, moral unity in the group whose standards are thus revived and applied. It is, for instance, of untold advantage to all righteous movements in the United States, that the nation traditionally exists to the ends of justice, freedom and humanity. This tradition means that there is already a noble and cherished ideal, no sincere appeal to which is vain; and we could as well dispense with the wisdom of the Constitution as with the sentiment of the Declaration of Independence.

On the same principle, it is a chief factor in the misgovernment of our cities that they are mostly too new and heterogeneous to have an established consciousness. As soon as the people feel their unity, we may hopefully look for civic virtue and devotion, because these things require a social medium in which to work. A man will not devote himself, ordinarily, where there is no distinct and human whole to devote himself to, no mind in which his devotion will be recognized and valued. But to a vital and enduring group devotion is natural, and we may expect that a self-conscious city, state, university or profession will prove to be a theatre of the magnanimous virtues.

16

Democracy and Distinction

What shall we say of the democratic trend of the modern world as it affects the finer sort of intellectual achievement? While the conscious sway of the masses seems not uncongenial to the more popular and obvious kinds of eminence, as of statesmen, inventors, soldiers, financiers and the like, there are many who believe it to be hostile to distinction in literature, art or science. Is there hope for this also, or must we be content to offset the dearth of greatness by the abundance of mediocrity?

This, I take it, is a matter for *a priori* psychological reasoning rather than for close induction from fact. The present democratic movement is so different from anything in the past that historical comparison of any large sort is nearly or quite worthless. And, moreover, it is so bound up with other conditions which are not essential to it and may well prove transient, that even contemporary fact gives us very little secure guidance. All that is really practicable is a survey of the broad principles at work and a rough attempt to forecast how they may work out. An inquiry of this sort seems to me to lead to conclusions somewhat as follows.

First, there is, I believe, no sound reason for thinking that the democratic spirit or organization is in its essential nature hostile to distinguished production. Indeed, one who holds that the opposite is the case, while he will not be able to silence the pessimist, will find little in fact or theory to shake his own faith.

Second, although democracy itself is not hostile, so far as we can make out its nature by general reasoning, there is much that is so in the present state of thought, both in the world at large and, more particularly, in the United States.

In this, as in all discussions regarding contemporary tendency, we need to discriminate between democracy and transition. At present the two

From "Democracy and Distinction," chapter 15 of *Social Organization: A Study of the Larger Mind* (1909; reprint New York: Schocken, 1963), 157–76.

go together because democracy is new; but there is no reason in the nature of things why they should remain together. As popular rule becomes established it proves capable of developing a stability, even a rigidity, of its own; and it is already apparent that the United States, for instance, just because democracy has had its way there, is less liable to sudden transitions than perhaps any other of the great nations.

It is true that democracy involves some elements of permanent unrest. Thus, by demanding open opportunity and resisting hereditary stratification, it will probably maintain a competition of persons more general, and as regards personal status more unsettling, than anything the world has been used to in the past. But personal competition alone is the cause of only a small part of the stress and disorder of our time; much more being due to general changes in the social system, particularly in industry, which we may describe as transition. And moreover, competition itself is in a specially disordered or transitional state at present, and will be less disquieting when a more settled state of society permits it to be carried on under established rules of justice, and when a discriminating education shall do a large part of its work. In short, democracy is not necessarily confusion, and we shall find reason to think that it is the latter, chiefly, that is opposed to distinction.

The view that popular rule is in its nature unsuited to foster genius rests chiefly on the dead-level theory. Equality not distinction is said to be the passion of the masses, diffusion not concentration. Everything moves on a vast and vaster scale: the facility of intercourse is melting the world into one fluid whole in which the single individual is more and more submerged. The era of salient personalities is passing away, and the principle of equality, which ensures the elevation of men in general, is fatal to particular greatness. "In modern society," said De Tocqueville, the chief begetter of this doctrine, "everything threatens to become so much alike that the peculiar characteristics of each individual will soon be entirely lost in the general aspect of the world."[1] Shall we agree with this or maintain with Plato that a democracy will have the greatest variety of human nature?[2]

Perhaps the most plausible basis for this theory is the levelling effect

1. De Tocqueville, *Democracy in America,* vol. ii, book iv, chap. 7. But elsewhere he expresses the opinion that this levelling and confusion is only temporary. See, for example, book iii, chap. 21.
2. Plato, *Republic,* book viii.

ascribed by many to the facilities for communication that have grown up so surprisingly within the past century . . . I have said much upon this matter, holding that we must distinguish between the individuality of choice and that of isolation, and giving reasons why the modern facility of intercourse should be favorable to the former.

To this we may add that the mere fact of popular rule has no inevitable connection, either friendly or hostile, with variety and vigor of individuality. If France is somewhat lacking in these, it is not because she is democratic, but because of the race traits of her people and her peculiar antecedents; if America abounds in a certain kind of individuality, it is chiefly because she inherited it from England and developed it in a frontier life. In either case democracy, in the sense of popular government, is a secondary matter.

Certainly, America is a rather convincing proof that democracy does not necessarily suppress salient personality. So far as individuality of spirit is concerned, our life leaves little to be desired, and no trait impresses itself more than this upon observers from the continent of Europe. "All things grow clear in the United States," says Paul Bourget, "when one understands them as an immense act of faith in the social beneficence of individual energy left to itself."[3] The "individualism" of our social system is a commonplace of contemporary writers. Nowhere else, not even in England, I suppose, is there more respect for non-conformity or more disposition to assert it. In our intensely competitive life men learn to value character above similarity, and one who has character may hold what opinions he pleases. Personality, as Mr. Brownell points out in contrasting the Americans with the French, is the one thing of universal interest here: our conversation, our newspapers, our elections are dominated by it, and our great commercial transactions are largely a struggle for supremacy among rival leaders.[4] The augmenting numbers of the people, far from obscuring the salient individual, only make for him a larger theatre of success; and personal reputation—whether for wealth, statesmanship, literary achievement, or for mere singularity—is organized on a greater scale than ever before. One who is familiar with any province of American life, as for example, that of charitable and penal reform, is aware that almost every advance is made through the embodiment of timely ideas in one or a few energetic individuals who set an example for the country to follow. Experience with numbers, instead of showing the insignificance of the individual, proves that if he has faith and a worthy aim there

3. Paul Bourget, *Outre-Mer,* English translation, p. 306.
4. See the final chapter of his *French Traits.*

is no limit to what he may do; and we find, accordingly, plenty of courage in starting new projects. The country is full of men who find the joys of self-assertion, if not always of outward success, in the bold pursuit of hazardous enterprises.

If there is a deficiency of literary and artistic achievement in a democracy of this kind, it is due to some other cause than a general submergence of the individual in the mass.

The dead-level theory, then, is sufficiently discredited as a general law by the undiminished ascendency of salient individualities in every province of activity. The enlargement of social consciousness does not alter the essential relation of individuality to life, but simply gives it a greater field of success or failure. The man of genius may meet with more competition, but if he is truly great a larger world is his. To imagine that the mass will submerge the individual is to suppose that one aspect of society will stand still while the other grows. It rests upon a superficial, numerical way of thinking, which regards individuals as fixed units each of which must become less conspicuous the more they are multiplied. But if the man of genius represents a spiritual principle his influence is not fixed but grows with the growth of life itself, and is limited only by the vitality of what he stands for. Surely the great men of the past—Plato, Dante, Shakespeare and the rest—are not submerged, nor in danger of being; nor is it apparent why their successors should be.

The real cause of literary and artistic weakness (in so far as it exists) I take to be chiefly the spiritual disorganization incident to a time of rather sudden transition. How this condition, and others closely associated with it, are unfavorable to great æsthetic production, I shall try to point out under the four heads, confusion, commercialism, haste and zeal for diffusion.

With reference to the higher products of culture, not only the United States, but in some degree contemporary civilization in general, is a confused, a raw, society, not as being democratic but as being new. It is our whole newspaper and factory epoch that is crude, and scarcely more so in America than in England or Germany; the main difference in favor of European countries being that the present cannot so easily be separated from the conditions of an earlier culture. It is a general trait of the time that social types are disintegrated, old ones going to pieces and new ones not perfected, leaving the individual without adequate discipline either in the old or in the new.

Now works of enduring greatness seem to depend, among other things, on a certain ripeness of historical conditions. No matter how gifted an individual may be, he is in no way apart from his time, but has to take that and make the best of it he can; the man of genius is in one point of view only a twig upon which a mature tendency bears its perfect fruit. In the new epoch the vast things in process are as yet so unfinished that individual gifts are scarce sufficient to bring anything to a classical completeness; so that our life remains somewhat inarticulate, our literature, and still more our plastic art, being inadequate exponents of what is most vital in the modern spirit.

The psychological effect of confusion is a lack of mature culture groups, and of what they only can do for intellectual or æsthetic production. What this means may, perhaps, be made clearer by a comparison drawn from athletic sports. We find in our colleges that to produce a winning foot-ball team, or distinguished performance in running or jumping, it is essential first of all to have a spirit of intense interest in these things, which shall arouse the ambition of those having natural gifts, support them in their training and reward their success. Without this group spirit no efficient organization, no high standard of achievement, can exist, and a small institution that has this will easily surpass a large one that lacks it. And experience shows that it takes much time to perfect such a spirit and the organizations through which it is expressed.

In quite the same way any ripe development of productive power in literary or other art implies not merely capable individuals but the perfection of a social group, whose traditions and spirit the individual absorbs, and which floats him up to a point whence he can reach unique achievement. The unity of this group or type is spiritual, not necessarily local or temporal, and so may be difficult to trace, but its reality is as sure as the principle that man is a social being and cannot think sanely and steadfastly except in some sort of sympathy with his fellows. There must be others whom we can conceive as sharing, corroborating and enhancing our ideals, and to no one is such association more necessary than the man of genius.

The group is likely to be more apparent or tangible in some arts than in others: it is generally quite evident in painting, sculpture, architecture and music, where a regular development by the passage of inspiration from one artist to another can almost always be traced. In literature the connections are less obvious, chiefly because this art is in its methods more disengaged from time and place, so that it is easier to draw inspiration from distant sources. It is also partly a matter of temperament, men of somewhat solitary imagination being able to form their group out of remote personalities, and so to be almost independent of time and place. Thus Thoreau lived with the Greek and Hindoo classics, with the old English poets, and with the suggestions of nature; but even he owed much to contemporary influences, and the more he is studied the less solitary he appears. Is not this the case also with Wordsworth, with Dante, with all men who are supposed to have stood alone?

The most competent of all authorities on this question—Goethe—was a full believer in the dependence of genius on influences. "People are always talking about originality," he says, "but what do they mean? As soon as we are born the world begins to work upon us, and this goes on to the end. And after all what can we call our own except energy, strength and will? If I could give an account of all that I owe to great predecessors and contemporaries, there would be but a small balance in my favor."[5] He even held that men of genius are more dependent upon their environment than others; for, being thinner-skinned, they are more suggestible, more perturbable, and peculiarly in need of the right sort of surroundings to keep their delicate machinery in fruitful action.

No doubt such questions afford ground for infinite debate, but the underlying principle that the thought of every man is one with that of a group, visible or invisible, is sure, I think, to prove sound; and if so it is indispensable that a great capacity should find access to a group whose ideals and standards are of a sort to make the most of it.

Another reason why the rawness of the modern world is unfavorable to great production is that the ideals themselves which a great art should express share in the general incompleteness of things and do not present themselves to the mind clearly defined and incarnate in vivid symbols. Perhaps a certain fragmentariness and pettiness in contemporary art and literature is due more to this cause than to any other—to the fact that the aspirations of the time, large enough, certainly, are too much obscured in smoke to be clearly and steadily regarded. We may believe, for example, in democracy, but it can hardly be said that we *see* democracy, as the middle ages, in their art, saw the Christian religion.

From this point of view of groups and organization it is easy to understand why the "individualism" of our epoch does not necessarily pro-

5. Goethe, *Conversations with Eckermann*, May 12, 1825.

duce great individuals. Individuality may easily be aggressive and yet futile, because not based on the training afforded by well-organized types—like the fruitless valor of an isolated soldier. Mr. Brownell points out that the prevalence of this sort of individuality in our art and life is a point of contrast between us and the French. Paris, compared with New York, has the "organic quality which results from variety of types," as distinguished from variety of individuals. "We do far better in the production of striking artistic personalities than we do in the general medium of taste and culture. We figure well, invariably, at the Salon. . . . Comparatively speaking, of course, we have no *milieu*."[6]

The same conditions underlie that comparative uniformity of American life which wearies the visitor and implants in the native such a passion for Europe. When a populous society springs up rapidly from a few transplanted seeds, its structure, however vast, is necessarily somewhat simple and monotonous. A thousand towns, ten thousand churches, a million houses, are built on the same models, and the people and the social institutions do not altogether escape a similar poverty of types. No doubt this is sometimes exaggerated, and America does present many picturesque variations, but only a reckless enthusiasm will equal them with those of Europe. How unspeakably inferior in exterior aspect and in many inner conditions of culture must any recent civilization be to that, let us say, of Italy, whose accumulated riches represent the deposit of several thousand years.

Such deposits, however, belong to the past; and as regards contemporary accretions the sameness of London or Rome is hardly less than that of Chicago. It is a matter of the epoch, more conspicuous here chiefly because it has had fuller sweep. A heavy fall of crude commercialism is rapidly obscuring the contours of history.

In comparison with Europe America has the advantages that come from being more completely in the newer current of things. It is nearer, perhaps, to the spirit of the coming order, and so perhaps more likely, in due time, to give it adequate utterance in art. Another benefit of being new is the attitude of confidence that it fosters. If America could

6. Brownell, *French Traits*, pp. 385, 387, 393.

hardly have sustained the assured mastery of Tennyson, neither, perhaps, could England an optimism like that of Emerson. In contrast to
the latter, Carlyle, Ruskin and Tolstoi—prophets of an older world—
are shadowed by a feeling of the ascendency and inertia of ancient and
somewhat decadent institutions. They are afraid of them, and so are
apt to be rather shrill in protest. An American, accustomed to see human nature have pretty much its own way, has seldom any serious
mistrust of the outcome. Nearly all of our writers—as Emerson, Long-
fellow, Lowell, Whittier, Holmes, Thoreau, Whitman, even Haw-
thorne—have been of a cheerful and wholesome personality.[7]

On the other hand, an old civilization has from its mere antiquity
a richness and complexity of spiritual life that cannot be transplanted
to a new world. The immigrants bring with them the traditions of
which they feel in immediate need, such as those necessary to found
the state, the church and the family; but even these lose something of
their original flavor, while much of what is subtler and less evidently
useful is left behind. We must remember, too, that the culture of the
Old World is chiefly a class culture, and that the immigrants have
mostly come from a class that had no great part in it.

With this goes loss of the visible monuments of culture inherited
from the past—architecture, painting, sculpture, ancient universities
and the like. Burne-Jones, the English painter, speaking of the commercial city in which he spent his youth, says: . . . "If there had been one
cast from ancient Greek sculpture, or one faithful copy of a great Ital-
ian picture, to be seen in Birmingham when I was a boy, I should have
begun to paint ten years before I did . . . even the silent presence of
great works in your town will produce an impression on those who
see them, and the next generation will, without knowing how or why,
find it easier to learn than this one does whose surroundings are so
unlovely."[8]

Nor is American life favorable to the rapid crystallization of a new
artistic culture; it is too transient and restless; transatlantic migration
is followed by internal movements from east to west and from city to
country; while on top of these we have a continuous subversion of
industrial relations.[9]

Another element of special confusion in our life is the headlong
mixture of races, temperaments and traditions that comes from the

7. Poe is the only notable exception that occurs to me.
8. Burne-Jones, *Memorials of Edward Burne-Jones,* ii, pp. 100, 101.
9. Our most notable group of writers—flourishing at Concord and Boston about
1850—is, of course, connected with the maturing, in partial isolation, of a local type
of culture, now disintegrated and dispersed on the wider currents of the time.

new immigration, from the irruption by millions of peoples from the south and east of the Old World. If they were wholly inferior, as we sometimes imagine, it would perhaps not matter so much; but the truth is that they contest every intellectual function with the older stock, and, in the universities for instance, are shortly found teaching our children their own history and literature. They assimilate, but always with a difference, and in the northern United States, formerly dominated by New England influences, a revolution from this cause is well under way. It is as if a kettle of broth were cooking quietly on the fire, when some one should come in and add suddenly a great pailful of raw meats, vegetables and spices—a rich combination, possibly, but likely to require much boiling. That fine English sentiment that came down to us through the colonists more purely, perhaps, than to the English in the old country, is passing away—as a distinct current, that is—lost in a flood of cosmopolitan life. Before us, no doubt, is a larger humanity, but behind is a cherished spirit that can hardly live again; and, like the boy who leaves home, we must turn our thoughts from an irrevocable past and go hopefully on to we know not what.

In short, our world lacks maturity of culture organization. What we sometimes call—truly enough as regards its economic life—our complex civilization, is simple to the point of poverty in spiritual structure. We have cast off much rubbish and decay and are preparing, we may reasonably hope, to produce an art and literature worthy of our vigor and aspiration, but in the past, certainly, we have hardly done so.

Haste and the superficiality and strain which attend upon it are widely and insidiously destructive of good work in our day. No other condition of mind or of society—not ignorance, poverty, oppression or hate—kills art as haste does. Almost any phase of life may be ennobled if there is only calm enough in which the brooding mind may do its perfect work upon it; but out of hurry nothing noble ever did or can emerge. In art human nature should come to a total, adequate expression; a spiritual tendency should be perfected and recorded in calmness and joy. But ours is, on the whole, a time of stress, of the habit of incomplete work; its products are unlovely and unrestful and such as the future will have no joy in. The pace is suited only to turn out mediocre goods on a vast scale.

It is, to put the matter otherwise, a *loud* time. The newspapers, the advertising, the general insistence of suggestion, have an effect of din, so that one feels that he must raise his voice to be heard, and the whispers of the gods are hard to catch. Men whose voices are naturally low and fine easily lose this trait in the world and begin to shout like the rest. That is to say, they exaggerate and repeat and advertise and caricature, saying too much in the hope that a little may be heard. Of course, in the long run this is a fatal delusion; nothing will really be listened to except that whose quiet truth makes it worth hearing; but it is one so rooted in the general state of things that few escape it. Even those who preserve the lower tone do so with an effort which is in itself disquieting.

A strenuous state of mind is always partial and special, sacrificing scope to intensity and more fitted for execution than insight. It is useful at times, but if habitual cuts us off from that sea of subconscious spirit from which all original power flows. "The world of art," says Paul Bourget, speaking of America, "requires less self-consciousness—an impulse of life which forgets itself, the alternations of dreamy idleness with fervid execution."[10] So Henry James[11] remarks that we have practically lost the faculty of attention, meaning, I suppose, that unstrenuous, brooding sort of attention required to produce or appreciate works of art—and as regards the prevalent type of business or professional mind this seems quite true.

It comes mainly from having too many things to think of, from the urgency and distraction of an epoch and a country in which the traditional structures that support the mind and save its energy have largely gone to pieces. The endeavor to supply by will functions that in other conditions would be automatic creates a rush which imitation renders epidemic, and from which it is not easy to escape in order to mature one's powers in fruitful quiet.

There is an immense spiritual economy in any settled state of society, sufficient, so far as production is concerned, to offset much that is stagnant or oppressive; the will is saved and concentrated; while freedom, as De Tocqueville noted, sometimes produces "a small, distressing motion, a sort of incessant jostling of men, which annoys and disturbs the mind without exciting or elevating it."[12] The modern artist

10. Bourget, *Outre-Mer,* p. 25.
11. In his essay on Balzac.
12. De Tocqueville, *Democracy in America,* vol. ii, book i, chap. 10.

has too much choice. If he attempts to deal largely with life, his will is overworked at the expense of æsthetic synthesis. Freedom and opportunity are without limit, all cultures within his reach and splendid service awaiting performance. But the task of creating a glad whole seems beyond any ordinary measure of talent. The result in most cases—as has been said of architecture—is "confusion of types, illiterate combinations, an evident breathlessness of effort and striving for effect, with the inevitable loss of repose, dignity and style."[13] A mediæval cathedral or a Greek temple was the culmination of a long social growth, a gradual, deliberate, corporate achievement, to which the individual talent added only the finishing touch. The modern architect has, no doubt, as much personal ability, but the demands upon it are excessive; it would seem that only a transcendent synthetic genius of the calibre of Dante could deal adequately with our scattered conditions.

The cause of strain is radical and somewhat feverish change, not democracy as such. A large part of the people, particularly the farming class, are little affected by it, and there are indications that in America, where it has been greater than elsewhere, the worst is now over.

By commercialism, in this connection, we may understand a preoccupation of the ability of the people with material production and with the trade and finance based upon it. This again is in part a trait of the period, in part a peculiarity of America, in its character as a new country with stumps to get out and material civilization to erect from the ground up.

The result of it is that ability finds constant opportunity and incitement to take a commercial direction, and little to follow pure art or letters. A man likes to succeed in something, and if he is conscious of the capacity to make his way in business or professional life, he is indisposed to endure the poverty, uncertainty and indifference which attend the pursuit of an artistic calling. Less prosperous societies owe something to that very lack of opportunity which makes it less easy for artistic ability to take another direction.

An even greater peril is the debasing of art by an uncultured market. There seem to be plenty of artists of every kind, but their standard of success is mostly low. The beginner too early gets commercial employ-

---

13. Henry Van Brunt, *Greek Lines*, p. 225. Some of these phrases, such as "illiterate combinations," could never apply to the work of good architects.

ment in which he is not held up to any high ideal. This brings us back to the lack of a well-knit artistic tradition to educate both the artist and the public, the lack of a type, "the non-existence," as Mr. Russell Sturgis says, "of an artistic community with a mind of its own and a certain general agreement as to what a work of art ought to be." This lack involves the weakness of the criticism which is required to make the artist see himself as he ought to be. "That criticism is nowhere in proportion to the need of it," says Henry James, "is the visiting observer's first and last impression—an impression so constant that it at times swallows up or elbows out every other."

The antipathy between art and the commercial spirit, however, is often much overstated. As a matter of history art and literature have flourished most conspicuously in prosperous commercial societies, such as Athens, Florence, Venice, the communes of the thirteenth and fourteenth centuries, the trading cities of Germany, the Dutch Republic and the England of Elizabeth. Nothing does more than commerce to awaken intelligence, enterprise and a free spirit, and these are favorable to ideal production. It is only the extreme one-sidedness of our civilization in this regard that is prejudicial.

It is also true—and here we touch upon something pertaining more to the very nature of democracy than the matters so far mentioned—that the zeal for diffusion which springs from communication and sympathy has in it much that is not directly favorable to the finer sorts of production.

Which is the better, fellowship or distinction? There is much to be said on both sides, but the finer spirits of our day lean toward the former, and find it more human and exhilarating to spread abroad the good things the world already has than to prosecute a lonesome search for new ones. I notice among the choicest people I know—those who seem to me most representative of the inner trend of democracy—a certain generous contempt for distinction and a passion to cast their lives heartily on the general current. But the highest things are largely those which do not immediately yield fellowship or diffuse joy. Though making in the end for a general good, they are as private in their direct action as selfishness itself, from which they are not always easily distinguished. They involve intense self-consciousness. Probably men who follow the whispers of genius will always be more or less at odds with their fellows.

Ours, then, is an Age of Diffusion. The best minds and hearts seek joy and self-forgetfulness in active service, as in another time they might seek it in solitary worship; God, as we often hear, being sought more through human fellowship and less by way of isolate self-consciousness than was the case a short time since.

I need hardly particularize the educational and philanthropic zeal that, in one form or another, incites the better minds among our contemporaries and makes them feel guilty when they are not in some way exerting themselves to spread abroad material or spiritual goods. No one would wish to see this zeal diminished; and perhaps it makes in the long run for every kind of worthy achievement; but its immediate effect is often to multiply the commonplace, giving point to De Tocqueville's reflection that "in aristocracies a few great pictures are produced, in democratic countries a vast number of insignificant ones."[14] In a spiritual as well as a material sense there is a tendency to fabricate cheap goods for an uncritical market.

> Men and gods are too extense.[15]

Finally, all theories that aim to deduce from social conditions the limits of personal achievement must be received with much caution. It is the very nature of a virile sense of self to revolt from the usual and the expected and pursue a lonesome road. Of course it must have support, but it may find this in literature and imaginative intercourse. So, in spite of everything, we have had in America men of signal distinction—such, for instance, as Emerson, Thoreau and Whitman—and we shall no doubt have more. We need fear no dearth of inspiring issues; for if old ones disappear energetic minds will always create new ones by marking greater demands upon life.

The very fact that our time has so largely cast off all sorts of structure is in one way favorable to enduring production, since it means that we have fallen back upon human nature, upon that which is permanent and essential, the adequate record of which is the chief agent in giving life to any product of the mind.

14. De Tocqueville, *Democracy in America*, vol. ii, book i, chap. 11.
15. Emerson, "Alphonso of Castile."

17

Open Classes

With the growth of freedom classes come to be more open, that is, more based on individual traits and less upon descent. Competition comes actively into play and more or less efficiently fulfils its function[1] of assigning to each one an appropriate place in the whole. The theory of a free order is that every one is born to serve mankind in a certain way, that he finds out through a wise system of education and experiment what that way is, and is trained to enter upon it. In following it he does the best possible both for the service of society and his own happiness. So far as classes exist they are merely groups for the furtherance of efficiency through coöperation, and their membership is determined entirely by natural fitness.

This ideal condition is never attained on a large scale. In practice the men who find work exactly suited to them and at the same time acceptable to society are at the best somewhat exceptional—though habit reconciles most of us—and classes are never wholly open or wholly devoted to the general good.

The problem of finding where men belong, of adapting personal gifts to a complex system, is indeed one of extreme difficulty, and is in no way solved by facile schemes of any sort. There are, fundamentally, only two principles available to meet it, that of inheritance or caste and that of competition. While the former is a low principle, the latter is also, in many of its phases, objectionable, involving waste of energy and apt to degenerate into anarchy. There are always difficulties on either hand, and the actual organization of life is ever a compromise between the aspiration toward freedom and the convenience of status.

We may assume, then, that in contemporary life we have to do with a society in which the constitution of classes, so far as we have them, is partly determined by inheritance and partly by a more or less open

From "Open Classes," chapter 21 of *Social Organization: A Study of the Larger Mind* (1909; reprint New York: Schocken, 1963), 239–47.

1. I make frequent use of this word to mean an activity which furthers some general interest of the social group. It differs from "purpose" in not neccessarily implying intention.

competition, which is, again, more or less effective in placing men where they rightly belong.

If classes are open and men make their way from one into another, it is plain that they cannot be separate mental wholes as may be the case with castes. The general state of things becomes one of facile inter-course, and those who change class will not forget the ideas and associ-ations of youth. Non-hereditary classes may have plenty of solidarity and class spirit—consider, for instance, the mediæval clergy—and their activity may also be of a special and remote sort, like that of an astronomical society, but after all there will be something democratic about them; they will share the general spirit of the whole in which they are rooted. They mean only specialization in consciousness, where caste means separation.

The question whether there is or ought to be "class-consciousness" in a democratic society is a matter of definitions. If we mean a division of feeling that goes deeper than the sense of national unity and sepa-rates the people into alien sections, then there is no such thing in the United States on any important scale (leaving aside the race question), and we may hope there never will be. But if we mean that along with an underlying unity of sentiment and ideals there are currents of thought and feeling somewhat distinct and often antagonistic, the an-swer is that class-consciousness in this sense exists and is more likely to increase than to diminish. A country of newspapers, popular educa-tion and manhood suffrage has passed the stage in which sentiments or interests can flow in separate channels; but there is nothing to pre-vent the people forming self-assertive groups in reference to economic and social questions, as they do in politics.

Class-consciousness along these lines will probably increase with growing interest in the underlying controversies, but I do not antici-pate that this increase will prove the dreadful thing which some imag-ine. A "class-war" would indeed be a calamity, but why expect it? I see no reason unless it be a guilty conscience or an unbelief in moral forces. A certain sort of agitators expect and desire a violent struggle, because they see privilege defiant and violence seems to them the short-est way to get at it; and on the other hand, there are many in the enjoyment of privilege who feel in their hearts that they deserve noth-ing better than to have it taken away from them: but these are naïve views that ignore the solidity of the present order, which ensures that any change must be gradual and make its way by reason. Orderly struggle is the time-honored method of adjusting controversies among a free people, and why should we assume that it will degenerate into anarchy and violence at just this point? Will not feeling be rather better than worse when a vague sense of injustice has had a chance to try itself out in a definite and positive self-assertion?

It is to be remembered, moreover, that in a society where groups interlace as much as they do with us a conflict of class interests is, in great degree, not a conflict of persons but rather one of ideas in a common social medium—since many persons belong to more than one class. Only under conditions of caste would a class war of the sort predicted by some theorists be likely to come to pass. I am not sure that it would be more fantastic to expect a literal war between Democrats and Republicans than between the parties—hardly less united by common social and economic interests—of Labor and Capital.

It seems equally mistaken to say, on the one hand, that all class-consciousness is bad, or, on the other, that we ought above all things to gird ourselves for the class-struggle. The just view apparently is that we should have in this matter, as elsewhere, difference on a basis of unity. Class loyalty in the pursuit of right ends is good; but like all such sentiments it should be subordinate to a broad justice and kindness. If there is no class-consciousness men become isolated, degraded and ineffective; if there is too much, or the wrong kind, the group becomes separate and forgets the whole. Let there be "diversities of gifts but the same spirit."

The present state of things as regards fellowship and coöperation in special groups is, on the whole, one of deficiency rather than excess. The confusion or "individualism" that we see in literature, art, religion and industry means a want of the right kind of class unity and spirit. There is a lack of mutual aid and support not only among hand-workers, where it is much needed, but also among scholars, artists, professional men, writers and men of affairs. The ordinary business or professional man hardly feels himself a member of any brotherhood larger than the family; with his wife and children about him he stands in the midst of a somewhat cold and jostling world, keeping his feet as best he can and seeking a mechanical security in bank-account and life insurance—being less fortunate in this regard, perhaps, than the trades-unionist, who has been forced by necessity to stand shoulder-to-shoulder with his fellows and give and take sacrifice for the common good. And much the same is true of scholars and artists: they are likely not to draw close enough together to keep one another warm and foster the class ideals which lead the individual on to a particular kind of efficiency: there is a lack of those snug nests of special tradition and association in which more settled civilizations are rich.

Organization, of certain kinds, is no doubt more extensive and elaborate than ever before, and organization, it may be said, involves the interdependence, the unity, of parts. But will this be a conscious and moral unity? In a high kind of organization it will; but rapid growth may give us a system that is mechanical rather than, in the higher sense, social. When organization quickly extends there is a tendency to lower its type, as a rubber band becomes thinner the more you stretch it; the relations grow less human, and so may degrade instead of elevating the individual's relation to his whole. In a measure this has taken place in our life. The vast structure of industry and commerce remains, for the most part, unhumanized, and whether it proves a real good or not depends upon our success or failure in making it vital, conscious, moral. There is union on a low plane and isolation on a higher. The progress of communication has supplied the mechanical basis for a spiritual organization far beyond anything in the past; but this remains unachieved. On the whole, in the words of Miss Jane Addams, with whom this is a cherished idea, "The situation demands the consciousness of participation and well-being which comes to the individual when he is able to see himself 'in connection and coöperation with the whole'; it needs the solace of collective art inherent in collective labor."[2]

It is indeed probable that the growth of class fellowship will help to foster that spirit of art in work which we so notably lack, and the repose and content which this brings. There is truth in the view that a confused and standardless competition destroys art, which requires not only a group ideal but a certain deliberation, a chance to brood over things and work perfection into them. When the workman is more sure of his position, when he feels his fellows at his shoulder and knows that the quality of his work will be appreciated, he will have more courage and patience to be an artist. We all draw our impulse toward perfection not from vulgar opinion or from our pay, but from the approval of fellow craftsmen. The truth, little seen in our day, is that all work should be done in the spirit of art, and that no society is humanly organized in which this is not chiefly the case.

2. Jane Addams, *Democracy and Social Ethics*, p. 219.

It is also true that closer fellowship—dominated by good ideals—should bring the sympathetic and moral motives to diligence and efficiency into more general action, and relegate the "work or starve" motive more to the background. Some of us love our work and are eager to do it well; others have to be driven. Is this because the former are naturally a superior sort of people, because the work itself is essentially more inviting, or because the social conditions are such that sympathy and fellowship are more enlisted with it? Allowing something for the first two, I suspect the third is the principal reason. What work is there that would not be pleasant in moderate quantities, in good fellowship, and in the feeling of service? No great proportion, I imagine, of our task. Washing dishes is not thought desirable, and yet men do it joyfully when they go camping together.

Class organization is not, as some people assert, necessarily hostile to freedom. All organization is, properly, a means through which freedom is sought. As conditions change, men are compelled to find new forms of union through which to express themselves, and the rise of industrial classes is of this nature.

In fact, the question of freedom, as applied to class conditions, has two somewhat distinct aspects. There are:

1. Freedom to rise from one class into another, freedom of individual opportunity, or *carrière ouverte aux talents*. This is chiefly for the man of exceptional capacity and ambition. It is important, but not more so than the other, namely:

2. Freedom of classes, or, what is the same thing, of those individuals who have not the wish or power to depart from the sphere of life in which circumstance has placed them. It means justice, opportunity, humane living, for the less privileged groups as groups; not opportunity to get out of them but to be something in them; a chance for the teamster to have comfort, culture and good surroundings for himself and his family without ceasing to be a teamster.

The first of these has been much better understood in America than the second. That it is wrong to keep a man down who might rise is quite familiar, but that those who cannot rise, or do not care to, have also just claims is almost a novel idea, though they are evidently that majority for whom our institutions are supposed to exist. Owing to a too exclusive preoccupation with ideals of enterprise and ambition, a certain neglect, and even reproach, have rested upon those who do quietly the plain work of life.

Ours, if you think of it, is rather too much success on the tontine plan, where one puts all he has into a pool in the hope of being one of a few survivors to get what the rest lose; it would be better to take to heart that idea of Emerson's that each may succeed in his own way, without putting others down. It is a great thing that every American boy may aspire to be president of the United States, or of the Standard Oil Company, but it is equally important that he should have a chance for full and wholesome life in the more probable condition of clerk or mill hand. While we must admire the heroes of Samuel Smiles, we may remember that they do and should constitute only a small minority of the human race.

And the main guaranty for freedom of this latter sort is some kind of class organization which shall resist the encroachment and neglect of which the weaker parties in society are in constant danger. Those who have wealth, position, knowledge, leisure, may perhaps dispense with formal organization (though in fact it is those who are strong already who most readily extend their strength in this way), but the multitudes who have nothing but their human nature to go upon must evidently stand together or go to the wall.

Social Change and the Pragmatic Method

18

The Tentative Method

We see around us in the world of men an onward movement of life. There seems to be a vital impulse, of unknown origin, that tends to work ahead in innumerable directions and manners, each continuous with something of the same sort in the past. The whole thing appears to be a kind of growth, and we might add that it is an *adaptive* growth, meaning by this that the forms of life we see—men, associations of men, traditions, institutions, conventions, theories, ideals—are not separate or independent, but that the growth of each takes place in contact and interaction with that of others. Thus any one phase of the movement may be regarded as a series of adaptations to other phases.

That the growth of persons is adaptive is apparent to every one. Each of us has energy and character, but not for an hour do these develop except by communication and adjustment with the persons and conditions about us. And the case is not different with a social group, or with the ideas which live in the common medium of communicative thought. Human life is thus all one growing whole, unified by ceaseless currents of interaction, but at the same time differentiated into those diverse forms of energy which we see as men, factions, tendencies, doctrines, and institutions.

The most evident distinction among these growing forms is that between the personal and the impersonal. A man is a personal form of life; a fashion or a myth is impersonal. This seems obvious enough, but there are cases in which the line is not so plain, and it may be well to consider more precisely what we mean by "personal" in this connection, or rather in just what sense a form of human life can be impersonal.

An impersonal form, I should say, is one whose life history is not identified with that of particular persons. A myth, for example, has a

From "The Tentative Method," chapter 1 of *Social Process* (1918; reprint Carbondale and Edwardsville: Southern Illinois University Press, 1966), 3–18.

history of its own which you would never discover in the biography
of individuals, and although it exists in the minds of men it cannot be
seen intelligibly except by regarding it as a distinct whole for which
human thought is only a medium. When an American Indian, let us
say, repeated with unconscious variations the story of Hiawatha, he
did not know he was participating in the growth of a myth; that was
taking place in and through him but quite apart from his personal
consciousness. The same is true of the growth of language. We know
that the speech of any people has a vital unity, offering to the philolo-
gist a world of interesting structures and relations of which those who
use the language and contribute to its growth are as unaware as they
are of the physiology of their bodies. The difference between personal
and impersonal organisms, then, is above all practical, resting upon
the fact that many forms of life are not identified with personality and
cannot be understood, can hardly be seen at all, by one who will interest himself only in persons. They exist in the human mind, but to perceive them you must study this from an impersonal standpoint.

Observe the practical value, if we hope to do away with war, of
perceiving that the chief opponent of peace is something far more than
any one group of men, like the Prussian aristocracy, namely militarism,
an international organism existing everywhere in the form of aggressive ideals, traditions, and anticipations. If we can learn to see this,
and see how we ourselves, perhaps, are contributing to it by our ignorance of foreign nations and our lack of generous ideals for our own,
we are in a position to oppose it effectually.

We live, in fact, in the very midst of a rank growth of social structures of which, since they are impersonal and do not appeal to our
interest in personality, we are mainly unaware. We can see that such
a growth has taken place in the past, and there is no reason to suppose
that it has ceased. The development of religious institutions during the
past thirty years has involved gradual changes in belief about such
matters as immortality, salvation, and the relation of God to man, of
which we have not been aware because they have not been the work
of definite thought and discussion, for the most part, but have been
borne in upon us by the mental currents of the time. We do not even
now know precisely what they are; but they are real and momentous,
and it is of such changes that the development of institutions chiefly
consists.

It is noteworthy that however impersonal a phase of social growth
may be it appeals to our interest as soon as we see that it has a life
history, as one may find amusement in following the history of a word
in one of the books of etymology. There is something in the course of

any sort of life that holds our attention when we once get our eye upon it. How willingly do we pursue the histories of arts, sciences, religions, and philosophies if some one will only show us how one thing grows out of another.

To say that a social form is impersonal does not mean that it is dead. A language or a myth is verily alive; its life is human life; it has the same flesh and blood and nerves that you and I have, only the development of these is organized along lines other than those of personal consciousness. When I speak, or even when I think, language lives in me, and the part that lives in me is acting upon other parts living in other persons, influencing the life of the whole of which I am unconscious. And the same may be said of tradition, of the earlier and less conscious history of institutions, and of many obscure movements of contemporary life which may prove important notwithstanding their obscurity.

It is evident that the personal and the impersonal forms must overlap, since the same life enters into both. If you took away all the persons there would be nothing left, the other systems would be gone too, because their constituents are the same. What we may not so readily admit (because of our special interest in personality) is that persons are equally without a separate existence, and that if you take away from a man's mind all the unconscious and impersonal wholes there would be nothing left—certainly no personality. The withdrawal of language alone would leave him without a human self.

Between persons, on the one hand, and those forms of life that are wholly impersonal, on the other, there are many intermediate forms that have something of both characteristics. A family is perhaps as personal as any group can be, because its members so commonly identify their personality with it, but it may easily have an organic growth of its own to which its members contribute without knowing. Every family has in greater or less degree a moral continuity from generation to generation through which we inherit the influence of our great grandfathers, and there is none of which a history might not be written, as well as of the Stuarts or Hohenzollerns, if we thought it worth while.

A small, closely knit community, like a primitive clan, or like a Jewish colony in a Russian village, has a corporate life of much the same personal character as the family; that is, the group comprehends almost the whole personality of the individuals, and is not too large or too complex for the individual to comprehend the group. Larger communities and even nations are also thought of as aggregates of persons, but they have a life history that must be seen as a whole and can never be embraced in any study of persons as such.

Most of the voluntary associations of our modern life are of a character chiefly impersonal; that is they tend to a specialization by which one interest of the individual is allied with the similar interests of others, leaving his personality as a whole outside the group. The ordinary active citizen of our day joins a dozen or more organizations, for profit, for culture, for philanthropy, or what-not, into each of which he puts only a fragment of himself, and for which he feels no serious responsibility. It is very commonly the case, however, that one or a few individuals—zealous employees or unpaid enthusiasts for the cause—do identify themselves with the life of the association and put personality into it. And this may happen with those social growths which we have noticed as peculiarly impersonal—even with language, as when an enthusiast sets out to revive Irish or promote Volapük.

May we not say, indeed, that whenever two persons associate we have a new whole whose life cannot altogether be understood by regarding it merely as the sum of the two? This is clearly the case with husband and wife, and no doubt, in measure, with other relations.

If we inquire more closely into the interaction and growth of these forms of life we come upon what I will call the tentative process. This is no other than what is vaguely known to popular thought as the process of evolutionary "selection," or the survival of the fittest, and is also described as the method of trial and error, the pragmatic method, the growth of that which "works" or functions, and by other terms similar to these. Perhaps as simple a description as any is to say that it is a process of experiment which is not necessarily conscious. That is, the trial of various activities and the guidance of behavior by the result of the trial may require no understanding of what is taking place.

The growth of social forms is for the most part roughly analogous to that of the wild-grape vine which has extended itself over trellises

and fences and into trees in my back yard. This vine has received from
its ancestry a certain system of tendencies. There is, for example, the
vital impulse itself, the general bent to grow. Then there is its habit
of sending out straight, rapidly growing shoots with two-branched tendrils at the end. These tendrils revolve slowly through the air, and
when one touches an obstacle, as a wire or branch, it hooks itself about
it and draws up in the form of a spiral spring, pulling the shoot up
after it. A shoot which thus gets a hold grows rapidly and sends out
more tendrils; if it fails to get a hold it by and by sags down and ceases
to grow. Thus it feels its way and has a system of behavior which
insures its growth along the line of successful experiment.

So in the human world we find that forms of life tending to act in
certain ways come into contact with situations which stimulate some
of their activities and repress others. Those that are stimulated increase, this increase acts upon the structures involved in it—usually
to augment their growth—and so a "selective" development is set in
motion. Intelligence may have a part in this or it may not; nothing is
essential but active tendencies and conditions which guide their operation.

You may sometimes see one vine growing upon another, involving
the mutual adaptation of two living forms. In human life this is the
usual condition, the environment being not something fixed but another plastic organism, interacting in turn with still other organisms,
giving rise to an endless system of reciprocal growth. One form of life
feels about among the various openings or stimuli offered by another,
and responds to those which are most congruous with its own tendencies. The two experiment with each other and discover and develop
some way, more or less congenial, of getting along. This is evidently
true of persons, and the principle applies equally to groups, ideas, and
institutions.

We have, at any given moment, a complex of personal and impersonal wholes each of which is charged with energy and tendency in
the form of heredity and habit coming from its past. If we fix our
attention upon any particular whole—a person, a party, a state, a doctrine, a programme of reform, a myth, a language—we shall find it in
the act of making its way, of growing if it can, in the direction of its
tendencies. As we have seen, it is alive, however impersonal, and has
human flesh, blood, and nerves to urge it on. It already has adapted
structure—hands and feet as Luther said of the Word of God—because if it had not developed something of the sort, some fitness to
live in the general stream of human life, we should not in fact find it
there. As its means of further growth it has a repertory of available

activities; and these, consciously or otherwise, are tried upon the situation. If not guided by something in the nature of intelligence they act blindly, and may nevertheless act effectively. In general some one or some combination of these activities will work better in the situation than others, finding more scope or stimulus of some sort, and will grow accordingly; the energies of the whole, so far as they are available, tending to find an outlet at this point. Thus the more a thing works the more it is enabled to work, since the fact that it functions draws more and more energy to it. And the whole to which it belongs, in thus continuing and enhancing the successful activity, behaves very much as if it were conducting a deliberate experiment. The enhanced activity also involves changes in the whole and in the situation at large; and thus we move on to new situations and new operations of the same principle.

Take, for illustration, the growth of a man at any point of his career; let us say a youth starting out to make his living. He has energies and capacities of which he is for the most part but vaguely aware. Young people wave their instincts and habits about for something to catch on very much as a vine does its tendrils. Suggestions as to possible lines of work, drawn from what he sees about him, are presented to his mind and, considering these with such light as he may have, he seeks a job. He selects as among his opportunities, and at the same time his opportunities, in the form of possible employers, select as between him and other seekers. Having undertaken a job he may find that he cannot do the work, or that it is too repugnant to his inclinations, in which case he presently drops it and tries another. But if he succeeds and likes it his energy more and more flows into it, his whole mind is directed toward it, he grows in that sense. And his success usually secures to him a larger and larger part to play in his chosen field, thus opening new opportunities for growth in the same direction. Life is constantly revealing openings which we could not have anticipated. It is like paddling toward the outlet of a lake, which you cannot locate until you are almost in it. We think that our course must extend in one of two directions; but further advance shows that there is a third more practicable than either. A little idea that we have overlooked or deemed insignificant often grows until it renders obsolete those we thought great.

In the case of a group under personal leadership the process is not

greatly different. A political party, a business enterprise, a social settlement, a church, a nation, develops by means of a mixture of foresight
and unforeseen experience. It feels its way, more or less intelligently,
until it finds an opening, in the form of policies that prove popular,
unexploited markets, neglected wrongs, more timely doctrines, or the
like; and then, through increased activity at the point of success, develops in the propitious direction.

Fashion well illustrates the tentative growth of an impersonal form.
Thus fashions in women's dress are initiated, it appears, at Paris, this
city having a great prestige in the matter which it has achieved by some
centuries of successful leadership. In Paris there are a large number of
professional designers of dress who are constantly endeavouring to
foresee the course of change, and to produce designs that will "take."
They compete with one another in this, and those who succeed gain
wealth and reputation for themselves and the commercial establishments with which they are connected. Although they initiate they by
no means have the power to do this arbitrarily, but have to adapt
themselves to vague but potent tendencies in the mind of their public.
It is their business to divine these and to produce something which
will fit the psychological situation. At the seasons when new styles are
looked for the rival artists are ready with their designs, which they try
upon the public by causing professional models, actresses, or other
notabilities to appear in them. Of the many so presented only a few
come into vogue, and no designer can be certain of success: no one
can surely foresee what will work and what will not. But the designs
that win in Paris spread almost without opposition over the rest of the
fashionable earth.

In the sphere of ideas "working" is to be understood as the enhanced thought which the introduction of an idea into the mental situation may stimulate. An idea that makes us think, especially if we think
fruitfully, is a working idea. In order to do this it must be different
from the ideas we have, and yet cognate enough to suggest and stimulate a synthesis. When this is the case the human mind, individual or
collective, is impelled to exert itself in order to clear the matter up and
find an open way of thinking and acting. Thus it strives on to a fresh
synthesis, which is a step in the mental growth of mankind.

Consider, for example, the working of the idea of evolution, of the
belief that the higher forms of life, including man, are descended from
lower. A pregnant, widely related idea of this sort has a complex
growth which is ever extending itself by selection and adaptation. We
known that various lines of study had united, during the earlier half
of the nineteenth century, to make it appear to bold thinkers that evo-

lution from lower forms was not improbable. This idea found a point of fruitful growth when, in the thought of Darwin especially, it was brought into contact with the geological evidence of change and with the knowledge of heredity and variation accumulated by breeders of domestic species. Here it worked so vigorously that it drew the attention and investigation first of a small group and later of a great part of the scientific thought of the time. Other ideas, like that of Malthus regarding the excess of life and the struggle for existence, were coordinated with it, new researches were undertaken; in short, the public mind began to function largely about this doctrine and has continued to do so ever since.

Just what is it that "works"? The idea implies that there is already in operation an active tendency of some sort which encounters the situation and whose character determines whether it will work there, and if so, how. In the case of the vine it is the pre-existing tendency of the tendrils to revolve in the air, to bend themselves about any object they may meet, and then to draw together like a spiral spring, which causes the vine to work as it does when it meets the wire. Indeed, to explain fully its working many other tendencies would have to be taken into account, such as that to grow more rapidly at the highest point attained, or where the light is greatest, and so on. In fact the vine has an organism of correlated tendencies whose operation under the stimulus of the particular situation is the working in question.

When we speak of human life we are apt to assume that the existing tendency is some conscious purpose, and that whatever goes to realize this is "working," and everything else is failure to work. In other words, we make the whole matter voluntary and utilitarian. This is an inadequate and for the most part a wrong conception of the case. The working of a man, or of any other human whole, in a given situation is much more nearly analogous to that of the vine than we perceive. Although conscious purpose may play a central part in it, there is also a whole organism of tendencies that feel their way about in the situation, reacting in a complex and mainly unconscious way. To put it shortly, it is a man's character that works, and of this definite purpose may or may not be a part.

In a similar way any form of human life, a group, institution, or idea, has a character, a correlation of complex tendencies, a *Motiv*, genius, soul or whatever you may choose to call it, which is the outcome of its past history and works on to new issues in the present situation. These things are very little understood. How a language will behave when it has new forms of life to interpret will depend, we understand, upon its "genius," its historical organism of tendencies, but I presume the operation of this is seldom known in advance. And likewise with our country as it lives in the minds of the people, with our system of ideas about God and the church, or about plants and animals. These are real forms of life, intricate, fascinating, momentous, sure to behave in remarkable ways, but our understanding of this branch of natural history is very limited. The popular impression that nothing important can take place in human life without the human will being at the bottom of it is an illusion as complete as the old view that the universe revolved about our planet.

Here is an example from Ruskin of the working of two styles of architecture in contact with each other. He says that the history of the early Venetian Gothic is "the history of the struggle of the Byzantine manner with a contemporary style [Gothic] quite as perfectly organized as itself, and far more energetic. And this struggle is exhibited partly in the gradual change of the Byzantine architecture into other forms, and partly by isolated examples of genuine Gothic taken prisoner, as it were, in the contest; or rather entangled among the enemy's forces, and maintaining their ground till their friends came up to sustain them." The reality of such struggles and adaptations cannot be gainsaid by any one acquainted with the history of art, nor the fact that they are the outworking of complex antecedent tendencies. But I suppose that all the individual builder perceived of this conflict was that men from the north were making window-mouldings and other details in new forms which he could use, if they pleased him, instead of other forms to which he had been accustomed. Of either style as an organic whole with more or less energy he probably know nothing. But they were there, just as real and active as two contending armies.[1]

One may sometimes discover in his own mind the working of complex tendencies which he has not willed or understood. When one first plans a book he feels but vaguely what material he wants, and collects notes somewhat at random. But as he goes on, if his mind has some synthetic energy, his thought gradually takes on a system, complex yet unified, having a growth of its own, so that every suggestion in this department comes to have a definite bearing upon some one of the many points at which his mind is striving to develop. Every one who has been through anything of this sort knows that the process is largely

---

1. Compare the chapter on "Gothic Palaces" in Ruskin's *Stones of Venice*.

unintentional and unconscious, and that, as many authors have testi-
fied, the growing organism frequently develops with greatest vigor in
unforeseen directions. If this can happen right in our own mind, with
matters in which we have a special interest, so much the more can it
with lines of development to which we are indifferent.

As a matter of psychology the evident fact underlying this "working"
is that mental development requires the constant stimulus of fresh suggestions, some of which have immensely more stimulating power than
others. We know how a word or a glance from a congenial person,
the quality of a voice, a poetic or heroic passage in a book, a glimpse
of strange life through an open door, a trait of biography, a metaphor,
can start a tumult of thought and feeling within us where a moment
before there was only apathy. This is "working," and it seems that
something like it runs all through life. It is thus that Greek literature
and art have so often awakened the minds of later peoples. The human
spirit cannot advance far in any separate channel: there must be a
group, a fresh influence, a kindred excitement and reciprocation.

These psychical reactions are more like the kindling of a flame, as
when you touch a match to fine wood, than they are like the composi-
tion of mechanical forces. You might also call it, by analogy, a kind
of sexuality or mating of impulses, which unites in a procreative whole
forces that are barren in separation.

This kindling or mating springs from the depths of life and is not
likely to be reduced to formulas. We can see, in a general way, that
it grows naturally out of the past. Our primary need is to live and
grow, and we are kindled by something that taps the energies of the
spirit where they are already pressing for an outlet. We are easily kindled in the direction of our instincts, as an adolescent youth by the
sight of a pretty girl, or of our habits, as an archæologist by the discovery of a new kind of burial urn.

It is in this way, apparently, that all initiation or variation takes
place. It is never produced out of nothing; there is always an antecedent system of tendencies, some of which expand and fructify under
fresh suggestions. Initiation is nothing other than an especially productive kind of working, one that proves to be the starting-point for a
significant development. A man of genius is one in whom, owing to
some happy combination of character and situation, old ideas are kindled into new meaning and power. All inventions occur through the

mating of traditional knowledge with fecundating conditions. A new type of institution such as our modern democracy, is but the expansion, in a propitious epoch, of impulses that have been awaiting such an epoch for thousands of years.

But let us confess that we have no wisdom to explain these motions in detail or to predict just when and how they will take place. They are deep-rooted, organic, obscure, and can be anticipated only by an imagination that shares their impulse. There is no prospect, in my opinion, of reducing them to computation. The statement, "that grows which works," is true and illuminating, but reveals more questions than it solves. Perhaps this is the main use of it, that it leads us on to inquire more searchingly what the social process actually is. It has, I think, an advantage over "adaptation," "selection," or "survival of the fittest" in that it gives a little more penetrating statement of what immediately takes place, and also in that it is not so likely to let us rest in mechanical or biological conceptions.

19

Intelligence in Social Function

The test of intelligence is the power to act successfully in new situations. We judge a man to be intelligent when we see that in going through the world he is not guided merely by routine or second-hand ideas, but that when he meets a fresh difficulty he thinks out a fresh line of action appropriate to it, which is justified by its success. We value the faculty because it does succeed, because in the changing world of human life we feel a constant need for it. In animal existence, where situations repeat themselves day after day, and generation after generation, with practical uniformity, a successful method of behavior may be worked out by unintelligent adaptation, and may become fixed in instinct or habit, but the power to deal effectively with intricate and shifting forces belongs to intelligence alone.

It is, then, essentially a kind of foresight, a mental reaction that anticipates the operation of the forces at work and is prepared in advance to adjust itself to them. How is this possible when the situation is a new one whose working cannot have been observed in the past?

The answer is that the situation is new only as a whole, and that it always has elements whose operation is familiar. Intelligence is the power to anticipate how these elements will work in a novel combination: it is a power of grasp, of synthesis, of constructive vision.[1]

It does not dispense with experience. A man who can take hold of a new undertaking and make it go will commonly be a man who has prepared himself by previous undertakings of a similar character: the more pertinent experience he has had the better. If he is opening a business agency in a strange city he will require a general acquaintance with the business, such as he might gain at the home office, and will do well also to learn all he can in advance about the city into which

From "Intelligence in Social Function," chapter 29 of *Social Process* (1918; reprint Carbondale and Edwardsville: Southern Illinois University Press, 1966), 351–62.

1. The most satisfactory account I know of the stages of synthesis in the development of intelligence, from the simplest assimilation of stimulus and consequence—as when a burnt child dreads the fire—to the most complex purposive action—as in the development and application of science—is found in L. T. Hobhouse's *Mind in Evolution*, chaps. 5–14.

he goes. But beyond this he will need the power to take a fresh, understanding view of the situation as he actually finds it, the state of the market, the people with whom he deals and the like, so as to perceive their probable working in relation to his own designs.

Intelligence, then, is based on memories, but makes a free and constructive use of these, as distinguished from a mechanical use. By an act of mental synthesis it grasps the new combination as a going whole and foresees how it must work. It apprehends life through an inner organizing process of its own, corresponding to the outward process which it needs to interpret, but working in advance of the latter and anticipating the outcome.

You might say that memory supplies us with a thousand motion-picture films showing what has happened in given sets of circumstances in the past. Now, when a new set of circumstances occurs the unintelligent mind picks out a film that shows something in common with it and, expecting a repetition of that film, guides its course accordingly. The intelligent mind, however, surveying many old films, is content with none of them, but by a creative synthesis imagines a new film answering more closely to the new situation, and foreshowing more nearly what will happen. It is a work of art, depicting what never was on sea or land, yet more like the truth than anything actually experienced.

I conceive that no mechanical theory of intelligence can be other than illusive. It is essentially a process of dealing with the unknown, of discovery. After its operations have taken place they may, perhaps, be formulated; but they can be predicted in advance only by the parallel operation of another intelligence. Behavior which can be formulated in advance is not, in any high sense, intelligent.

Even the intelligence, however, works by a tentative method; it has to feel its way. Its superiority lies in the fewness and effectiveness of its experiments. Our mental staging of what is about to happen is almost never completely true, but it approaches the truth, in proportion as we are intelligent, so that our action comes somewhere near success, and we can the more easily make the necessary corrections. Napoleon did not always foresee how military operations would work out, but his prevision was so much more nearly correct than that of other generals that his rapid and sure experiments led to almost certain victory. In a similar manner Darwin felt his way among observations and hypotheses, proving all things and holding fast what was good, going slowly but surely up a road where others could make no headway at all. It is the same, I believe, with composers, sculptors, painters, and poets: their occasionally rapid accomplishment is the fruit of a long discipline in trial and error.

This selection and organization in the intelligent mind is also a participation in the social process. As the mental and the social are merely phases of the same life, this hardly needs proof, but an illustration will do no harm.

Suppose, then, I am considering whether to send my son away from home to a certain college. Here is a problem for my intelligence, and it is also a social problem, a situation in a drama wherein my son and I and others are characters, my aim being to understand and guide its development so that it may issue as I wish. I bring before my mind all that I have been able to learn about the teachers at the college, the traditions and surrounding influences, as well as the disposition and previous history of the boy, striving all the time to see how things will develop if I do send him, and how this will be related to my own wishes for his welfare. The better I can do this the more likely I am to act successfully in the premises. The whole procedure is a staging in my mind of a scene in the life of society.

The process that goes on in a case like this is the work not only of my own private mind but of a social group. My information comes to me through other people, and they share in forming my ideas. Quite probably I discuss the matter with my friends; certainly with my wife: it may be matter for a family council. Intelligence works through a social process.

It is easy, then, to pass from what seems to be an act of merely private intelligence through a series of steps by which it becomes distinctly public or societal. The deliberations of a family council differ only in continuity of organization from those of a wide nation, with newspapers, legislatures, and an ancient constitution. There is nothing exclusively individual about intelligence. It is part of our social heritage, inseparably bound up with communication and discussion, and has always functioned for that common life which embraces the most cogent interests of the individual. The groups in which men have lived—the family, the tribe, the clan, the secret society, the village community, and so on to the multiform associations of our own time—have had a public intelligence, working itself out through discussion and tradition, and illuminating more or less the situations and endeavors of the group.

It is, indeed, a chief function of the institutions of society to provide an organization on the basis of which public intelligence may work effectively. They preserve the results of past experiment and accumulate them about the principal lines of public endeavor, so that intelligence working along these lines may use them. They supply also specialized symbols, traditions, methods of discussion and decision, for industry, science, literature, government, art, philosophy and other departments of life. The growth of intelligence and the growth of a differentiated social system are inseparable.

The movement of this larger or public intelligence is a social process of somewhat the same character as the less conscious processes. It is tentative, adaptive, has periods of conflict and of compromise, and results in progressive organization. The difference is just that it is more intelligent; that thinking and planning and forecasting play a greater part in it, and that there is not so much waste and misdirection. Its development requires a special psychological method, including the initiation of ideas, discussion, modification, and decision; which of course is absent on the lower plane of life.

It is essential, if we are to have a public intelligence, that individuals should identify themselves with the public organism and think from that point of view. If there is no consciousness of the whole its experiments and adaptations cannot be truly intelligent, because, as a whole, it makes no mental synthesis and prevision. A society of "economic men," that is, of men who regarded all questions only from the standpoint of their individual pecuniary loss or gain, could never be an intelligent whole. If it worked well, as economists formerly believed that it would, this would be an unforeseen and unintended result, not a direct work of intelligence. In fact, during the nineteenth century England and America went largely upon the theory that a general intelligence and control were unnecessary in the economic sphere—with the result that all competent minds now perceive the theory to be false.

On the other hand, the act of larger intelligence need not take place all at once or in the mind of only one individual. It is usually co-operative and cumulative, the work of many individuals, all of them, in some measure, thinking from the point of view of the whole and building up their ideas and endeavors in a continuing structure.

Thus it may be said that in all modern nations the political life is partly intelligent, because none of them, perhaps, is without a line of patriots who, generation after generation, identify their thoughts with the state, discuss aims and methods with one another, and maintain a tradition of rational policy. It is so with any organism which attracts the allegiance of a continuous group. The church, as a whole and in its several branches, has a corporate intelligence maintained in this way, and so have the various sciences; also, in a measure, political parties, the fine arts, and the more enduring forms of industrial organization. Human nature likes to merge itself in great wholes, and many a corporation is served, better, perhaps, than it deserves, by men who identify their spirits with it.

It would be a false conception of intelligence to regard it as something apart from sentiment and passion. It is, rather, an organization of the whole working of the mind, a development at the top of a process which remains an interrelated whole. This is true of its individual aspect; for our sentiments and passions furnish in great part the premises with which intelligence works; they are the pigments, so to speak, with which we paint the picture. And so with the collective aspect; discussion is far more than an interchange of ideas; it is also an interaction of feelings, which are sometimes conveyed by words and sometimes by gesture, tones, glances of the eye, and by all sorts of deeds. The obscure impulses that pass from man to man in this way have quite as much to do with the building of the collective mind as has explicit reasoning. The whole psychic current works itself up by complex interaction and synthesis. And the power of collective intelligence in a people is not to be measured by dialectic faculty alone; it rests quite as much upon those qualities of sense and character which underlie insight, judgment, and belief. Intelligence, in the fullest sense, is wisdom, and wisdom draws upon every resource of the mind.

There is no way of telling whether a people is capable of intelligent self-direction except by observing that they practise it. It may be true that certain races or stocks do not have political capacity in sufficient measure to meet the needs of modern organization, and will fail to produce stable and efficient societies. It is a matter of experiment, and our more optimistic theories may prove to be unsound.

For similar reasons no dividing-line can be drawn between what is intelligent and what is ethical, however clearly they may be separated in particular cases. That is, the intelligent view of situations is a synthetic view which, if it is only synthetic enough, embracing in one whole all the human interests at stake, tends to become an ethical view. Righteousness is the completest intelligence in action, and we are constantly finding that what appears intelligent to a narrow state of mind is quite the opposite when our imaginations expand to take in a wider range of life. There can be an unmoral kind of intelligence which is very keen in its way, as, for that matter, there can be an unintelligent kind of morality which is very conscientious in its way; but the two tend to coincide as they become more complete. The question of our higher development is all one question, of which the intellectual and moral sides are aspects. We get on by forming intelligent ideals of right, which are imaginative reconstructions and anticipations of life, based upon experience. And in trying to realize these ideals we initiate a new phase of the social process, which goes on through the usual interactions to a fresh synthesis.

It seems that intelligence, as applied to social life, is essentially dramatic in character. That is, it deals with men in all their human complexity, and is required to forecast how they will act in relation to one another and how the situation as a whole will work out. The most intelligent man is he who can most adequately dramatize that part of the social process with which he has to deal. If he is a social worker dealing with a family he needs not only to sympathize with the members individually, but to see them as a group in living interaction with one another and with the neighbors, so that he may know how any fresh influence he may bring to bear will actually work. If he is the labor-manager of a factory he must have insight to see the play of motive going on among the men, their attitude toward their work, toward the foreman and toward the "office," the whole group-psychology of the situation. In the same way a business man must see a proposed transaction as a living, moving whole, with all the parties to it in their true human characters. I remember talking with an investigator for one of the great commercial agencies who told me that in forming his judgment of the reliability of a merchant he made a practice, after an interview with him, of imagining him in various critical situations and picturing to himself how such a man would behave—of dramatizing him. I think that we all do this in forming our judgments of people.

Or what is the stock-market but a continuous drama, successful participation in which depends upon the power to apprehend some phase of it as a moving whole and foresee its tendency? And so with statesmanship; the precise knowledge of history or statistics will always and rightly be subordinate to the higher faculty of inspired social imagination.

The literary drama, including fiction and whatever other forms have a dramatic character, may be regarded as intelligence striving to interpret the social process in art. It aims to present in comprehensible form some phase of that cyclical movement of life which otherwise is apt to seem unintelligible.

When the curtain rises we perceive, first of all, a number of persons, charged with character and reciprocal tendency, each one standing for something and all together constituting a dynamic situation. We feel ourselves in the stress of life; conflict is implicit and expectation aroused. The play proceeds and the forces begin to work themselves out; there are interactions, mutual incitements and adjustments, with a development both of persons and of the situation at large. At length the interacting powers arrange themselves more or less distinctly about a central question, and presently ensues that struggle for which our expectation is strung; some decisive clash of human forces, which satisfies our need to see the thing fought out, and releases our excitement, to subside, perhaps, in reflection. And presently we have the *dénouement,* a final and reconciling situation, a completer and more stable organization of the forces that were implicit in the beginning.

Conflict is the crisis of drama, as it is of the social process, and there is hardly any great literature, whether dramatic in form or not, which is not a literature of conflict. What would be left of the Bible if you took away all that is inspired by it; from the Psalms, for instance, all echoes of the struggles of Israel with other nations, of upper with lower classes, or of the warring impulses within the mind of the singer? The power of the story of Jesus centres about his faith, his courage, his lonely struggle, his apparent failure, which is yet felt to be a real success—the Cross. And so one might take Homer, Dante, Shakespeare's tragedies, Faust, as well as a thousand works of the second order, finding conflict at the heart of all. Without this we are not greatly moved.

Each type of society has particular forms of the drama setting forth what it apprehends as most significant in its own life. Savages dramatize battle and the chase, while plays of our own time depict the conflict of industrial classes, of old ideas and conventions with new ones, and of the individual with circumstances. The love game between the sexes—a sort of conflict however you look at it—is of perennial interest.

Forms like the play and the novel should be the most effective agents of social discussion; and, in fact, the more searching, in a social and moral sense, are the questions to be discussed, the more these forms are in demand. In an ordinary political campaign, where there is little at issue beyond a personal choice of candidates or some clash of pecuniary interests, the usual appeals through newspaper editorials, interviews, and speeches may suffice. But when people begin to be exercised about really fundamental matters, such as the ethics of marriage, the ascendancy of one social class over another, the contact of races or the significance of vice and crime, they show a need to see these matters through novels and plays. The immense vogue of literature of this sort in recent years is good democracy; in no other way is it possible to present such questions with so much of living truth, and yet so simplified as to make a real impression.

In recent time there has been a great enlargement of the intelligent process, which will doubtless continue in the future. As regards mechanism, this is based on the extension and improvement of communication, of printing, telegraphy, rapid travel, illustration, and the like. These disseminate information and make a wider and quicker discussion possible. At the same time there appears to have been an advance in the power of organized intelligence to interpret life and bring sound judgment to bear upon actual situations. No one would dispute the truth of this as regards our dealings with the material world, not is there much doubt that it is in some degree true in the sphere of social relations. We understand better how life works and should be able to impress a more rational and humane character on the whole process. At any rate this, I suppose, is what we are all striving for.

But no achievement of this sort is likely to affect the preponderance of the unintelligible. You might liken society to a party of men with lanterns making their way by night through an immeasurable forest. The light which the lanterns throw about each individual, and about the party as a whole, showing them how to guide their immediate steps, may increase indefinitely, illuminating more clearly a larger area; but there will always remain, probably, the plutonian wilderness beyond.

20

Social Science

We have seen that social intelligence is essentially an imaginative grasp of the process going on about us, enabling us to carry this forward into the future and anticipate how it will work. It is a dramatic vision by which we see how the agents now operating must interact upon one another and issue in a new situation. How shall we apply this idea to social science? Shall we say that that too is dramatic?

There would be nothing absurd in such a view. All science may be said to work by a dramatic method when it takes the results of minute observation and tries to build them into fresh wholes of knowledge. This, we know, takes creative imagination; the intelligence must act in sympathy with nature and foresee its operation. The work on the evolution of life for which Darwin is most famous may justly be described as an attempt to dramatize what mankind had come to know about plants and animals. He took the painfully won details and showed how they contributed to a living process whose operation could be traced in the past, and possibly anticipated for the future. And, indeed, so homogeneous is life, the phases he found in this process—divergence, struggle, adaptation—are much the same as have always been recognized in the drama.

Darwin regarded the study of fossils as a means to the better understanding of life upon earth, as a way to *see what is going on,* and in like manner the precise observation of individuals and families in sociology is preparatory to a social synthesis whose aim also is to see what is going on.

The routine conception of science as *merely* precise study of details is never a sound one, and is particularly barren in the social field. If we are to arrive at principles or have any success at all in prediction we must keep the imagination constantly at work. And even in detailed studies we must dramatize more or less to make the facts intelligible. An investigator of juvenile delinquency who was not armed with insight as well as schedules would not report anything of much value.

From "Social Science," chapter 33 of *Social Process* (1918; reprint Carbondale and Edwardsville: Southern Illinois University Press, 1966), 395–404.

There are marked differences, however, between biology and sociology, considered as studies of process, of which I will note especially two. One is that in biology essential change in types is chiefly slow and not easily perceptible. For the most part we have to do with a moving equilibrium of species and modes of life repeating itself generation after generation. It took a Darwin to show, by comparing remote periods, that nature was really evolving, dramatic, creative.

In social life, on the other hand, change is obvious and urgent; so that the main practical object of our science is to understand and control it. The dramatic element, which in biology is revealed only to a titanic imagination, becomes the most familiar and intimate thing in experience. Any real study of society must be first, last, and nearly all the time a study of process.

Again, the sciences that deal with social life are unique in that we who study them are a conscious part of the process. We can know it by sympathetic participation, in a manner impossible in the study of plant or animal life. Many indeed find this fact embarrassing, and are inclined to escape it by trying to use only "objective" methods, or to question whether it does not shut out sociology and introspective psychology from the number of true sciences.

I should say that it puts these studies in a class by themselves: whether you call them sciences or something else is of no great importance. It is their unique privilege to approach life from the point of view of conscious and familiar partaking of it. This involves unique methods which must be worked out independently. The sooner we cease circumscribing and testing ourselves by the canons of physical and physiological science the better. Whatever we do that is worth while will be done by discarding alien formulas and falling back upon our natural bent to observation and reflection. Going ahead resolutely with these we shall work out methods as we go. In fact sociology has already developed at least one original method of the highest promise, namely that of systematic social surveys.

The reason that students of the principles of sociology (as distinguished from those whose aim is immediately practical) are somewhat less preoccupied with the digging out of primary facts than with their interpretation, is simply that, for the present, the latter is the more difficult task. We have within easy reach facts which, if fully digested and correlated, would probably be ample to illuminate the whole subject. It is very much as in political economy, whose principles have been worked out mainly by the closer and closer study and interpretation of facts which, as details, every business man knows.

Knowledge requires both observation and interpretation, neither being more scientific than the other. And each branch of science must be worked out in its own way, which is mainly to be found in the actual search for truth rather than by *a priori* methodology. Sociology has as ample a field of verifiable fact as any subject, and it is not clear that the interpretations are more unsettled than they are elsewhere. The chief reason why it has developed late and still appears uninviting to many is the very abundance and apparent confusion of the material, which seems to take away the hope of simple, sure, and lasting results. One purpose in our study of principles is to restore this hope and give order to this abundance. And while there are certainly special difficulties, as in all sciences, our own is coming to afford, I think, as great intellectual attraction as can be found in other studies, along with a human and social character peculiar to itself. It will be strange if an increasing proportion of good minds do not give themselves to it.

While I ascribe the utmost importance to precision in preparing the data for social science, I do not think its true aim is to bring society within the sphere of arithmetic. Exact prediction and mechanical control for the social world I believe to be a false ideal inconsiderately borrowed from the provinces of physical science. There is no real reason to think that this sort of prediction or control will ever be possible.

Much has been made of the fact that human phenomena, when studied statistically on a large scale, often show a marked numerical uniformity from year to year; and some have even inferred that human spontaneity is an illusion, and that we are really controlled by mathematical laws as precise as those which guide the course of the planets. But I take it that such uniformities as are to be observed in births, marriages, suicides, and many other human phenomena do not indicate underlying principles analogous to the laws of gravitation or chemical reaction. They merely show that under a given social condition the number of persons who will choose to perform certain definite acts within the year may remain almost the same, or may be increased or diminished by certain definite changes, such as the advent of war or economic hardship. They no more prove that human conduct is subject to numerical law than does the fact that I eat three meals a day, or that I shall spend more money if my salary is raised, and less if it is diminished.

In other words statistical uniformities do not show that it is possible to predict numerically the working of intelligence *in new situations,* and of course that is the decisive test. Where exact prediction is possible the whole basis of it I take to be the fact that the general social situation remains the same, or is changed in ways which do not involve new problems of choice in the field studied. In short, the more the question is one of intelligence the less the numerical method can cope with it.

Uniformity in the suicide rate, so far as it exists, shows that the causes of suicide, whatever they may be, are operating in about the same degree from year to year, that the social situation is static, or rather in moving equilibrium. It reveals no law of suicide beyond the fact that it is connected in some definite way with the social situation in general. It does not help you to understand why Saul Jones killed himself, or to predict whether Jonathan Smith will or not. All you know is that if the general current of human trouble goes on about the same, the number of cases is not likely to vary much.

Serious attempts to understand suicide and to predict its prevalence under various conditions are based, if they are intelligent, upon psychological theories of an imaginative character. Thus Dürkheim, in his book upon the subject, develops the idea of "altruistic" suicide, and enables us to understand how a disgraced army officer, for example, might be driven to it by social pressure. To such studies statistics is only an adjunct.

In the case of marriage you may be able to predict with some accuracy the effect of the simpler sort of economic changes, such as larger or smaller crops, but, if so, it is because marriage is a familiar problem, settled in much the same way by one generation after the other, on the basis of lasting instincts or conventions. You cannot, in the same way, anticipate the outcome of the next presidential campaign, or of any other transaction in which the human mind is confronting a fresh situation.

The only instrument that can in any degree meet the test of prediction, where new problems of higher choice confront the mind, is the instructed imagination, which, by a kind of inspired intelligence, may anticipate within itself the drama of social process, and so foresee the issue. That this supreme act of the mind, never more than partly successful, even in the simplest questions, can ever become, on a large scale, sure, precise, and demonstrable before the event, there is no evidence or probability. So far as we can now see or infer, social prediction, in the higher provinces, must ever remain tentative, and I suspect that all the sciences which deal with the life process are subject to a similar limitation. Darwin's suggestion regarding the "free-will" of the dinosaur would seem to indicate that this was his opinion.[1]

Intelligent social prediction is contradictory to determinism, because, instead of ignoring the creative will, it accepts it and endeavors by sympathy to enter into it and foresee its working. If I predict an artistic or humanitarian movement, it is partly because I feel as if I myself, with whatever freedom and creative power is in me, would choose to share in such a movement.

The possibility of social science rests upon the hypothesis that social life is in some sense rational and sequent. It has been assumed that this can be true only if it is mechanically calculable. But there may easily be another sort of rationality and sequence, not mechanical, consistent with a kind of freedom, which makes possible an organized development of social knowledge answering to the organic character of the social process. The life of men has a unity and order of its own, which may or may not prove to be the same in essence as that which rules the stars. It seems to include a creative element which must be grasped by the participating activity of the mind rather than by computations. How far it can be known and predicted is a matter for trial. The right method is the one that may be found to give the best results. Apparently it is not, except in subordinate degree, the numerical method.

A sociologist must have the patient love of truth and the need to reduce it to principles which all men of science require. Besides this, however, he needs the fullest sympathy and participation in the currents of life. He can no more stand aloof than can the novelist or the poet, and all his work is, in a certain sense, autobiographic. I mean that it is all based on perceptions which he has won by actual living. He should know his groups as Mr. Bryce came to know America, with a real intimacy due to long and considerate familiarity with individuals, families, cities, and manifold opinions and traditions. He cannot be a specialist in the same way that a chemist or a botanist can, because he cannot narrow his life without narrowing his grasp of his subject. To attempt to build up sociology as a technical tradition remote from the great currents of literature and philosophy, would, in my opinion, be

1. "I rather demur to *Dinosaurus* not having 'free will,' as surely we have" (*More Letters of Charles Darwin*, vol. I, p. 155).

a fatal error. It cannot avoid being difficult, but it should be as little abstruse as possible. If it is not human it is nothing.

I have often thought that, in endowment, Goethe was almost the ideal sociologist, and that one who added to more common traits his comprehension, his disinterestedness and his sense for organic unity and movement might accomplish almost anything.

The method of social improvement is likely to remain experimental, but sociology is one of the means by which the experimentation becomes more intelligent. I think, for example, that any one who studies the theory of social classes—the various kinds, the conditions of their formation and continuance, their effect in moulding the minds of those who belong to them, and the like—using what has been written upon the subject to stimulate his own observation and reflection, will find that the contemporary situation is illumined for him and his grasp of the trend of events enhanced.

By observation and thought we work out generalizations which help us to understand where we are and what is going on. These are "principles of sociology." They are similar in nature to principles of economics, and aid our social insight just as these aid our insight into business or finance. They supply no ready-made solutions but give illumination and perspective. A good sociologist might have poor judgment in philanthropy or social legislation, just as a good political economist might have poor judgment in investing his money. Yet, other things equal, the mind trained in the theory of its subject will surpass in practical wisdom one that is not.

At bottom any science is simply a more penetrating perception of facts, gained largely by selecting those that are more universal and devoting intensive study to them—as biologists are now studying the great fact of heredity transmission. In so far as we know these more general facts we are the better prepared to work understandingly in the actual complexities of life. Our study should enable us to discern underneath the apparent confusion of things the working of enduring principles of human nature and social process, simplifying the movement for us by revealing its main currents, something as a general can follow the course of a battle better by the aid of a map upon which the chief operations are indicated and the distracting details left out. This will not assure our control of life, but should enable us to devise measures having a good chance of success. And in so far as they fail we should be in a position to see what is wrong and do better next time.

I think, then, that the supreme aim of social science is to perceive the drama of life more adequately than can be done by ordinary observation. If it be objected that this is the task of an artist—a Shakespeare, a Goethe, or a Balzac—rather than of a scientist, I may answer that an undertaking so vast requires the co-operation of various sorts of synthetic minds; artists, scientists, philosophers, and men of action. Or I may say that the constructive part of science is, in truth, a form of art.

Indeed one of the best things to be expected from our study is the power of looking upon the movement of human life in a large, composed spirit, of seeing it in something of ideal unity and beauty.

21

The Tentative Character of Progress

I cannot accept the view that progress is nothing more or other than the growth of intelligent control. No doubt this is a large part of it; an enlightened and organized public will is, perhaps, our most urgent need; but, after all, life is more than intelligence, and a conception that exalts this alone is sure to prove inadequate. Progress must be at least as many-faceted as the life we already know. Moreover, it is one of those ideas, like truth, beauty and right, which have an outlook upon the infinite, and cannot, in the nature of the case, be circumscribed by a definition.

The truth is that it is often one of the requisites of progress that we trust to the vague, the instinctive, the emotional, rather than to what is ascertained and intellectual. The spirit takes on form and clarity only under the stress of experience: its newer outreachings are bound to be somewhat obscure and inarticulate. The young man who does not trust his vague intuitions as against the formulated wisdom of his elders will do nothing original.

The opinion sometimes expressed that social science should set forth a definite, tangible criterion of progress is also, I think, based on a false conception of the matter, derived, perhaps, from mechanical theories of evolution. Until man himself is a mechanism the lines of his higher destiny can never be precisely foreseen. It is our part to form ideals and try to realize them, and these ideals give us a working test of progress, but there can be nothing certain or final about them.

The method of our advance is, perhaps, best indicated by that which great individuals have used in the guidance of their own lives. Goethe, for example, trusted to the spontaneous motions of his spirit, studying these, however, and preparing for and guiding their expression. Each of his works represented one of these motions, and he kept it by him for years to work upon when the impulse should return. So the collective intelligence must wait upon the motions of humanity, striving to

From "The Tentative Character of Progress," chapter 34 of *Social Process* (1918; reprint Carbondale and Edwardsville: Southern Illinois University Press, 1966), 405–9.

anticipate and further their higher working, but not presuming to impose a formal programme upon them.

The question whether, after all, the world really does progress is not one that can be settled by an intellectual demonstration of any kind. It is possible to prove that mankind has gained and is gaining in material power, in knowledge, and in the extent and diversity of social organization; that history shows an enlarging perspective and that the thoughts of men are, in truth, "broadened with the process of the suns": but it is always possible to deny that these changes are progress. We seem to mean by this term something additional, a judgment, in fact, that the changes, whatever they may be, are on the whole *good*. In other words progress, as commonly understood, is essentially a moral category, and the question whether it takes place or not is one of moral judgment. Nothing of this kind is susceptible of incontrovertible demonstration, because the moral judgment is not bound by definite intellectual processes, nearly the same in all minds, but takes in the most obscure and various impulses of human nature.

Suppose you compare the state of the first white settlers in America, narrow and hard, physically, mentally, and socially, with the comparatively easy and spacious life of their descendants at the present time; or contrast the life of a European peasant, dwelling in mediæval ignorance and bondage, with that of the same peasant and his family after they have emigrated to the United States and come to a full share in its intelligence and prosperity. It may seem clear to most people that these changes, which are like those the world in general has been undergoing, are for the better; but the matter is quite debatable. The simpler lot of the pioneer and the peasant can easily be made to appear desirable, and there are, and no doubt always will be, those who maintain that we are no better off than we were.

Development, I should say, can be proved. That is, history reveals, beyond question, a process of enlargement, diversification, and organization, personal and social, that seems vaguely analogous to the growth of plant and animal organisms; but whether we are to write our moral endorsement on the back of all this is another matter. Is it better to be man or the marine animal, "resembling the larvæ of existing Ascidians,"[1] from which he is believed to have descended? In the end it comes down to this: is life itself a good thing? We see it

1. Darwin, *Descent of Man*, chap. 4.

waxing and shining all about us, and most of us are ready to pronounce that it is good; but the pessimist can always say: "To me it is
an evil thing, and the more of it the worse." And there is no way of
convincing him of error.

In short, the reality of progress is a matter of faith, not of demonstration. We find ourselves in the midst of an onward movement of
which our own spirits are a part, and most of us are glad to be in it,
and to ascribe to it all the good we can conceive or divine. This seems
the brave thing to do, the hopeful, animating thing, the only thing that
makes life worth while, but it is an act rather of faith than of mere
intelligence.

I hold, then, that progress, like human life in every aspect, is essentially
tentative, that we work it out as we go along, and always must; that
it is a process rather than an attainment. The best is forever indefinable; it is growth, renewal, onwardness, hope. The higher life seems
to be an upward struggle toward a good which we can never secure,
but of which we have glimpses in a hundred forms of love and joy. In
childhood, music, poetry, in transient hours of vision, we know a fuller, richer life of which we are a part, but which we can grasp only in
this dim and flitting way. All history is a reaching out for, a slow,
partial realization of, such perceptions. The thing for us is to believe
in the reality of this larger life, seen or unseen, to cling to all persons
and activities that help to draw us into it, to trust that though our
individual hold upon it relax with age and be lost, yet the great Whole,
from which we are in some way inseparable, lives on in growing splendor. I may perish, but We are immortal.

I look with wonder and reverence upon the great spirits of the past
and upon the expression of human nature in countless forms of art
and aspiration. It seems to me that back of all this must be a greater
Life, high and glorious beyond my imagination, which is trying to
work itself out through us. But this is in the nature of religion, and I
do not expect to impose it upon others by argument.

As regards the proximate future I see little to justify any form of
facile optimism, but conceive that, though the world does move, it
moves slowly, and seldom in just the direction we hope. There is something rank and groping about human life, like the growth of plants in
the dark: if you peer intently into it you can make out weird shapes,
the expression of forces as yet inchoate and obscure; but the growth
is toward the light.

22

A Primary Culture for Democracy

One who looks even a little beneath the surface of things may see that there is no question more timely than that of culture, and none which has more need of fresh and fundamental conceptions. It is by no means a question merely of the decoration of life or of personal enjoyment; it involves the whole matter of developing large-minded members for that strong and good democracy which we hope we are building up. Without such members such a democracy can never exist, and culture is essential to the power and efficiency, as well as to the beauty, of the social whole.

We may all agree, I imagine, that culture means the development of the human and social, as distinct from the technical, side of life. Our recent growth, so far at least as it is realized in our institutions, has been mainly technical, the creation of an abundant economic system and a marvelous body of natural science, neither of them achievements of a sort to center attention upon what is broadly human.

It is true that along with these has come a growth of humane sentiment and aspiration, of a spirit Christian and democratic in the largest sense of those words; but this remains in great part vague and ineffectual. To give it clearness and power is one of the aims of the culture we need.

There is also, I am sure, a growing *demand* for culture. In the course of the greatest struggle of history, which is also a struggle for righteous ideals, the people everywhere have learned that the social order needs reconstruction, and that the popular will has power to transform it, as has actually been seen in molding nations to efficiency in war. All this gives rise, especially in the young, to large and radical thinking, which permeates the armies, the press, the labor unions, and other popular associations; and among the first results of this thinking is a demand for a new sort of liberal education, through which all members of the coming order shall get a wider outlook, a higher and clearer

From "A Primary Culture for Democracy," in *Papers and Proceedings: Thirteenth Annual Meeting, American Sociological Society* (Chicago: University of Chicago Press, 1918), 1–10.

idealism, and so be prepared to create that free, righteous, and joyful system of life to which they aspire.

Indeed our democracy, in spite of its supposed materialism, has long had at heart the ideal of culture. Culture has been a god that we somewhat ignorantly worshiped. We are not satisfied with beholding the multiplication of material things, nor even with the hope of greater justice in their distribution; we want joy, beauty, hope, higher thoughts, a larger life, a fuller participation in the great human and divine whole in which we find ourselves. Even those popular movements which formulate their aims in material terms are not really materialistic but get their strongest appeal from the belief that these aims are the condition of a fuller spiritual life.

Another reason for turning our thoughts to culture is that the economic outlook demands it. We are apparently entering upon a period of cheap, standardized production upon an enormous scale, which will multiply commodities and perhaps increase leisure but will make little demand upon the intelligence of the majority of producers and offer no scope for mental discipline. Work is becoming less than ever competent to educate the worker, and if we are to escape the torpor, frivolity, and social irresponsibility engendered by this condition, we must offset it by a social and moral culture acquired in the schools and in the community life.

Our culture must be a function of our situation as a whole. Just as the arts, like literature, painting, and sculpture, cannot be merely traditional but must spring fresh and creative from the living spirit of the time, so also must culture, which is likewise an expression of the general life. It may be contrasted with, perhaps opposed to the apparent trend of things; but if so it is only because it is rooted in a deeper trend. If it does not function in the whole it is nothing.

I am in sympathy with those who cling to the great humanistic traditions of the past. There can be no real culture that is altogether new; it can only be a fresh growth out of old stems; but it must be that; it must be new in the sense that it is wholly reanimated by the spirit of our own time. Any attempt to impose an old culture upon us merely because the educated class cherish it, or because it can be supported by general arguments having no reference to our actual needs, must fail. Through control of institutions the classicist, or the scientist, or the religionist may for a time force the forms of an old learning upon a new generation; but before long all that does not vigorously function in the life of the day will slough off and be forgotten.

Certainly no culture can be real for us that is not democratic. This does not mean, however, that it must be superficial, or commonplace, or uniform. These are traits which the enemies of democracy have endeavored to fix upon it, but which do not belong to its essence. Democracy is at bottom a more humane, inclusive, and liberal organization of life, and certainly a democratic culture will be one based on large and kindly conceptions, meeting the needs of the plain people as well as of the privileged classes, and worked out largely through the schools and other popular institutions. Because culture has in the past been inaccessible to the masses and still is so in great part, we must make it our very special business to bring it within their reach; but the idea that such a culture must lack refinement and distinction has no basis in sound theory and will be refuted as fast as we make democracy what it can and should be.

An undemocratic humanism, in our time, is not humanism at all but an academic retreat out of which no living culture can come—just as a dead-level democracy without humane depth and richness of life is not true democracy. Finer achievements get their vitality from the sympathy of a group, and an idealistic democracy, which includes a unique mingling of races, classes, and nationalities, should achieve a culture as rich in human significance as any the world has seen.

We should recognize, however, that such traditional culture as we have is not democratic for the most part, but involves the inheritance, through an upper class, of the conceptions of an outworn society. The very word "culture" is in somewhat bad odor with people of democratic sympathies, because it suggests a parasitic leisure. Nothing could be more timely than that the plain people should take up the idea, reinterpret it from their point of view, and give it a chief place on the program of reform.

A living culture is not only an organic part of life as a whole, but it is a complex thing in itself. It must embrace, I think, two main aspects: a common or primary culture of knowledge and sentiment diffused through the whole people, and a variety of more elaborate culture processes, informed with the common spirit but developed by small groups in diverse fields of achievement. I mean by the former, to which I shall confine myself in this paper, such elements of culture as American children might get, in the schools or otherwise, before they have passed the age of compulsory attendance, or say sixteen years. This must supply the soil and atmosphere in which all our higher life is to grow, while the more specialized culture will give room for classical studies, sciences, philosophy, fine arts—what you will; nothing human need be lacking.

The aim of a common culture, I should say, must be a humane

enlargement of the thought and spirit of the people, including especially primary social knowledge and ideals; inculcated in no merely abstract form but appealing to the imagination and assimilated with experience. The currents of such a culture will flow, in large degree, outside the channels of public guidance and formal institutions, working upon us through newspapers, popular literature, the drama, motion pictures, and the like. They will get much of their form and direction, however, from the common schools and other community institutions, and since these are within our control they call for peculiar attention.

Of the studies now pursued in our primary schools those most plainly suited to be the means of culture are language and history, because they deal directly with the larger human life; but it cannot be assumed that they are actually fulfilling the culture function. They do so in proportion as they impart the higher traditions and ideals of our country and of the world at large, awakening in boys and girls a hearty participation in this greater life.

Language studies should make the individual a member of the continuing organism of thought and enable his spirit to grow by interaction with it. For our people this means self-expression in the English language and a beginning appreciation of its literature. These studies should be disciplinary, requiring precision of understanding and expression, but they should also be joyous, for culture has no worse enemy than the sort of teaching that makes drudgery of them. Noble sentiment is of their essence, and if that is not imparted nothing worth while is.

Other languages, modern and ancient, belong to the more specialized culture, not to that of the whole people. They are essential to many kinds of higher leadership and production, and children who are believed to be destined for such functions may well begin their study in childhood; to ask more for them would be fanatical.

It might perhaps be thought that history would be a study of the humane development of mankind in the past, bringing home to our knowledge and sympathy the common life and upward struggle of the people, and so leading to an understanding of the social questions of our own day. But it is not that in any great degree at the present time, and there is little prospect that it will be in the near future. Although some teachers of history, perhaps many of them, are striving to reanimate their subject in accordance with modern social conceptions, it is my impression that this movement is only beginning, and that the study of history, as actually practiced in the schools, conduces little, if at all, to understanding of, or interest in, matters of social and economic betterment. I question whether this study can make its full contribution to culture without an almost revolutionary change in its underlying conceptions and in the training of its teachers.

The central thing in a study of the past common to all American children should no doubt be the history of our own country, conceived in a social spirit as our part in the universal struggle for humane ideals of life, political democracy and federation, economic opportunity, social freedom, and higher development of every sort. It should be easy to treat American history in this way and to keep it in constant relation to the ideals and endeavors of our own day.

No aspect of history is better suited to the uses of culture than is the economic aspect, the age-long striving for material support, comfort, and leisure, along with the development and mutations of social classes, leading to our own problems of social justice. These are cultural because, on the one hand, they appeal to actual interest and daily observation, while, on the other, they lead directly to the most urgent questions of humane progress. One does not need to be an economic determinist to hold that here is one broad road to participation in the larger currents of life. The fact that history has slighted these things, and that men may pass as experts in it who have made no serious study of them, is itself explicable only by historical causes. Has not the pursuit of history become a kind of institution which, like many of our institutions, is still ruled by ideas impressed upon it in a former undemocratic state of society?

The very lowliness and homeliness of the daily life of the masses are one cause for its being somewhat neglected by research, and we must reckon also with the unconscious influence of an upper-class point of view unfavorable to studies that call in question the existing social order. I have sometimes fancied that our friends the historians, being for the most part accomplished men of the world, had for that reason a certain predilection for the upper circles of society, both past and present.

However this may be, it is clear that on grounds of culture every child ought to know something of the struggles of the unprivileged masses to gain a share of the opportunity and outlook achieved by a privileged few. Our middle and upper economic classes are still, for the most part, limited to a view of such matters that is both undemocratic and uncultured, and which the schools do little to correct.

It seems then that instruction in sociology and economics, of a simple and concrete kind, must be part of a universal democratic culture. How this should be related to history is perhaps an open question, but certainly the latter, as it is now understood, is wholly inadequate.

When all these studies are informed by a common spirit it may be possible to unite them.

So intimate and so animating is our relation to nature that natural science may well claim a place in any scheme for a basic humane culture. I would in fact include enough of this to impress the mind with the rule of law in nature and enable it to understand the experimental method by which man discovers this law and adapts it to his ends.

I must add that any school culture depends for its reality upon the personality of those who impart it. If the teachers and textbook writers were overflowing with those large views and sentiments that are culture, the students would invariably get them. This in turn depends somewhat upon that more adequate recognition by the public of the place of teachers as leaders and exemplars of cultures, from which intelligent selection and support would flow. The whole question is one we cannot solve by any mere change in the curriculum, but is implicated with the spirit and organization of the community.

Indeed our basic culture is likely to come quite as much from the social experiences of the school and community life as from culture studies. Culture is the larger mind that comes from the larger life, and the most direct and universal access to this is through association and co-operation with other people. No movements now going on promise more in this way than do those which aim at a livelier community spirit and expression in all the towns and neighborhoods of the land. When every locality has its center for social intercourse and discussion; its consciousness of its own past and ideals for the future; its communal music, sports, and pageants; its municipal buildings with noble architecture, painting, and sculpture; its local organization ready to take up voluntarily any responsibilities which the state or the nation may impose—then the child who learns to share in these things will not fail to get from them a social and spiritual enlargement.

The school especially can and should provide a group life, ideal, as far as possible, in its forms and spirit, participation in which will involve in the most natural way the elements of social, moral, and even religious culture. As states of the human spirit democracy, righteousness, and faith have much in common and may be cultivated by the same means, namely by the group activities of the school, such as socialized class work, athletics, self-government, plays, and the like, into which the boys and girls eagerly put themselves, and from which they may get training for a larger life. And this larger mind should by no means be allowed to lapse with graduation but should be cherished in the reunions and festivals of the local Alma Mater.

I feel that what I have said deals only with the more immediate and perhaps the more superficial factors in the growth of a primary culture. The studies, the teachers, the social activities of the schools and the community, are all expressions of an underlying current of life which molds their character for better or worse and can only gradually be changed. It would be fatuous not to see that this current is largely unfavorable to the development of any real culture, either primary or secondary. The influence in our society which is organized and dominant is commercialism; the elements of culture are for the most part scattered, demobilized, and impotent. The very idea and spirit of it are starved and crowded out.

If we divide the sources of culture into two parts, those that derive from tradition and those that come to us more directly from participation in life, we shall find that the former especially are deficient. Perhaps the first requisite of progress is to face the fact that we are, as a people, in a state of semi-barbarism as regards participation in that heritage which comes only by familiarity with literature and the arts. And since this is lacking in the people at large, including the bulk of the educated classes, our schools, which are nothing if not an expression of the people, do not readily supply it. The wealthy and energetic men who have general control of education mean well, but their whole life-history, in most cases, has been such that words like culture, art, and literature can be little more to them than empty sounds, and whatever provision they make for them can hardly fail to be somewhat perfunctory and superficial.

I do not mean that culture is irreconcilable with commercial activities or with technical training in the schools. On the contrary, periods of commercial expansion have usually been those when arts and literature flourished most; and technical training, if moderate in its demands and enlarged by a constant sense of the social whole to which it contributes, may itself involve a most essential kind of culture. But our commercialism has been exorbitant and exclusive; and our technical training is rarely of a sort which makes the student feel his membership in the larger whole. Both must be transformed by a social spirit and philosophy before they can join hands with culture.

These are the underlying reasons for the unsatisfactory state of our schools and for the extreme difficulty of introducing any culture spirit into them. American education, on the culture side, is deadened by formalism from the first grade in the primary schools to and including the graduate departments of our universities. In spite of much sound theory and honest effort on the part of teachers the stifling gases of commercialism have passed from the general atmosphere into academic halls and devitalized almost everything having no obvious economic purpose. I doubt if there has on the whole been any progress in this way, perhaps rather a retrogression, during my own time.

When I contemplate the state of culture in our colleges I cannot wonder that it does not flourish in the elementary schools. Thus, to take only one indication, I have reason to think that serious spontaneous reading is far less common among university students than it was forty years ago. This is my own observation, confirmed by others and corroborated by the evidence of a veteran bookseller, who told me that he sold fewer books of general literature to, say, 5,000 students at the time of our conversation than he did to one-fourth of that number in the Victorian era.

I find the outlook somewhat more cheerful as regards that sort of culture which we get as a by-product of co-operation with our fellows. This is a plant which grows untended in a free and friendly life; and I think that democracy is giving our feelings, our manners, and our social perceptions an enlargement which is truly, in its way, a kind of culture. That consideration, helpfulness, and ready sociability which, it appears, have endeared our soldiers to the villages of France are a part of our civilization and may well prove to be the first fruits of a new sort of culture. Let us cherish and diffuse this spirit in every possible way, especially through that school and community organization of which I have spoken. It is not only a fine thing in itself but will help us to appreciate and acquire that transmitted culture, akin to it in essence, which we now so sadly lack.

On the whole, our present condition as regards a popular culture, though unsatisfactory, is not unpromising. We have energy, good-will, and a sincere though vague idealism. We may expect these to work gradually upon all departments of life, our schools, our communities, our economic institutions, and the general atmosphere of the country, slowly bringing to pass a culture which will certainly be fresh, democratic, and human, and need not be deficient in those things that have to be learned from the past.

If I have not undertaken a discussion of the diversified higher culture, it is not because I doubt that democracy can and will develop in this direction. I say again that our ideal does not allow uniformity or limitation of any kind, but calls for utmost opportunity working out in utmost richness of life. In the way of culture, as in technical training, our higher schools should offer the best that the world has achieved, and should also foster specialized culture groups to kindle and support the individual in his struggle for a larger life.

Index of Names

Subject Index

19936981R00155

Made in the USA
Lexington, KY
13 January 2013